P9-EDU-172

Other McGraw-Hill Reference Books of Interest

ISDN
Concepts, Facilities, and Services

Gary C. Kessler

McGraw-Hill, Inc.
New York   St. Louis   San Francisco   Auckland   Bogotá
Caracas   Hamburg   Lisbon   London   Madrid
Mexico   Milan   Montreal   New Delhi   Paris
San Juan   São Paulo   Singapore
Sydney   Tokyo   Toronto

Library of Congress Cataloging-in-Publication Data

Kessler, Gary C.
   ISDN : concepts, facilities, and services / Gary C. Kessler.
      p.   cm.
   ISBN   0-07-034242-3
   1. Integrated services digital networks. I. Title.
   TK5103.7.K47   1990   67442
   621.382—dc20   90-5818
                                                         CIP

   2 3 4 5 6 7 8 9 0   DOC/DOC   9 5 4 3 2 1 0

ISBN 0-07-034242-3

The sponsoring editor for this book was Theron Shreve, the editing supervisor was Nancy Young, and the production supervisor was Dianne L. Walber. This book was set in Century Schoolbook. It was composed by McGraw-Hill's Professional & Reference Division composition unit.

Printed and bound by R. R. Donnelley & Sons Company.

For information about our audio products, write us at:
Newbridge Book Clubs, 3000 Cindel Drive, Delran, NJ 08370

This book is dedicated to my wife and friend, Carol,
and to my children, Joshua and Sarah

Contents

Contents ix

Preface

This book is a first introduction to some of the many aspects of the Integrated Services Digital Network (ISDN). It is intended for those who must learn about ISDN but feel intimidated by all of the technical jargon commonly found in the current literature. This book defines ISDN terms and explain concepts, allowing the reader to better understand the standards and current literature, as well as vendor's implementation and application specifications.

This book broadly explains what ISDN is, defines relevant terms and concepts, describes pertinent standards and protocols, and discusses some of the current ISDN issues, services, trials, and products. In that way, it serves as a first step in learning about the many aspects of ISDN.

It can be argued that consumers are not interested in technology, but rather in solutions to their problems. In data and telecommunications today, these issues are becoming increasingly inseparable. To truly understand all of the available communications solutions and choose the correct strategy for a given environment and application, there must also be some understanding of the underlying technology. This book will help the reader to get started on that understanding of ISDN.

Gary C. Kessler

Acknowledgments

Many people helped me prepare this book. I would like to give particular thanks to E. Raymond Hapeman of Bellcore, who was responsible for writing a large part of Chap. 6 on ISDN user-network signaling.

Dr. Bruce J. Chalmer, Robert L. Dayton, Jeffrey C. Frost, Dr. David A. Train, and Larry E. Walters reviewed various drafts and portions of this book and made many valuable comments adding to its readability, usefulness, and technical correctness. Brian King turned my rough drawings into the artwork that is used in this book. I thank them and appreciate their time and skill. I would also like to thank Jay Ranade for his encouragement and patience, as well as the production staff at McGraw-Hill, especially Nancy Young.

Many companies provided me with product and other information. Special thanks are due to Ms. Lois Kitson of the AT&T Consultant Liaison Program and to Dr. Paul Polishuk of IGI Consulting for all of their assistance. People from other companies, including Fujitsu Network Switching of America, Inc., Hayes Microcomputer Products, Inc., ICL North America, NEC America, Inc., Newbridge Networks, Inc., and Northern Telecom, Inc., also helped me obtain product and service information, and their assistance is greatly appreciated.

I also thank my students of the last several years who, through their questions and comments, have helped me to better understand ISDN and have frequently taught me.

Finally, I must thank my family, who did not know what I was really getting into when I committed to write this book but were supportive and helpful nevertheless.

How to Use This Book

Chapter 1 provides an overview of data communications topics. Understanding the issues in this chapter is essential for a good understanding of ISDN technology and how an ISDN can work. Chapter 2 provides definitions and terms necessary for the understanding of ISDN standards, services, and products. Chapter 3 describes the categories of available ISDN services, per the current standards. These three chapters provide a foundation for the rest of the book.

Chapters 4 and 5 describe the Physical Layer and Data Link Layer protocols, respectively. Although these chapters do not go into intimate detail on the procedures associated with the protocols, they are technical in nature. These chapters are oriented more toward implementors and product developers than casual end users and can be used as the basis for a much more rigorous treatment about the protocols' operation. These chapters may be skipped by those readers uninterested in the protocols without losing comprehension of the later chapters.

Chapter 6 describes the interface between the user and the network. This chapter describes the basic procedures in which voice and data calls are established and terminated and the use of supplementary services. This chapter is aimed at developers and users alike.

Chapter 7 describes Signaling System No. 7 (SS7), the common channel signaling network associated with ISDN. This chapter describes common channel signaling network concepts, SS7 protocols, and SS7 services. The beginning of the chapter may be skipped by those readers who are not interested in the SS7 protocol layers without losing comprehension about SS7 services.

Chapters 8 through 10 are nontechnical and address different aspects of ISDN. Chapter 8 describes the future of some current data and telecommunications services in the ISDN era, ISDN applications, and the different ISDN markets. Chapter 9 describes the evolution of ISDN trials in the United States and throughout the world. Finally, Chapter 10 presents an overview of some of the ISDN products that have been announced.

The book has several appendices. Appendix A provides a list of abbreviations and acronyms that are used throughout the book and/or are important to ISDN. Appendix B lists all of the CCITT ISDN recommendations. Appendix C lists all messages and information elements used in the ISDN user-network interface. Appendix D gives the addresses of various standards organizations, where most of the standards mentioned in this book may be obtained. It is followed by a glossary of ISDN-related terms.

Introduction

Imagine a network that would break down the walls of classrooms, letting teachers, students, and staff directly access computer-based resources and other communications facilities. This network could enhance communications between teachers and staff, allowing students to gain more of their teachers' time for instruction, personal attention, and an enriched curriculum. Computer-aided instruction (CAI) and computer-based teaching and grading could be enhanced, allowing better tailor-made courses and tracking of an individual student's progress. Teleconferencing could provide courses to the sick or homebound student, courses to students spread over a wide geographic area, and continuing education for teachers and other staff members. Community- or state-wide databases could allow the sharing of scarce educational resources. Student attendance and teacher availability could all be tracked via centralized databases. PC-to-PC networking could be easily accomplished between buildings on a campus or between campuses.

Imagine a network that would make communications to, and between, entities of an insurance company easier. When calling a customer service agent, the customer's records could automatically appear on the agent's display; the display and the telephone call could both be forwarded to another agent, if necessary. Claims processing could be expedited by improving communications between the agent, customer, and claims adjuster. Independent agents could access insurance company databases to quickly examine different policy plans and costs. Communications between the home office, branch agencies, benefits office, and various customers could be more easily arranged. All offices in a given area could be tied together in a city-wide Centrex, bringing remote sites closer together. PC-to-PC networking, 3270-connectivity, access to X.25 packet networks, and Group 4 (digital) facsimile transmission could all be supported.

Imagine a network that would streamline the operation of a hospital, allowing more efficient delivery of health care. The network could provide communications between major medical centers, community hospitals, and doctors' offices. Central databases and medical artificial intelligence (AI) systems could be made more generally available, even to health care centers with limited financial resources. Databases could make the posting and tracking of patient care, as well as billing, easier and more accurate. Furthermore, this information would be available to the patient's private physician and to this (or another) hospital in case of a subsequent readmission or transfer to another facility. Teleconferencing and electronic mail could enhance staff training and communications, making new medical technologies and protocols more generally available. Inventory control and access to needed equipment could be more simply handled using a centralized computer-based system. Outpatient monitoring could be only a telephone call away, regardless of the patient's location, allowing faster response to potential emergencies, shorter hospital stays, and faster recovery times.

Imagine a network that would bring simultaneous voice and data applications to the home. A central computer could control telephone ringing, temperature, lighting on a room-by-room basis, and the operation of home appliances. This computer, in turn, could be controlled remotely by the user via the network. Other services might include call forwarding, call waiting, and special telephone ring signals, all tailored dynamically by the user depending upon the telephone number of the *calling* party. Two-way television and easy access to data and video services could all be available. Banking, insurance, and utility companies could design applications to take advantage of this network to provide better and more efficient service to the customer in the home.

While these scenarios may sound idealistic and futuristic, they are very real possibilities with the implementation of ISDN. More than 100 ISDN trials or service implementations comprising more than 100,000 lines already exist today in Canada, England, France, Japan, the United States, West Germany, and other countries.

ISDN is here. The capabilities mentioned in the paragraphs above are all possible; it remains only for the applications and products to be designed to take advantage of this communications technology.

I.1 A DEFINITION OF ISDN

An Integrated Services Digital Network (ISDN) may be viewed as many things, depending upon the perspective of the viewer. The International Telegraph and Telephone Consultative Committee (CCITT), which is largely responsible for today's international ISDN standards, defines an ISDN as:

> . . . a network, in general evolving from a telephony Integrated Digital Network (IDN), that provides end-to-end digital connectivity to support a wide range of services, including voice and non-voice services, to which

users have access by a limited set of standard multi-purpose user-network interfaces. (From CCITT Recommendation I.110, 1988.)

As the definition implies, an ISDN really is, in fact, many things. In its simplest form, an ISDN is merely an enhancement to the telephone local loop that will allow both voice and data to be carried over the same twisted pair. In a more comprehensive view, an ISDN is a network that can provide a myriad of data and telecommunications services. It is a fully digital network, where all devices and applications present themselves in a digital form. That is, information from the telephone, personal computer, stereo, television, PBX, mainframe, and ISDN coffee pot are all seen as bit streams by the network switch. Therefore, all of the information can be switched and transported by the same network equipment.

I.2 THE FORCES BEHIND ISDN

Telephone networks around the world have been evolving toward the use of digital transmission facilities and switches for many years. Many critics of ISDN have claimed that this evolution in technology is the primary motivating factor to build ISDNs, thus creating a solution without a problem. There are, in fact, several forces driving the move to ISDN. Among them are:

- The growing demand for domestic and international digital communications service for voice and data, particularly as businesses become more geographically disperse and dependent upon international cooperation
- The demand for increased network simplicity, flexibility, and control at economical prices
- The advantage of separating the evolution of customer premises equipment (CPE) from the evolution of network equipment, thus allowing users to purchase the equipment best suited to their applications regardless of the network hardware and to protect their investment

An ISDN, by itself, will not accomplish all of these goals. Associated with the network and its services are the requirements for standards describing the functions of, and access to, the network. Standards will:

- Support universality of services and portability of equipment
- Reduce costs as standard chip sets can be mass produced
- Increase the potential market by introducing new, affordable services

I.3 ISDN INTEGRATED ACCESS

The ISDN will have a common set of rules so that different types of user equipment can request the appropriate set of services from the network. The ISDN is integrated not only in the sense that a single network will provide these many kinds of services but also in the sense that a single set of interface rules will govern all devices requesting service from the network.

In the current state of data and telecommunications, users need a different physical and logical interface to each network that they access for the different services that they require (Fig. I-1). For example, a user accessing the public telephone network (PTN) requires a connection to the central office (C.O.) and telephone equipment that follows the correct protocols for accessing that network.

If the user wants a packet switching data service, an additional set of wires will have to be brought out from the C.O. or packet network provider. The customer premises equipment will have to support the X.25 (or other packet network) protocol.

If the user also wants telex service, additional wires must be brought out to the customer site and new equipment placed that adheres to the telex network protocol. Access to a community antenna TV (CATV) service requires yet another physical interface (coaxial cable) and a device that can convert the cable signal to one that is understood by the TV set. Each new service requires an additional communications path, different protocols, and different network facilities.

Initially, ISDNs will eliminate the problem of all of the different access methods by providing a single (integrated) set of wires and access protocols to the network (Fig. I-2). Indeed, each of the services might still be provided by a separate subnetwork, but the user will only see a single access port and single set of protocols to request service. If there are multiple subnetworks embedded within the ISDN, they will be transparent to the user. When ISDNs are fully implemented, the ISDN itself can provide all of the different services (Fig. I-3). Little

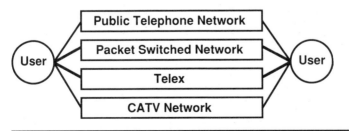

Figure I.1 Current model of communications; users have different interfaces to different network services.

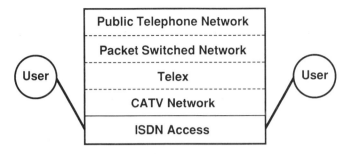

Figure I.2   Interim ISDN model showing ISDN's integrated access to possibly multiple networks.

Figure I.3   Long-term ISDN model, providing integrated access and integrated services from a single network.

will change from the customer's point of view, however; there will still be a single access port and access protocol set.

I.4 ISDN DIGITAL SERVICES

The ISDN access path acts as a "digital pipe" to the customer's premises (Fig. I-4). Regardless of the service and equipment type, the connection between the customer and the C.O. is a digital facility. The only question is how large the digital pipe will be and what services can be accommodated.

An ISDN must provide services at a level comparable to what is available today. This includes, naturally, voice and data services, as well as many other low-speed services such as security monitoring and telemetry applications. Ultimately, additional services will be offered at very high data rates, such as video services, videotext, and teleconferencing.

I.5 WHAT ISDN IS AND ISN'T

The ISDN standards provide the rules for the user interface to the network; they do not describe the network itself. The standards also de-

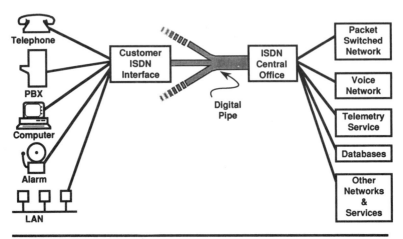

Figure I.4   ISDN "digital pipe."

scribe the services that may be offered by an ISDN; they do not describe their implementation or applications that use the services.

In many ways, ISDN is not really a communications revolution. The telephone companies in the United States and throughout the world have been designing, building, and using digital switching and transmission facilities for over 25 years. Thus, a digital network providing many services is consistent with the current network evolution. The revolution that will occur will be by the users and in the way they perceive the "telephone company" as a communications service provider. The majority of people today use the telephone network only for the occasional telephone call. A massive consumer reeducation will be necessary in the ISDN era; a single network will provide not only telephone service but many other services, including:

- Remote control of home devices
- Home meters that can send billing information automatically to a utility company while the utility company monitors use of critical resources
- The ability for a user to simultaneously call a catalog store (via their telephone), examine a picture of an item (via their television), and authorize the purchase of an item (via their personal computer)
- Customized pay-per-view sports, news, educational, and other types of television programming

ISDN is a strategy to provide users with these additional communications services. After some initial expense, the digital network should be less costly for the end user than the current analog one. Therefore, over time, customers should be able to obtain greater service at a price comparable to today's relatively limited service set. Economics, then, will be the real test for early residential and business ISDN customers: Are the myriad services worth the initial cost, do the consumers know how to use all of these services, and can anyone (initially) afford them?

New applications, hardware, and software must be developed for ISDN implementation to succeed; without new applications, how will customers justify the cost of the conversion to a new network? The common Catch-22 problem of any new technology then arises: Customers will be reluctant to purchase ISDN without new applications and better services, and vendors will be reluctant to design new products and applications without a guaranteed ISDN market. Another important question looms, as well: Where will the necessary infusion of research and development funds come from?

ISDN is not just a European or North American idea or a scheme of only academic interest or a ploy of the telephone companies to generate more revenue. It is a global strategy being actively pursued in North and South America, Europe, Asia, and the Pacific.

I.6 WHERE TO FROM HERE

This book will look at ISDN from the perspective of the user and the services that the user can obtain from the network. It will also examine the protocols used across the user-network interface and the network signaling system. Applications for ISDN, the future of current communications strategies, and the ISDN market will also be discussed. Finally, the evolution of ISDN trials and commercial offerings in the United States and around the world and an overview of ISDN products will be presented.

1

Data Communications Background for ISDN

This chapter will review some of the data communications topics relevant to ISDN. It is not intended to provide in-depth analyses or motivation; readers should refer to a data communications text for more detailed information (see "References" at the end of the book for suggested texts).

1.1 COMMUNICATIONS BASICS

1.1.1 Analog and Digital Signals

One of the most important concepts to understand in data communications is the difference between analog and digital signals (Fig. 1.1). An analog signal is one that is continuous and may take on any value within a given range of values. Examples of analog signals are human voice, video, and music. Analog signals are sometimes referred to as *broadband,* or modulated, signals.

A digital signal is one that may take on only a discrete set of values within a given range. Binary signals, in particular, are digital signals that may take on only two values, 0 or 1. Digital signals are sometimes referred to as *baseband,* or unmodulated, signals.

The distinction between analog and digital signals is important. Sound is produced when air is set in motion by a vibrating source, such as the vocal cords or the strings of a guitar. When the vibrating source pushes out, the air particles around it are compressed; when the source pulls back, the air particles are pulled apart. This pressing and pulling of air particles causes a chain reaction through the air

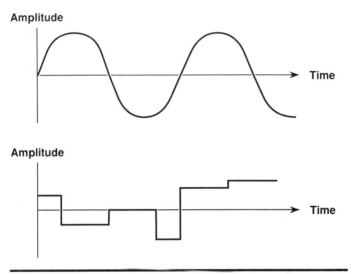

Figure 1.1   Analog (top) and digital (bottom) signals.

away from the original source, generating a sound wave. Sound waves are analog signals, where each in-and-out vibration is called a *cycle*. The frequency of the signal is measured in hertz (Hz), or cycles per second. A sound wave with a frequency of 261.63 Hz, for example, is the musical note middle C.

Human voice comprises a particular type of analog signal, a mixture of sinusoidal (sine) waves. The telephone network has been designed specifically to handle analog human voice signals. An ISDN network will only carry digital signals, although we will still want to send human voice through the network. Later discussion in this chapter will describe how human voice is carried in a digital network.

1.1.2   Amplifiers and Repeaters

The analog telephone network contains amplifiers to boost the signals so that they can be carried over long distances. Unfortunately, all copper media (e.g., twisted pair and coaxial cable) act as an antenna to pick up electrical signals from the surrounding environment. This noise can come from many sources, such as fluorescent lights, electric motors, and power lines. An amplifier, by the nature of its function, boosts the signal (e.g., the human voice) and background noise equally. The effects of noise, then, are additive in an analog network; the noise boosted by one amplifier becomes input to the next amplifier.

Amplifiers in the analog network are poorly suited for digital signals. Digital signals are represented as square waves, although they leave the transmitter in a rounded-off form, looking much like an analog signal. An amplifier, then, would accept a poorly formed digital signal plus any noise on the line, and output a louder, degraded signal.

Digital networks use signal regenerators (or repeaters) instead of amplifiers. A signal regenerator accepts the incoming digital signal and then creates a new outgoing signal. Repeaters are typically placed every 6000 feet (ft) or so in the long distance digital network. Since the signal is regenerated, the effects of noise are not additive from repeater to repeater.

1.1.3 Structure of the Telephone Network

Figure 1.2 shows the major components of the public switched telephone network (PSTN) in North America. The implementation of this hierarchical network was started in the 1930s and essentially completed in the 1950s; it has undergone continual modifications as technology and population demographics have changed.

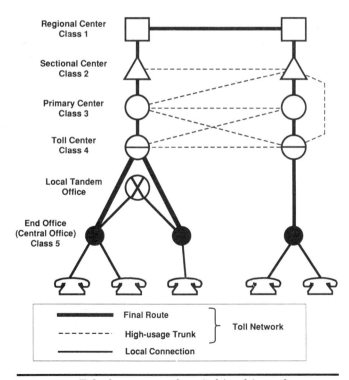

Figure 1.2   Telephone network switching hierarchy.

The ten-digit telephone numbers commonly used in North America expedite call routing within this switching hierarchy; the first three digits identify the area code, the next three digits identify the end office, and the last four digits identify the end user.

An end user, such as a residential or business customer, is directly connected to a telephone network end office, also called a class 5 or central office (C.O.). Users are typically connected to the C.O. over a single twisted wire pair called the *local loop*.

The class 4 (toll) offices can serve two functions. As a toll switch, a class 4 office is part of the long distance (toll) network. Alternatively, a class 4 office can act as a tandem switch to interconnect those class 5 offices having sufficient interoffice traffic to justify direct trunks. Local tandem office switches can also handle overflow traffic on direct trunks between end offices. The distinction between toll and tandem became particularly important in the United States after the divestiture of AT&T resulted in the separation of communications resources within the network.

Routing between C.O.s will always use the fewest number of switching offices possible to minimize the cost of carrying the traffic. The actual route selected will depend upon such factors as the distance between the two C.O.s, the current network traffic level, and time of day.

A connection between two users who are physically connected to the same C.O. requires only the involvement of that single switching office. Where two subscribers are connected to different central offices and the two class 5 offices are attached to the same class 4 office, that toll center can make the connection. When the C.O.s are further apart, other switching offices are used, although it is not necessary that class 5, 4, or 3 offices always connect through the next higher level of switch. A higher-class switch can perform all lower-class switching functions; a class 5 office, for example, can be served by a class 4, 3, 2, or 1 office.

The final (primary) route structure shown in Fig. 1.2 is supplemented by an alternate routing structure. To minimize heavy traffic loads at the higher levels and signal degradation when the route involves many trunks and switching offices, high-usage trunks may be used between any class switching offices where economically justified.

There are approximately 19,000 class 5 offices in the United States and 200 million local loops. There are also about 900 class 4, 204 class 3, 63 class 2, and 10 class 1 offices.

The Modification of Final Judgement (MFJ), signed by Judge Harold H. Greene in January 1982, represented the settlement of the U.S. Government's 1974 antitrust suit against AT&T. The MFJ was the basis of the breakup of AT&T and the Bell operating telephone companies. AT&T's Plan of Reorganization (POR), filed in December

1982, provided the new structure and organization of the U.S. telephone industry after January 1, 1984.

According to the POR, AT&T retained long distance communication services and communications equipment manufacturing businesses, as well as other assets such as Bell Laboratories. The 19 Bell Operating Companies (BOCs) were organized into seven Regional BOCs (RBOCs). All Bell System assets were assigned to either AT&T or an RBOC, meaning that joint ownership of switching equipment was no longer allowed. Thus, AT&T kept the toll network switches (class 1 to 4 offices and some tandem switches) and the RBOCs kept local switching equipment (class 5 and some tandem offices).

The service areas of the BOCs have been subdivided into approximately 160 local access and transport areas (LATAs). An additional 18 LATAs are served by independent telephone companies (ITCs), non-Bell-affiliated providers such as General Telephone and United Telecommunications. The BOCs and ITCs are limited to handling intra-LATA (inside the LATA) traffic; thus they are called local exchange carriers (LECs).

Inter-LATA (between LATA) traffic is handled by the interexchange carriers (IECs), such as AT&T, MCI, and U.S. Sprint. There are a few exceptions to this rule; several high-traffic corridors have been defined, such as in the New York City area, where the LEC provides some inter-LATA service. The toll network is owned by the IECs.

1.1.4 Passband and Bandwidth

Before analyzing the requirement of transmitting human voice in a digital form, we must first define the bandwidth associated with voice and the telephone local loop.

Recall that the frequency of an analog signal is the number of complete sine waves (or vibrations) sent every second and is measured in cycles per second. The passband of a channel is the range of frequencies that can be carried by that channel; the bandwidth is merely the width of the passband. For example, one television channel may use the 470.5- to 476.5-million-hertz (MHz) passband while another television channel uses the 800- to 806-MHz passband, but both channels have a bandwidth of 6 MHz.

Human voice can produce tones in the approximate passband of 50 to 15,000 Hz (15 kilohertz, 15 kHz), for a bandwidth of 14.95 kHz. The ear can hear sounds in the 20- to 20,000-Hz passband (19.98-kHz bandwidth).

1.1.5 The Telephone Local Loop

The passband of the telephone local loop is roughly 300 to 3400 Hz. This may be surprising, considering that the human voice produces sounds between 50 and 15,000 Hz. How can a channel with a bandwidth of 3.1 kHz carry the information of a channel with a 14.95-kHz bandwidth?

In fact, the local loop is not meant to carry just any analog signal but is optimized for human voice. It can be shown that the major portion of the relative energy of the human voice signal is in the passband from about 200 to 3500 Hz. This is the frequency range where the bulk of the power, intelligibility, and recognizability of the voice signal occurs. Thus, the 300- to 3400-Hz passband is adequate for quality human voice transmissions.

Note that a channel with a bandwidth of 3.1-kHz cannot carry all of the information in the ear's passband. Voice can be limited to a 3.1-kHz band because the ear can obtain most of the necessary information from that narrow band.

Consider the case of music, which is intended to be pleasing to a larger frequency spectrum of the ear. A transmission facility carrying music, then, must use a larger bandwidth than voice. Think about what happens when someone plays a musical instrument over the telephone; it sounds flat and tinny because it is missing all frequency components below 300 and above 3400 Hz.

The primary reason that the telephone network uses the narrow 3.1-kHz band rather than the entire 15 kHz of voice is that the narrow band allows more telephone conversations to be carried over a single physical channel. This is particularly important for the trunks connecting telephone switching offices. Filters and load coils in the network cut out the voice signals below 300 and above 3400 Hz on a single connection; the wire itself is capable of carrying much higher frequencies.

1.1.6 Multiplexing

Multiplexing in a network allows a single resource to be shared by many users. In particular, multiplexers in the telephone network allow many voice conversations to be carried over a single physical communications line.

Analog communications facilities typically use frequency division multiplexing (FDM) to carry multiple conversations. FDM divides the available frequency among all users and each user has its assigned channel for as much time as necessary (Fig. 1.3). In the case of voice, each conversation is shifted to a different passband with a bandwidth of at least 3.1 kHz. Since the bandwidth is held constant, the integrity of the user's information is maintained even though the passband has been altered.

FDM is a scheme that we are all familiar with. Television stations,

Frequency

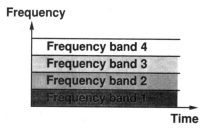

Time

Figure 1.3 Frequency division multiplexing.

for example, each require a 6-MHz passband and all TV channels share the available bandwidth of the air. The TV set in our house, then, acts like a demultiplexer to tune in only the passband (i.e., the channel) that we want to watch. This is also the same principle used for cable TV and radio channels.

Digital signals are typically multiplexed on a communications facility using time division multiplexing (TDM). Whereas FDM provides each user with part of the frequency spectrum for all of the time that the user requires, a TDM scheme provides each user with the entire frequency spectrum for a small burst of time (Fig. 1.4). In the figure, time slots are granted on a round-robin basis to the five users who share the channel.

1.2 DIGITAL TELEPHONY

1.2.1 The Move to a Digital Telephone Network

Prior to the early 1960s, the U.S. telephone network was an integrated analog network (IAN), meaning that all devices, facilities, and services were analog in nature. In fact, plain old telephone service

Frequency

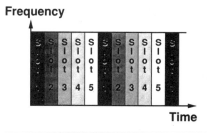

Time

Figure 1.4 Time division multiplexing.

(POTS) was all that was offered; the telephone network would carry analog utterances from one point in the network to another.[1]

While the telephone local loop is still predominantly analog today, the rest of the network has been undergoing a move toward using digital facilities for well over 25 years. The Bell system started looking into converting the network to digital in the 1950s. The first digital lines used in the United States were T1 carriers, introduced into the network in 1962 for traffic between telephone switching offices. T1 carriers use two wire pairs as opposed to the local loop's single pair.

The first digital switch, AT&T's No. 4ESS (Electronic Switching System), was introduced into the toll network in 1976. Northern Telecom, Inc., (NTI) introduced their digital toll switch, the DMS-200, in early 1980. Throughout the 1980s, digital switches have been introduced into central offices, as well. Northern Telecom's DMS-100 was introduced into the Bell system in 1981 and AT&T's No. 5ESS switch began service in March 1982; both of these are digital switches for the C.O. The majority of central offices in North America now use a digital switch.

The introduction of digital switches and carrier facilities allowed portions of the telephone network to operate more efficiently and meant that new types of digital services could be offered to some customers. Even if all switching offices and interoffice trunks in the network were digital today, the network still contains local loops that are optimized to carry human voice signals. The "analog" local loop, then, is the weakest link and POTS would continue to be the primary service available to most end users. An integrated digital network (IDN) is a network where all switches, interoffice trunks, local loops, and telephones are digital.

There are a number of reasons for converting network facilities from analog to digital, but the overriding one is economy. Digital facilities and digital devices are less expensive to design, build, and maintain than comparable analog devices. Indeed, the microprocessor revolution of the last 20 years has caused the price of digital devices in all facets of life to plummet, while the price of analog devices has remained relatively stable. There are also moving parts in an electromechanical switch, while digital switches perform their switching electronically via internal table exchanges. Once the network has been converted to digital, it is a natural step, not a quantum leap, to observe that many types of different services may be carried by this network.

---

[1]POTS refers to the limited set of services offered by a telephone company. Since ISDN represents the other extreme of service offerings, some industry observers have referred to its as pretty amazing new stuff, or PANS.

1.2.2 Digitizing Voice and Pulse Code Modulation

To carry human voice in a digital form, the voice signal is sampled 8000 times per second. This is a result of Harry Nyquist's Sampling Theorem, which states that to be able to accurately reproduce an analog signal from a series of samples, sampling must occur at twice the highest frequency of the signal. The human voice passband is taken to be between 0 and 4000 Hz to provide an appropriate guard band for protection between adjacent voice channels when multiplexing is performed. The maximum frequency, 4 kHz, requires a sample rate of 8000 times per second.

Each sample of the voice signal is converted to a digital bit stream. The process of converting the analog sample to a bit stream is pulse code modulation (PCM) and is performed by a device called a CODEC (COder-DECoder). The CODEC may be part of a digital switch, in which case the local loop between the telephone and switch carries analog signals. Alternatively, the CODEC may be placed in the telephone set, in which case the local loop carries digital signals.

Figure 1.5 shows the voice digitization scheme. The voice signal is sampled every 125 microseconds (μs), or once every 1/8000 second (s). This sampling is called pulse amplitude modulation (PAM). The amplitude of the PAM sample is mapped to a discrete value on the amplitude axis. The coding of the analog sample into a digital bit stream is the PCM step.

Note the nonlinearity of the PCM amplitude scale. The defined amplitude levels are closer together at lower volumes and farther apart at higher volumes; this is called *companding*. A nonlinear scale is used because it is more important to catch the subtleties and nuances when people are talking softly than when they are yelling. There are two main companding schemes used in digital telephony: the μ-law is used primarily in North America and Japan, while the A-law is used throughout most of the rest of the world.

The PCM companding algorithms specify 255 amplitude levels;

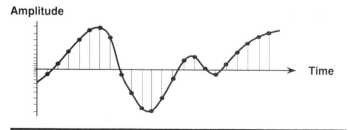

Figure 1.5 Pulse code modulation.

therefore, each voice sample is coded as an 8-bit stream. Since 8000 samples are taken each second, the bit rate of a single voice channel is 64,000 bits per second (bps). This is sometimes referred to as digital signaling level 0, or DS-0.

It should be noted that the analog voice signal cannot be mapped exactly onto the digital amplitude scale. Thus, the digitized signal is not an exact replica of the original signal; the difference is called the *quantization error*. Because of the large number of amplitude levels that are defined and the companding strategy, the quantization error is minimized and what little remains is easily compensated for by the listener.

1.2.3 The Digital TDM Hierarchy

As mentioned above, T1 carriers were the first digital carriers employed in the United States. A T1 carrier multiplexes 24 voice channels over a single transmission line using time division multiplexing. The basic unit of transmission is a *frame,* which contains one sample from each of the 24 channels. Since a sample is represented by 8 bits, a single frame contains 192 bits of user data. Each frame is preceded by a single framing bit; thus, a single T1 frame contains 193 bits. Since each frame contains one sample from each voice channel, there must be 8000 frames per second on the T1 channel. This yields a bit rate of 1.544 million bits per second (Mbps), which is also known as digital signaling level 1 (DS-1). Since 8000 of the bits are framing bits, the actual user data rate is 1.536 Mbps.

The T1 carrier multiplexes 24 voice channels using TDM. Several T1 carriers, in turn, can be multiplexed using TDM to form even higher-speed channels. The number of channels multiplexed together is defined by the digital TDM hierarchy. The T-carrier system follows the AT&T digital TDM hierarchy, used in North America, Japan, Taiwan, and South Korea (Table 1.1).

The other widely used TDM hierarchy is based upon the Conference

TABLE 1.1   AT&T North American Standard TDM Hierarchy

Digital Signal Level	Number of voice channels	Bit rate (Mbps)
DS-0	1	0.064
DS-1	24	1.544
DS-1C	48	3.152
DS-2	96	6.312
DS-3	672	44.736
DS-4	4,032	274.176

of European Postal and Telecommunications (CEPT) administrations standard (Table 1.2). The first level of the CEPT digital hierarchy multiplexes the equivalent of 32 voice-grade (64-kbps) channels, yielding a bit rate of 2.048 Mbps. One of the channels is used for signaling, one is for frame alignment, and the remaining 30 are used for actual user data. This is sometimes referred to as the E1 frame format.

T1 carriers predate digital switching. Therefore, in the early days of digital carriers, the switches were still analog. That meant that a CODEC had to be placed on both ends of every digital carrier between every pair of offices. Thus, one telephone connection might be routed through several switches, requiring that the coding/decoding process be performed several times. In a fully digital network, there will be a single coding and a single decoding step since the CODEC will be part of the end-user equipment. Even if the local loop is analog, the CODEC will be placed in the C.O., which would still only require a single coding and decoding operation.

1.2.4 Digital Signals on the Local Loop

A major stumbling block to sending digital signals between the C.O. and customer site is today's local loop. The local loop comprises a twisted pair of 22- to 26-gauge unshielded copper wire. The average length of a local loop in the United States is about 18,000 ft, or 18 kilofeet (kft).

Load coils are placed on the local loop to reduce the voice frequency attenuation (power loss) in the wire pair. While the load coils ensure that the voice signal is strong enough to travel the distance between the customer site and the C.O., they effectively limit the voiceband to approximately 300 to 3400 Hz. *Bridged taps* are also present on the local loop; they reduce installation time for new customer connections but also negatively affect digital transmission on the loop.

The problem with the analog local loop is that while 3.1 kHz is suf-

TABLE 1.2   Conference of European Postal and
Telephone Administrations' Standard TDM
Hierarchy

Level Number	Number of voice channels	Bit rate (Mbps)
0	1	0.064
1	30	2.048
2	120	8.448
3	480	34.368
4	1,920	139.264
5	7,680	565.148

ficient for carrying analog human voice signals, it is not sufficient for carrying the frequencies required to represent digital data. It can be shown that square waves are actually composed of a series of sine waves of different frequencies. Stable, recognizable square waves require frequency components much higher than 3400 Hz, making the local loop inadequate for digital communication.

The 300- to 3,400-Hz bandwidth limitation of the local loop is imposed by the network, not by the medium itself. In fact, unshielded twisted pair may be used in analog telephony applications with a bandwidth up to 250 kHz, which requires amplifiers every 16.5 to 19.8 kft (5 to 6 km), and in digital applications with bit rates up to 4 Mbps, which requires repeaters approximately every 6.5 kft (2 km). Therefore, digital communication over twisted pairs is possible once load coils and bridged taps are removed from the line. This unloaded local loop, if used for digital applications, is called a digital subscriber line (DSL).

It should be noted that some current local area network (LAN) products and standards use unshielded twisted pair at data rates up to 16 Mbps. The length of the wire, however, is limited to several hundred feet, well short of the local loop requirements of several miles.

1.2.5 Full-Duplex Communication on the Local Loop

Deloading the local loop would allow digital transmission. The next issue is how to accomplish simultaneous, two-way (full-duplex) communication over the loop.

Today's analog local loops already carry sounds in both directions at the same time. The voice signals from both parties are on the local loop simultaneously and, in addition, bridged taps, wire gauge changes, and splices can cause echo of the signal back to the transmitter. Full-duplex communication over the local loop is not a problem in analog applications. When people talk over the telephone, the brain merely filters out their words when they are echoed back. For data applications, modems typically split the bandwidth of the local loop in half to achieve full-duplex communication; the originating modem will usually transmit in the lower half of the passband and the answering modem will usually transmit in the upper half.

Splitting the bandwidth in half is not appropriate in a digital environment since digital signals cannot be confined to a given passband. Alternatively, the T1 approach could be adopted; two pairs of wire could be used, one for transmit and one for receive. This solution, however, is not a viable one for the local loop since tens of millions of miles of new cable would have to be installed in the United States alone.

Instead, two other approaches are used to achieve full-duplex digital communication over a two-wire DSL.

The first method is called time-compression multiplexing (TCM). TCM works as follows: if we wish a facility to operate at x-bps full-duplex, we can simulate that by operating the facility at $2x$-bps half-duplex, where each data stream travels in opposite directions over the shared channel. TCM requires facilities at both ends of the communications channel to constantly and quickly turn the line around, an operation called *ping-ponging*.

The half-duplex facility, in fact, really has to operate at a rate somewhat above $2x$ bps. In those systems employing TCM, most 56- and 64-kbps full-duplex signals are carried on a 144-kbps half-duplex channel, a ratio of 2.57:1 and 2.25:1, respectively. TCM was developed in the early 1980s for AT&T's Circuit Switched Digital Capability (CSDC) service and is used today over two-wire facilities in AT&T's Switched 56 and Northern Telecom's Datapath services. It was proposed, but will not be used, for ISDN local loops.

The second approach to achieving full-duplex communication over the DSL is to use a device called an echo canceller. An echo canceller does exactly what its name implies; the transmitter remembers what it is sending and "subtracts" the appropriate signal from the incoming transmission, thus eliminating the returning echo. This requires complex algorithms but, in fact, is the method of choice for use on ISDN local loops. Echo cancellation will be discussed again in Chap. 4.

1.3 TYPES OF SWITCHED NETWORKS

To fully understand and appreciate ISDN services, it is necessary to understand circuit switching and packet switching (*circuit mode* and *packet mode,* respectively, in the ISDN vernacular). Both switching techniques are in common use today and will be supported by an ISDN. Before discussing these two types of switching, it is useful to examine the characteristics of voice and data calls.

Voice calls are typically characterized by the following:

- *Delay sensitive:* Silence in human conversation conveys information, so the voice network cannot add (or remove) periods of silence.

- *Long hold time:* Telephone calls usually last for a relatively long time compared to the time necessary to set up the call; while it may take 3 to 11 s to set up a telephone call, the average call lasts for 5 to 7 minutes (min).

- *Narrow passband requirement:* As we have already seen, a 3.1-kHz passband is sufficient for human voice. Furthermore, increasing the bandwidth available for the voice call does not affect the duration of the call.

Data calls have different characteristics. They typically include:

- *Delay insensitive:* Most user data does not alter in meaning because of being delayed in the network for a few seconds; a packet containing temperature information from the bottom of Lake Champlain, for example, will not change in meaning because of a short delay in the network.

- *Short hold time:* Most data traffic is bursty; i.e., the bulk of the data is transmitted in a short period of time, such as in interactive applications. A 90-10 rule is often cited to demonstrate this: 90 percent of the data is transmitted in 10 percent of the time. Since data transmission will tend to be very fast, long call setup times yield inefficient networks.

- *Wide passband use:* Data can use all of a channel's available bandwidth; if additional bandwidth is made available for a data call, the duration of the call can decrease.

Figure 1.6 shows the general structure of a switched network. Hosts (end users) are connected to a network to gain communications pathways to each other. Nodes are switches within the network. In a switched network, the path between a pair of hosts is usually not fixed. Therefore, host 1 might connect to host 3 via nodes A, C, E, and D or via nodes A, B, and D.

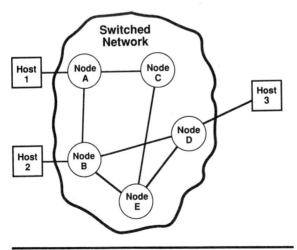

Figure 1.6 Components of a switched network.

In the telephone network, telephones could be considered hosts while switching offices are nodes. The network is switched because two end users do not have a permanent, dedicated path between them. Instead, a path is established on request and released at the end of the call. One primary difference between different types of switching networks is whether the physical path allocated through the network for a given call is shared with other calls or not.

1.3.1   Circuit Switching

Circuit switching is the most familiar type of switching to most people; the telephone network provides an excellent example of this type of network. In a circuit switched network, the communications pathway between two users is fixed for the duration of the call and is not shared by other users. Although several users may share one physical line by use of frequency division multiplexing, only one user is assigned to a single voiceband channel at any given time.

In circuit mode, a connection is obtained between two users by establishing a fixed pathway through the network. The route is established after the calling party initiates the call setup procedure by telling the network the address of the called party, i.e., after the user dials the telephone number.

The temporary connection through the network exists for the duration of the telephone call. During that period, the circuit is equivalent to a physical pair of wires connecting the two users. The physical circuit connection is dedicated to this call and is not shared by other users.

Circuit-mode connections are well suited for voice traffic. The dedicated pathway is required because of the delay-sensitive nature of voice calls. Also, the long call setup time is compensated for by the relatively long call hold time.

For similar reasons, circuit-mode connections are not as well suited for data calls. The bursty nature of data means that a long call setup procedure wastes time. Since the voice network is optimized for human voice, all channels are narrowband; again, this means that data calls will have a longer duration. Furthermore, dedicating a channel to bursty traffic means that the channel is idle much of the time. While data may be (and is) carried over circuit switched facilities, it is an inefficient use of those facilities and not optimal for data transmission.

1.3.2   Packet Switching

Packet switching was first described for data communications in the early 1960s. With it, there is no dedicated physical connection between two users; instead, users submit their messages to the network for delivery to another user. The connection between users, then, is logical rather than physical. Since physical channels are not dedicated to a specific end-to-end connection, they may be shared by many end-to-end logical connections. In this way, packet switching optimizes use of network resources by ensuring that needed physical channels are never idle, except in the absence of traffic. Packet switching is suitable only for delay-insensitive traffic. .

In packet switched networks, user messages are subdivided into units for transmission called *packets*. A packet has a fixed maximum size, usually 128 or 256 octets. The receiver has the responsibility to reassemble the original message from the incoming packets.

A packet-mode connection defines a logical pathway between two hosts through the packet network but does not dedicate any physical facilities to that connection. In this way, several packet-mode connections can share the physical resources, optimizing use of the network resources. When packets are received by a node, they are placed in buffers and sent on to the next node in the path at the next available opportunity. Having multiple users share a physical resource on an as-needed basis is a type of statistical time division multiplexing.

A potential problem with statistical TDM is that some transmissions will be delayed. For example, if two packets are ready for transmission on the same physical line at the same time, the node will send one of them and buffer (store) the other one. The delay is not a problem for data, however, since data is delay insensitive. Delay-sensitive applications, however, cannot use this scheme.

Packets are sent to a network node by the user (host) and then are forwarded through the network from node to node until they are delivered to the destination host. As we observed above, the transmitting node must store the packet until it can forward it to the next node. For this reason, packet switching is called a *store-and-forward* strategy.

When two hosts communicate over a packet switched network (PSN), they have a virtual circuit between them defining the logical host-to-host connection. A virtual circuit connection means that while packets are guaranteed to be delivered to the destination and to be delivered in sequence, no physical lines are dedicated to the connection between the two hosts. Even though all packets associated with a virtual circuit probably follow the same route through the network, no user "owns" a physical line. For example, in Fig. 1.6, a virtual circuit between host 1 and host 3 and a virtual circuit between host 2 and host 3 might well share the physical path between nodes B and D.

1.4 OPEN SYSTEMS INTERCONNECTION REFERENCE MODEL

During the 1960s and 1970s, companies such as Burroughs, Digital Equipment Corporation (DEC), Honeywell, and IBM defined network communications protocols for their computer products. Because of the proprietary nature of the protocols, however, the interconnection of computers from different manufacturers or even between different product lines from the same manufacturer was very difficult.

In the late 1970s, the International Organization for Standardization (ISO) developed the Reference Model for Open Systems Interconnection (OSI). The OSI model comprises a seven-layer architecture which will be the basis for open network systems of the future, allowing computers from any vendor to communicate with each other.

The goals of the OSI model are to expedite communication between equipment built by different manufacturers and to make applications independent of the hardware on which they operate. The layering of the OSI model provides transparency; that is, the operation of a single layer of the model is independent of the other layers.

Figure 1.7 shows the seven layers of the OSI model. Peer layers across the network communicate using *protocols*; adjacent layers in the same machine communicate via an *interface*. Network architectures (such as ISDN) specify the function of the layers, the protocol procedures for peer-to-peer communication, and the communication across the interface between adjacent protocol layers. Actual implementations and algorithms are not typically specified.

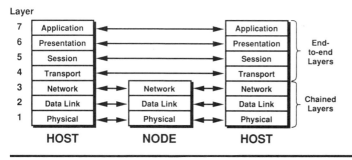

Figure 1.7   OSI Reference Model.

The lower three layers of the OSI model are:

- *Physical layer (layer 1):*   Specifies the electrical and mechanical characteristics of the protocol used to transfer bits between two adjacent devices in the network; common examples include EIA-232-D (formerly RS-232-C), V.24, and V.35.

Data link layer (layer 2): Specifies the protocol for error-free communication between adjacent devices across the physical link; common examples include IBM's Binary Synchronous Communications (BISYNC) and Synchronous Data Link Control (SDLC) protocols, DEC's Digital Data Communication Message Protocol (DDCMP), ISO's High-level Data Link Control (HDLC), and CCITT's Link Access Procedures Balanced (LAPB) and Link Access Procedures on the D-channel (LAPD).

- *Network layer (layer 3):* Specifies protocols for such functions as routing, congestion control, accounting, call setup and termination, and user-network communications.

The lower three layers of the OSI model are called the chained layers and comprise procedure for host-to-node and node-to-node communication. End users (hosts), as well as all switching devices (nodes) along the route between the hosts, must implement these protocol layers.

The upper four layers of the OSI model are:

- *Transport layer (layer 4):* Specifies the protocols and classes of service for error-free communication between hosts across the subnetwork

- *Session layer (layer 5):* Specifies process-to-process communication, error recovery, and session synchronization

- *Presentation layer (layer 6):* A set of general, non-application-specific user services relating to the presentation of user data, such as encryption and text compression

- *Application layer (layer 7):* Specifies the user interface to the network and a set of specific user applications, such as electronic mail and message handling systems, directory services, distributed transaction processing, virtual terminal emulation, network management, and file transfer services.

The upper four layers are called the end-to-end layers since they are implemented only in hosts. End-to-end information is transparent to the lower protocol layers.

1.4.1 Packet Switching and X.25

The CCITT standard ISDN protocols comprise only the chained layers. While an ISDN itself can provide many types of services using many types of protocols, the ISDN user-network interface is designed to be a common set of protocols for user access to the network, regardless of the required service. Therefore, the ISDN protocols comprising the user-network interface are only implemented at layers 1 through 3. These protocols are discussed in more detail in Chaps. 4 through 6.

CCITT Recommendation X.25 defines the interface between a user and a packet switched public data network (PSPDN). User hosts are called data terminal equipment (DTE) and the network nodes are called data circuit-terminating equipment (DCE). X.25 is very important to ISDNs; packet switching will be supported by ISDNs and X.25 is the most widely used packet switching protocol today. Recommendation X.25 defines three layers of protocols corresponding to a user-network interface:

- *Layer 1:*   Exchange bits between the DTE and DCE; the physical layer specified by X.25 is based on Recommendations X.21 and X.21 *bis.*

- *Layer 2:*   Ensures error-free communication between the DTE and DCE; the X.25 data link layer protocol is the Link Access Procedures Balanced (LAPB).

- *Layer 3:*   Provides rules for the establishment of virtual calls and the ability to have several simultaneous virtual calls on a single physical channel between the DTE and DCE; this Protocol is called the Packet Layer Protocol (PLP).

CCITT Recommendation X.75 is very similar to X.25. Originally written for internetworking between PSPDNs, it has taken on a more general role for internetworking many types of packet networks, including PSPDNs, ISDNs, and LANs.

This book will not specifically discuss packet switching or Recommendation X.25. A basic understanding of the X.25 architecture and packet switching, however, will enhance understanding of ISDN packet-mode operations.

2

ISDN Terms, Definitions, and Standards

An ISDN is a digital network that can provide many types of services to a user. The real thrust of the ISDN standards is not how the network operates but how the user communicates with the network and accesses network services. ISDN standards, then, define the interface between the user and the network. This interface is in the form of a set of protocols, including a message set used to request services.

Most people have heard many of the common terms used to describe ISDN, such as D-channel, B-channel, 2B + D, 23B + D, basic rate, primary rate, NT1, etc. This chapter will introduce and define many of the terms used in the standards, literature, and in vendors' ISDN product and service descriptions.

The use of these terms in this book is not intended to confuse or intimidate the reader. On the contrary, the terms have rather precise meanings and facilitate discussion about the network, its components, and its services. The concepts of ISDN are actually quite straightforward except for the new language that has been introduced to discuss them.

ISDN cannot succeed as a global communications strategy without standards. This chapter will conclude with a brief introduction to the organizations responsible for creating U.S. and international ISDN standards. It is impossible to understand any of the ISDN compatibility issues without some knowledge of the players in the ISDN standards game.

2.1 ISDN CHANNELS

In data communications, a *channel* is a conduit through which information flows. A channel can carry digital or analog signals comprising user data or network signaling information.

In today's telephone network, the local loop connection between the user and central office provides a single analog channel, used for different types of information. First, the loop is used to carry signals between the user's equipment and the network. The telephone, for example, places a current on the line to indicate that the handset has been taken off-hook. A dial tone from the network signals the user to enter the telephone number. Pulses or tones representing the dialed number, busy signals, and ringing signals also appear over the local loop. Second, the loop carries user information, which may be voice, audio, video, or binary data, depending upon the application. These two types of information flow could be said to represent two logical channels, one for signaling and one for user services.

In an ISDN, the local loop will only carry digital signals. Furthermore, the ISDN local loop will comprise several logical channels for signaling and user data. There are three basic types of channels defined for ISDN communications, differentiated by their function and bit rate (Table 2.1):

- *D-channel:* Carries signals between the user and the network; may also carry user data packets

- *B-channel:* Carries information for user services, including voice, audio, video, and digital data; operates at the DS-0 rate (64 kbps)

- *H-channel:* Same function as B-channels, but operates at bit rates above DS-0

The following sections describe these channels in more detail.

2.1.1 The D-Channel

All ISDN devices attach to the network using a standard physical connector and exchange similar messages with the network to request

TABLE 2.1   ISDN Channel Types

Channel	Purpose	Bit Rate
B	Bearer services	64 kbps
D	Signaling and packet mode data	16 kbps (BRI) 64 kbps (PRI)
H_0	Six B-channels	384 kbps
H_1	All available H_0 channels H_{11} (24B) H_{12} (30B)	1.536 Mbps 1.920 Mbps
H_2	Broadband ISDN (proposed) H_{21} H_{22}	32.768 Mbps 43-45 Mbps
H_4	Broadband ISDN (proposed)	132-138.240 Mbps

service. The contents of the signaling messages vary with the device type; an ISDN telephone, for example, will request different services than an ISDN television. User equipment exchanges service requests and other signaling messages with the network over the ISDN D-channel.

The D-channel's primary function is to carry user-network signaling messages. Since the exchange of signaling messages is unlikely to use all of the available bandwidth on the D-channel, extra bandwidth is available for users' packet data. Carrying packet-mode data is the secondary function of the D-channel.

The D-channel operates at either 16 or 64 kbps, depending upon the user's access interface, which is discussed below.

2.1.2   The B-Channel

Signals exchanged on the D-channel describe the characteristics of the service that the user is requesting. For example, an ISDN telephone may request a circuit-mode connection operating at 64 kbps for the support of a speech application. This profile of characteristics describes what is called a *bearer service*. Bearer services are granted by allocating a bearer channel, or B-channel.

The primary purpose of the B-channel, then, is to carry the user's voice, audio, data, and video signals. No service requests from the user are sent on the B-channel. B-channels always operate at 64 kbps, the bit rate required for digital voice applications.

The B-channel can be used for both circuit switching and packet switching applications. A circuit-mode connection can provide a transparent user-to-user connection or a connection specifically suited to one type of service (e.g., television or music). Packet-mode connections can support packet switching equipment using protocols such as CCITT Recommendation X.25.

The most important point to remember with respect to the use of the B- and D-channels is that devices use the D-channel to exchange signaling messages necessary to request services on the B-channel.

2.1.3   H-Channels

A user service with a bit rate higher than 64 kbps may be obtained by requesting higher-rate channels, or H-channels, which provide the bandwidth equivalent to a group of B-channels. Applications requiring bit rates above 64 kbps include fast facsimile, high-speed data, high-quality audio, teleconferencing, and video services.

The first step above a single B-channel is an H_0-channel, which has a data rate of 384 kbps, the equivalent bandwidth of six B-channels. An H_1-channel comprises all available H_0-channels across a single interface (operating at the T1 or E1 rate). An H_{11}-channel operates at 1.536 Mbps and is equivalent to four H_0-channels (24 B-channels) for compatibility with the North American digital hierarchy (T1 rate). An H_{12}-channel operates at 1.920 Mbps and is equivalent to five H_0-channels (30 B-channels) for compatibility with the CEPT digital hierarchy (E1 rate).

Future ISDN standards will define channels with even higher bit rates for broadband ISDN (B-ISDN) applications. B-ISDN channels are those that operate at speeds greater than H_1 rates. H_2- and H_4-channels have been proposed in CCITT recommendations.

The proposed H_2-channels will operate in the range of 32 to 45 Mbps and are roughly equivalent to the level 3 signaling rates of the digital hierarchies described earlier. For compatibility with the CEPT level 3 signaling rate of 34.368 Mbps, an H_{21}-channel has been proposed that will operate at 32.768 Mbps. For compatibility with the North American DS-3 rate of 44.736 Mbps, an H_{22}-channel is proposed that will operate in the range of 43 to 45 Mbps. The proposed H_4-channel rate will be in the range of 132 to 138.24 Mbps.

2.2 ISDN ACCESS INTERFACES

The concept of an access interface is a familiar one to most users of today's networks. Most residences, for example, have a single-line telephone and, accordingly, a single connection to the local central office. This single local loop can be said to comprise two logical channels, as described earlier, one for user-network signals and one for user data.

If a customer wants additional telephone lines, additional physical resources are brought out to the customer's site. A second local loop, for example, will provide a second phone line, or a trunk circuit can provide multiple lines between a customer's private branch exchange (PBX) and the C.O. Access to other networks and/or network services (e.g., a packet or telex network) can be provided by bringing additional lines to the customer's premises.

ISDN access interfaces differ somewhat from today's access interfaces. First, one goal of ISDN is to provide all services over a single network access connection, independent of the equipment or service type. Second, ISDN access interfaces comprise a D-channel for signaling and some number of B-channels for user data. This design allows multiple information flows simultaneously on a single physical interface and allows users to switch between the available services on demand.

ISDN standards currently define two different access interfaces to the network, called the basic rate interface (BRI) and primary rate interface (PRI). These access interfaces specify the rate at which the physical medium will operate and the number of available B-, D-, and H-channels (Table 2.2).

2.2.1 Basic Rate Interface

The BRI comprises two B-channels and one D-channel and is designated 2B + D. The BRI D-channel always operates at 16 kbps.

The BRI will typically be used in one of two ways. First, it can provide ISDN access between the residential customer and the ISDN central office. Alternatively, it can provide ISDN access between user equipment and an ISDN-compatible PBX in a business environment.

The user data rate on the BRI is 144 kbps (2 × 64 kbps + 16 kbps), although additional signaling for the physical connection requires that the BRI operate at a total bit rate of 192 kbps.

2.2.2 Primary Rate Interface

The PRI has a number of possible configurations. The most common designation in North America is 23B + D, meaning that the interface comprises 23 B-channels plus a single D-channel operating at 64 kbps. Optionally, the D-channel at a given interface may not be activated, allowing that time slot to be used as another B-channel, 24B. The 23B + D PRI is based upon the North American digital carrier hierarchy. It operates at a total bit rate of 1.544 Mbps (designated by the CCITT as 1544 kbps), of which 1.536 Mbps is user data.

A 30B + D PRI is also defined, based upon the CEPT digital hierarchy. This interface comprises 30 B-channels and a 64-kbps D-channel. It operates at 2.048 Mbps (designated by the CCITT as 2048 kbps), of which 1.984 Mbps is user data.

The PRI contains more channels than a typical end-user device can use. The PRI is, in fact, intended to provide access to the network by

TABLE 2.2   ISDN Basic and Primary Rate Interfaces

Interface	Structure	Total Bit Rate	User Data Rate
Basic Rate Interface (BRI)	2B + D$_{16}$	192 kbps	144 kbps
Primary Rate Interface (PRI)	23B + D$_{64}$ 30B + D$_{64}$	1.544 Mbps 2.048 Mbps	1.536 Mbps 1.984 Mbps

some sort of customer premises switching equipment, such as a PBX or host computer.

2.3 ISDN FUNCTIONAL DEVICES AND REFERENCE POINTS

Different devices may be present in the connection between customer premises equipment (CPE) and the network to which the CPE is attached. Consider the relatively simple example of a customer's connection to the telephone network. All of the subscriber's telephones are connected to a junction box in the customer's building; the local loop provides the physical connection between the junction box and the network switch. As far as the customer is concerned, the CPE is communicating directly with the switch; the junction box is transparent.

Other equipment may also be present. If a PC is attached to the telephone network, for example, a modem will replace the telephone. If the customer has a PBX, the telephones and modems will attach to the PBX, which will provide on-site switching; the PBX is, in turn, connected to the central office switch.

Protocols describe the rules governing communication between devices in a network. With all of the possible devices mentioned here, questions arise as to which protocols are to be used where and who is responsible for defining the protocols. The telephone, for example, uses a familiar protocol that is specified by the network; certain current represents the off-hook signal, special pulses or tones represent the dialed digits, etc.

A modem follows the same protocol as a telephone on the side that connects to the telephone network. It uses a different protocol, however, on the side that connects to a PC; EIA-232-D, and the Hayes command set, for example, are commonly used between a PC and external modem. The modem acts as a protocol converter so that signals output from the PC will be suitable for the analog telephone network.

The presence of a PBX adds another level of complexity. A telephone connected to a PBX follows protocols specified by the PBX manufacturer, which is why many PBX-specific telephones are not usable on the public telephone network. The PBX, in turn, must use network-specified protocols for the PBX-to-network communication.

These same ideas are extended to ISDN. The ISDN standards define several different types of devices. Each device type has certain functions and responsibilities but may not represent an actual physical piece of equipment. For that reason, the standards call them *functional devices*.

Since the ISDN recommendations describe several functional device types, there are several device-to-device interfaces, each requiring a communications protocol. Each of these device interfaces is called a *reference point.*

The paragraphs below describe the different functional devices and reference points, which are shown in Figure 2.1.

2.3.1 ISDN Functional Devices

The ISDN central office is called the local exchange (LE). ISDN protocols are implemented in the LE, which is also the network side of the ISDN local loop. Other LE responsibilities include maintenance, physical interface operation, and providing requested user services.

Some manufacturers further break down the functions of the LE into two subgroups called local termination (LT) and exchange termination (ET). The LT handles those functions associated with the termination of the local loop, while the ET handles switching functions. For simplicity and generality, this book will usually refer only to the LE and avoid specific references to LT or ET except where necessary.

Network termination type 1 (NT1) equipment represents the termination of the physical connection between the customer site and the LE. Line performance monitoring, timing, power transfer, and the multiplexing of the B- and D-channels are the responsibility of the NT1.

Network termination type 2 (NT2) equipment are those devices providing customer site switching, multiplexing, and concentration. This includes PBXs, LANs, mainframe computers, terminal controllers, and other CPE for voice and data switching. An NT2 will be absent in some ISDN environments, such as residential ISDN service.

Terminal equipment (TE) are end-user devices, such as an analog or

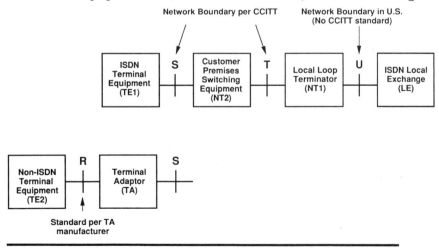

Figure 2.1 ISDN functional devices and reference points.

digital telephone, X.25 data terminal equipment (DTE), ISDN workstation, or integrated voice/data terminal (IVDT). Terminal equipment type 1 (TE1) are those devices that use the ISDN protocols and support ISDN services, such as an ISDN telephone or workstation. Terminal equipment type 2 (TE2) are non-ISDN-compatible devices, such as an analog telephone in use on today's telephone network.

A terminal adaptor (TA) allows a non-ISDN device (TE2) to communicate with the network. TAs have particular importance in today's ISDN marketplace; nearly every device in use in today's data and telecommunications environment is TE2. TAs allow analog telephones, X.25 DTEs, PCs, and other non-ISDN devices to use the network by providing any necessary protocol conversion.

The reader should note that a single physical piece of equipment can take on the responsibilities of two or more of the functional devices defined here. For example, a PBX might actually perform NT1 (local loop termination) and NT2 (customer site switching) functions; this combination is sometimes referred to as NT12.

2.3.2   ISDN Reference Points

The previous paragraphs describe ISDN functional devices. The ISDN reference points define the communication between the different devices. The importance of the different reference points is that different protocols may be used at each reference point. Four protocol reference points are commonly defined for ISDN, called R, S, T, and U.

The R reference point is between non-ISDN terminal equipment (TE2) and a terminal adaptor. The TA will allow the TE2 to appear to the network as an ISDN device, just as a modem allows a terminal or PC to communicate over today's telephone network. There are no set standards for the R reference point; the TA manufacturer determines how the TE2 and TA communicate with each other. Existing public standards, such as EIA-232-D (formerly RS-232-C) or V.35, or proprietary solutions, such as placing a board inside of a PC or terminal, may be used.

The S reference point is between the ISDN user equipment (i.e., TE1 or TA) and the network termination equipment (NT2 or NT1). The T reference point is between customer site switching equipment (NT2) and the local loop termination (NT1). CCITT ISDN recommendations specifically address protocols for the S and T reference points. In the absence of the NT2, the user-network interface is usually called the S/T reference point.

One of the most controversial aspects of ISDN between 1984 and 1988 was the definition of the transmission standard across the local loop between the NT1 and the LE, called the U reference point. The

CCITT considers the physical NT1 device to be owned by the network administration; that makes the local loop part of the network. Therefore, the CCITT views the S and T reference points as the user-network boundary. CCITT recommendations do not address internal network operations, so they have no standard for transmission across the local loop.[1]

The U.S. Federal Communications Commission (FCC), however, does not adopt this view about the local loop. Since the NT1 is on the customer's site, the FCC considers it to be CPE. Since network equipment (the LE) is on one side of the U reference point and user equipment (the NT1) is on the other, it is clearly the local loop that represents the user-network boundary according to the FCC. Furthermore, operation across the user-network boundary in the United States must be described by a public standard and, in fact, is the subject of a U.S. national standard from the American National Standards Institute (ANSI). Since the CCITT has not created any recommendations for this connection, the ANSI U reference point standard may well have international significance.

Although not shown in the figure or described further in this book, some manufacturers define a V reference point between the LT and ET within the local exchange. This reference point is an implementation-dependent feature of the C.O. switch that is transparent to the user and will not be discussed further in this book.

2.4 ISDN STANDARDS ORGANIZATIONS

2.4.1 The CCITT

The organization primarily responsible for producing ISDN standards is the International Telegraph and Telephone Consultative Committee (CCITT, or Comité Consultatif International Télégraphique et Téléphonique). The CCITT is one of the committees operating under the auspices of the International Telecommunication Union (ITU), an agency of the United Nations. Although the United Nations dates back only to 1945, the CCITT and ITU can trace their formal beginnings back as far as the mid-1860s.

The work of the CCITT is performed by 15 study groups (SGs) (Table 2.3). Standards, called Recommendations, are formally adopted at plenary sessions held every four years and are published in a set of books that are referred to by the color of their cover; 1988 recommendations are contained in the Blue Books, 1984 in the Red Books, 1980 in the Yellow Books, and 1976 in the Orange Books, for example. The

---

[1]In fact, the CCITT does not refer to the U reference point; they mention the R, S, and T reference points and the *transmission line*.

CCITT STUDY GROUPS

Designation	Title
I	Definition, operation and quality of service aspects of telegraph, data transmission and telematic services
II	Operation of telephone network and ISDN
III	General tariff principles including accounting
IV	Transmission maintenance of international lines, circuits and chains of circuits; maintenance of automatic and semi-automatic networks
V	Protection against dangers and disturbances of electromagnetic origin
VI	Outside plant
VII	Data communications networks
VIII	Terminal equipment for telematic services
IX	Telegraph networks and terminal equipment
X	Languages and methods for telecommunications applications
XI	ISDN and telephone network switching and signaling
XII	Transmission performance of telephone networks and terminals
XV	Transmission systems
XVII	Data transmission over the telephone network
XVIII	Digital networks including ISDN

official U.S. representative to the CCITT is the State Department, although many other organizations have representatives at the various working group meetings including network providers, switch manufacturers, equipment vendors, and user groups.

CCITT Study Group XVIII has responsibility for digital networks including ISDN. Among other things, they are responsible for writing the I-series recommendations defining ISDN and specifying appropriate services and protocols. Figure 2.2 shows the general organization of the I-series recommendations. CCITT I-series and other ISDN-related recommendations are listed in App. B of this book.

CCITT involvement with ISDN started over 20 years ago. In 1968, a CCITT study group meeting convened to discuss the integration of switching and transmission. The meeting was so successful that the CCITT formed a special study group devoted to this topic (Study Group Special D), which later became Study Group XVIII.

Study Group D dealt with integrated digital networks (IDN) and integrated services networks (ISN); the former is a network that contains digital switches and transmission facilities from end to end and the latter is a network that offers many types of services from a single

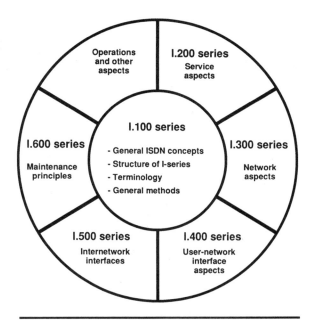

Figure 2.2 Organization of CCITT I-series (ISDN) recommendations.

network. In 1971, another CCITT meeting was convened to discuss these terms. Several countries wanted the word *digital* added to the ISN term since integrated services can, conceivably, be offered by an analog network, which was not the subject of Study Group XVIII's work. Other countries felt that integration of services was only feasible in a digital environment, thus adding the word was redundant. The compromise was to coin the term *integrated services (digital) network*. Eventually the parentheses were dropped, yielding the term that we have today.

Under the direction of Study Group XVIII, CCITT leadership in organizing and developing ISDN standards grew. The first set of ISDN recommendations were formally published in 1984 (Red Books), followed by updated standards in 1988 (Blue Books).

Other CCITT study groups also participate in the ISDN standards process. For example, Study Group VII is responsible for data communications networks (X-series recommendations) and Study Group XI deals with ISDN and telephone network switching and signaling (Q-series recommendations). For this reason, several I-series recommendations are also assigned Q-, X-, or other series' recommendation numbers. Support of X.25 terminals on an ISDN, for example, is described in both Recommendation I.462 and Recommendation X.31;

these two standards are identical. Similarly, ISDN signaling messages on the D-channel are listed as both Recommendations I.451 and Q.931.

In this book, CCITT recommendations will be referred to by the series and number where they are actually published. An I-series or other designation, if any, will be given in parentheses.

2.4.2 ANSI

As mentioned earlier, CCITT recommendations do not address all aspects of ISDN. In particular, the local loop operation (U reference point) for the BRI is not the topic of any CCITT recommendation; it is addressed in the United States by the American National Standards Institute (ANSI). ANSI itself does not create standards but rather coordinates and sanctions the activities of appropriate organizations that do write standards. The organization accredited by ANSI to produce the U.S. National Standards for Telecommunications (ANSI T1-series) is the Exchange Carriers' Standards Association (ECSA).

Perhaps the best-known ANSI ISDN standards body was the T1D1 subcommittee. The T1 committee was reorganized in early 1988 and the T1D1 subcommittee was disbanded; the current structure of the T1 committee is shown in Table 2.4. The former T1D1.1 (Architecture and Services) and T1D1.2 (Switching and Signaling Protocols) task

TABLE 2.4   Organization of the ANSI T1 Committee

Subcommittee	Responsibility
T1E1 Network Interfaces	T1E1.1: Analog Access T1E1.2: Wideband Access T1E1.3: Connector and Wiring Assignments T1E1.4: Digital Subscriber Loop (DSL) Access T1E1.5: Editorial
T1M1 Internetwork Operations, Administration, Maintenance and Provisioning	T1M1.1: Internetwork Planning and Engineering T1M1.2: Internetwork Operations T1M1.3: Testing and Operations Support Systems and Equipment T1M1.5: OAM & P Architectures, Interfaces and Protocols
T1Q1 Performance	T1Q1.1: 4 kHz Voice and Voiceband Data T1Q1.3: Digital Packet and ISDNs T1Q1.4: Digital Circuit T1Q1.5: Wideband Program
T1S1 Services, Architectures and Signaling	T1S1.1: Architecture and Services T1S1.2: Switching and Signaling Protocols T1S1.3: Common Channel Signaling T1S1.4: Individual Channel Signaling
T1X1 Digital Hierarchy and Synchronization	T1X1.3: Synchronization Interfaces T1X1.4: Metallic Hierarchical Interfaces T1X1.5: Optical Hierarchical Interfaces T1X1.6: Tributary Analysis
T1Y1 Specialized Subjects	T1Y1.1: Specialized Video and Audio Services T1Y1.2: Specialized Voice and Data Processing T1Y1.4: Environmental Stds. for Exchange and Interexchange Networks

groups were moved into the T1S1 subcommittee, and T1D1.3 (ISDN physical layer) was renamed and renumbered as T1E1.4. U.S. national ISDN standards are published in the T1.600-series.

2.4.3   Other Standards Organizations

The International Organization for Standardization (ISO) creates standards in many areas. In networking, ISO standards include the OSI Reference Model, the High-level Data Link Control (HDLC) bit-oriented protocol, international LAN standards, and OSI protocols. ANSI is the U.S. representative to ISO.

In the United States, AT&T has long published standards for manufacturers wanting to interface their equipment to the public telephone network. Although local telephone service is no longer offered by AT&T, they manufacture the majority of C.O. switches used by the local telephone companies in the United States today. AT&T technical bulletins and other publications remain industry standards for both local telephone service from the C.O. and long distance services via AT&T's toll network. AT&T continues to play an important role in ANSI and CCITT standards development.

After the breakup of AT&T, Bell Communications Research (Bellcore) was formed as the research and development arm of the seven Regional Bell Operating Companies (RBOCs) in the United States. Bellcore participates in the ANSI and CCITT standards process and also defines implementation standards and requirements for the BOCs. They produce Technical Advisory documents (TA-series) which, after industry review, become Technical Requirements (TR-series) for implementation. The United States Telephone Association (USTA) performs a somewhat similar function for the independent telephone companies in the United States.

The National Institute for Standards and Technology (NIST), formerly the National Bureau of Standards (NBS), has taken a lead role in North America for defining ISDN applications. NIST sponsors periodic meetings to guide manufacturers in creating standards for applications that are of most interest to users.

Other organizations also create ISDN standards, although some of those standards are proprietary and/or network specific. MCI, U.S. Sprint, Northern Telecom, Siemens, GTE, and others, for example, are creating ISDN standards for their products. These organizations also actively participate in the creation of public ISDN standards.

3

ISDN Services

The evolution of the telephone network over the last hundred years has been driven by the need to provide voice services. Telephone switches and transmission facilities, using the available technology, were analog in nature. Thus, the telephone network and voice service were well suited for each other.

Computers changed this since they produce digital signals that are not well suited for an analog network. With the invention of the transistor, integrated circuits, and microprocessors, digital control has become a part of all facets of life. Over the last 20 years, the price of everything digital has dropped tremendously in products ranging from computers to watches to digital stereos.

Inexpensive, yet highly reliable, digital components have led to digital telephone switches and transmission lines. Falling prices of digital equipment, coupled with the better use of bandwidth and higher reliability, led to the evolution toward a digital telephone network. The increased number of services that can be provided by this digital network is the impetus behind ISDN.

From the customer's viewpoint, a fully digital network can provide a myriad of user services since all devices attached to the network merely send bits (Fig. 3.1). Digital technology is not limited to the telephone network or to the telephone companies; it has found its way into the business and residential environments as well. The Business Model uses a point-to-point primary rate interface. A private branch exchange (PBX) provides the business customer with a local distribution system and the potential to connect many users to a private local network as well as to the public wide area ISDN. The Residential Model uses a point-to-multipoint basic rate interface. This would allow residential customers to have two simultaneous B-channel connections providing multiple service operations, such as viewing a pic-

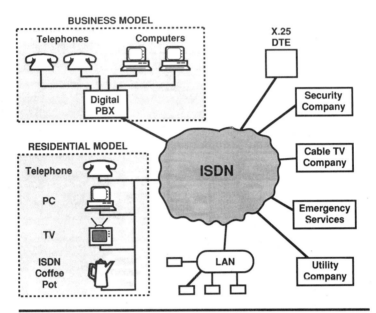

Figure 3.1   Services available from an ISDN.

ture of suites in a hotel on the television while talking over the telephone to the travel agent. As applications and new ISDN devices evolve, the customers' requirements from the communications network will also evolve.

3.1 SERVICE REQUIREMENTS

An ISDN must have many capabilities to be able to handle the different services expected of it, some of which are not available on today's network. The network must have the ability to:

- Handle voice, audio, interactive or bulk data, facsimile, compressed video, and full-motion video
- Efficiently transport both continuous traffic (e.g., bulk data, voice, video, and facsimile) and bursty traffic (e.g., interactive data)
- Allocate bandwidth on a demand basis
- Allow fast call establishment and termination
- Handle a wide range of transmission speeds and call hold times
- Guarantee low bit error rates, low end-to-end message delay, and low message misdelivery and nondelivery rates
- Provide various levels of communication security

TABLE 3.1   Residential Service Requirements

Service	Required Bandwidth	ISDN Channel Type			Switching Facility		
		B	H	D	Circuit Switched	Packet Switched	Channel Switched
Telephone	8, 16, 32, 64 kbps	•			•		
Alarm systems	10-100 bps			•		•	
Utility metering	0.1-1 kbps			•	•	•	
Energy management	0.1-1 kbps			•	•	•	
Interactive information svcs.	4.8-64 kbps	•		•		•	
Electronic mail	4.8-64 kbps	•		•		•	
Broadcast video	96 Mbps		•				•
Switched video	96 Mbps		•				•
Interactive video	96 Mbps		•		•		•

Tables 3.1 and 3.2 list some of the anticipated service requirements for residences and businesses. Each listed service identifies bandwidth requirements, applicability of the B-, H-, or D-channels, and switching facility requirements.

Alarms, metering, and energy management are telemetry services that could easily be accomplished using a packet network. Rather than having someone walk house to house every 3 months to read the water meter, for example, would it not be simpler (and cheaper and more accurate) for the water department to send an electronic "read water meter" message to every house? This service could also allow utility companies to measure large resource users on a real-time basis and dynamically react to anticipated surpluses and shortfalls. Alarms could be tied into the network to send appropriate messages for different types of emergencies, automatically summoning fire, police, or medical assistance. Interactive information services provide some value-added service, above and beyond the mere transport of bits. This

TABLE 3.2   Business Service Requirements

Service	Required Bandwidth	ISDN Channel Type			Switching Facility		
		B	H	D	Circuit Switched	Packet Switched	Channel Switched
Telephone	8, 16, 32, 64 kbps	•			•		
Interactive data communications	4.8-64 kbps	•		•		•	
Electronic mail	4.8-64 kbps	•		•		•	
Bulk data transfer	4.8-64 kbps	•			•		
Facsimile/graphics	4.8-64 kbps	•			•		
Slow scan TV	56-64 kbps	•			•		
Videoconferencing	1.544 Mbps		•				•

could include such services as electronic banking, electronic yellow pages, and opinion polling.

The requirements listed above almost all refer to the ability of an ISDN to provide a large set of digital services, much like the services of today's networks. One advantage of the ISDN strategy is that all of the services can be offered from a single network.

An additional important ISDN service is that of incoming call management. Services such as call forwarding, call waiting, and acceptance of reverse charging can be tailored by a customer based upon the calling party's telephone number. These call management features are not really new since customers may subscribe to many of these features today. In the ISDN environment, however, call management capabilities that are currently available only in the C.O. will be brought out to the customer and will operate under the user's control.

3.2   ISDN SERVICES AND ATTRIBUTES

As alluded to earlier, an ISDN user device obtains a bearer channel by requesting service over the D-channel. When a user requests a particular service from the network, the request message over the D-channel contains a set of parameters identifying the desired service.

ISDN services are categorized based upon their scope and the source of the service (Fig. 3.2). *Bearer services* are those that allow the user to send information from one device on the network to another. They allow information transfer and involve only lower layer functions (i.e., layers 1 through 3 of the OSI model).

The users may agree between each other to use any higher-layer protocol(s) across the requested connection. Use of higher layers is transparent to the ISDN and the network makes no effort to assure compatibility between the higher layers. For example, the language and topic of conversation could be considered higher-layer functions

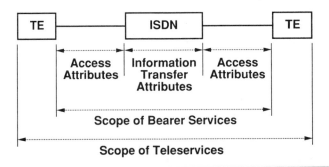

Figure 3.2   Bearer and teleservices.

between two users of the telephone network. The network itself, however, has no knowledge of the language being spoken nor does it prevent an English-speaking user from calling a French-speaking user.

Teleservices are a value-added service provided by the network, above and beyond the mere transport of bits. Teleservices can provide end-to-end (user-to-user) communication and they are characterized by their lower-layer attributes (i.e., the bearer service) and higher-layer attributes (i.e., the value-added service). Examples of teleservices include facsimile, teletex, videotex, and message handling systems.

3.2.1 Bearer Services

Bearer services supported by an ISDN are described in CCITT Recommendation I.210 and the I.230-series recommendations. They are defined in terms of *access attributes, information transfer attributes,* and *general attributes.* Access attributes are those characteristics describing how a user accesses network functions or facilities. Information transfer attributes are those characteristics associated with the transfer of information across the network. General attributes describe other characteristics of the service, such as supplementary services, quality-of-service parameters, and internetworking.

The next several sections and Tables 3.3 through 3.5 list the set of information transfer, access, and general attributes defined by the CCITT. The tables look formidable because they show all possible attribute values, but these bearer services embody the essence of ISDN. The sections below will define all of the entries. Appropriate CCITT recommendations are listed to provide the reader with a source for more detailed information.

3.2.2 Information Transfer Attributes

Table 3.3 shows the seven information transfer attributes. These attributes describe characteristics of the connection between users across the ISDN.

Bearer services can be offered in one of two *information transfer modes,* circuit and packet. *Circuit mode* is analogous to a connection over a circuit switched network and provides a dedicated end-to-end connection for delay-sensitive applications, such as voice, audio, video, and real-time data. *Packet mode* is analogous to a connection via a packet switched data network. The discussion in Chap. 1 gives more details about circuit and packet switching.

The *information transfer rate* is the throughput required for the requested connection across the network. The rate is specified in bits per

TABLE 3.3   Bearer Service Information Transfer Attributes

Attribute	Possible values of attributes						
Information transfer attributes							
1. Information transfer mode	Circuit						Packet
2. Information transfer rate	Bit rate (kbps)						Throughput (packets/sec)
	64	2 x 64	384	1536	1920	Other values (FFS)	(FFS)
3. Information transfer capability	Unrestricted Digital Info.	Speech	3.1 kHz audio	7 kHz audio	15 kHz audio	Video	Other value (FFS)
4. Structure	8 kHz integrity	Service data unit integrity		TSSI	RDTD	Unstructured	
5. Establishment of communication	Demand		Reserved		Permanent		
6. Symmetry	Unidirectional		Bidirectional symmetric		Bidirectional asymmetric		
7. Communication configuration	Point-to-point		Multipoint		Broadcast (FFS)		

second for circuit-mode service and in packets per second for packet-mode service. Information transfer rates of 64, 384, 1536, and 1920 kbps correspond to B-, H_0-, H_{11}-, and H_{12}-channels, respectively. The 2 × 64-kbps service is intended for use on the BRI and allows a user to access both B-channels on a single call; it does not provide a single 128-kbps channel. Other circuit-mode bit rates, as well as the packet-mode throughput, are left for further study (FFS).

Information transfer capability refers to the type of information that is being transferred across the network. *Unrestricted digital information (UDI)* is a bit stream where any bit pattern may appear in an octet. UDI is the default for packet-mode transfer.[1]

Speech and *3.1-kHz audio* both describe a transfer capability using a single voice-grade channel. The reason for distinguishing between the two services is that it may be cost effective for the network to use compression and encoding techniques that are appropriate only for human speech. Nonspeech applications (e.g., use of a modem) of the voiceband use the bandwidth differently than voice does and might be rendered useless if the signal is altered using voice compression techniques. *Seven-* and *15-kHz audio* provide a similar quality voice service as that of commercial monaural and stereo radio stations, respectively. *Video* service is for visual information transfer; current channel speeds limit this service to slow-scan video and teleconferenc-

---

[1]Unrestricted digital information is the opposite of *restricted digital information (RDI)*, a 64-kbps bit stream where all-zero octets are not permitted. T1 carriers, for example, need to have a sufficient number of 1 bits so that frame synchronization is maintained. One common strategy to guarantee this minimum number of 1 bits is to set the eighth bit of every octet to 1; this approach, called *bit robbing*, yields an effective data rate of only 56 kbps over a 64-kbps channel. Bit robbing will not be necessary on 64-kbps "clear" ISDN channels, but RDI transfer capability is an ISDN service option to support this type of equipment for an interim period of time. An RDI bearer service was an option in the 1984 standards but was removed from the 1988 standards. Recommendation I.464 discusses support for RDI.

ing applications. Speech is the default information transfer capability for circuit-mode service; other capabilities are for further study.

The ISDN will provide a guarantee that transmitted data will be delivered to the destination; the *structure* attribute specifies the unit of transmission to which this guarantee applies. *Service data unit integrity* implies that the packet or message (i.e., the data unit of transmission) will be delivered to the destination in the same form as it was given to the network by the sender. *Data sequence integrity,* the network's guarantee that the data units will arrive in sequence, is for further study. Service data unit integrity is the default for packet mode.

Eight-kHz integrity means that all bits transmitted within a single 125-μs interval will be delivered within a corresponding 125-μs interval at the destination. Digital voice, for example, requires that a single sample be taken precisely every 125-μs (every 1/8000 s). This is the circuit-mode default structure.

Time slot sequence integrity (TSSI) applies to the 2 × 64-kbps access or any other service comprised of an aggregate of access channels. TSSI means that information is delivered at the receiving side in the same order as submitted at the transmitting side. *Restricted differential time delay (RDTD)* is typically used with 8-kHz integrity to further specify that information will be delivered to the receiving side within 50 milliseconds (ms) of being submitted at the transmitting side. *Unstructured* means that no structure is implied by the given service.

Establishment of communication describes when the requested service should be granted. *Demand* means that the user is requesting the service at the time that it is needed and that the network should grant the service immediately. This is analogous to the way in which a dial-up connection is established over today's telephone network and is the default value for this attribute.

Reserved means that a user can request a service and specify a later time that the service should actually be granted. One of the issues associated with the implementation of this option is what to do at the appointed time if all channels are busy; is the request dropped, does the network postpone the request until a channel is free, or does the network clear one of the in-use channels and reallocate that channel to this request?

Permanent establishment is analogous to a leased line. It provides the requested service for a subscribed period of time.

The *symmetry* attribute alludes to whether the flow of information is one way or two way and whether the speed in both directions is the same or not. *Unidirectional* means that transmission is one way, with no reverse communication; examples include TV and radio broadcasts. *Bidirectional* means that transmission can occur in both directions simultaneously. *Bidirectional symmetric* means that both users transmit at the same information transfer rate, as would be expected when two telephones are connected to each other. *Bidirectional asymmetric* means that the transfer rates are different in the two directions; for example, when one computer is sending huge data files to another computer but is only receiving occasional acknowledgments in reply.

The *communication configuration* describes the configuration of the connection between the end users of this service. *Point to point* describes a service involving two users, such as a simple telephone call. *Multipoint* describes a service initiated by one user to several other users, such as a conference call. *Broadcast* would allow a single user to transmit to a group of users; this option is for further study.

3.2.3 Access Attributes

Access attributes, shown in Table 3.4, describe the characteristics of the connection between a user and the network itself. These attributes, then, provide information about the channel type and protocols that a user will use to access the network. Access attributes provide no indication about how the network should carry the user's information or how the end-to-end connection should be established.

The first access attribute indicates the *access channel and rate* over which user access to the network should be granted. The user may request service on a D- (16 kbps for the BRI, 64 kbps for the PRI), B-, H_0-, H_{11}-, or H_{12}-channel; use of other channels is for further study.

There is some debate as to what types of services should be available on which channels. While the B-channel can be used for packet-mode transfers, many observers point out that this application is a waste of the B-channel's bandwidth. Packet switching is used for bursty traffic; why, then, dedicate a 64-kbps channel for intermittent use? At the same time, there is consideration by some vendors about the feasibility of using H-channels for wideband packet-mode services for high-speed, bulk data transfers.

TABLE 3.4   Bearer Service Access Attributes

Attribute	Possible values of attributes						
Access attributes							
8. Access channel and rate	D (16 kbps)	D (64 kbps)	B	H_0	H_{11}	H_{12}	Others (FFS)
9.1— Signaling access 9.3 protocol layers 1-3	I.430/I.431	LAPD	I.451		X.25 LAPB		X.25 PLP
	Rate adaption: I.461, I.462, I.463, I.465						
	Others (FFS)						
9.4— Information access 9.6 protocol layers 1-3	I.430/I.431	HDLC	LAPD		X.25 LAPB		X.25 PLP
	G.711 PCM	G.721 ADPCM	I.451 (FFS)				T.70 Telex/FAX
	Rate adaption: I.460, I.461, I.462, I.463, I.465						
	Others (FFS)						

Recall that the bearer service conforms to OSI *layers 1 through 3*. The access protocols describe which specific protocols may be used for the requested service. *Signaling access protocols* refer to those used for user-network signaling, while *information access protocols* are used for information exchange between users. The layers 1 through 3 protocols may be specified for each type of access and there are many options.

At the physical layer (layer 1), CCITT Recommendations I.430 and I.431 describe the frame formats, signaling, and electrical characteristics of the basic rate interface and primary rate interface, respectively. Chapter 4 describes these protocols in more detail.

Recommendation G.711 defines pulse code modulation (PCM), the digital voice coding scheme described in Chap. 1. Recall that there are two companding algorithms used to define the scale on the amplitude axis, called the µ-law and A-law. A telephone that uses one companding scheme will clearly not be usable on a network using the other scheme. Furthermore, when a µ-law network has a gateway to an A-law network (for international calls), it is the responsibility of the µ-law network to perform the µ-law-to-A-law conversion at its gateway. CCITT Recommendation G.711 describes both companding schemes, as well as the conversion from one to the other.

Recommendation G.721 describes adaptive differential pulse code modulation (ADPCM), a digital voice compression algorithm. ADPCM converts an 8-bit PCM sample to a 4-bit ADPCM code, meaning that voice can be transmitted at a rate of 32 kbps instead of 64 kbps.

Link Access Procedures on the D-channel, or the LAPD protocol, is the data link layer (OSI level 2) protocol used on the ISDN D-channel; it can also be used on the B-channel. Recommendation I.451 defines the level 3 protocol used on the D-channel to request user services. LAPD (also known as I.441 or Q.921) and I.451 (also designated Q.931) are described more in Chaps. 5 and 6, respectively.

Non-ISDN protocols may also be supported by the network:

- The X.25 LAPB protocol (layer 2) and/or Packet Layer Protocol (layer 3) may be used as signaling or information access protocols.

- The ISO HDLC bit-oriented protocol may also be used as a layer 2 information access protocol.

- CCITT Recommendation T.70 specifies a set of protocols supporting teletex and facsimile services; the T.70 Minimal Network Layer Protocol may be used as a layer 3 information access protocol.

Finally, Recommendations I.460, I.461, I.462, I.463, and I.465 specify the rate adaption and multiplexing algorithms for the B-channel. Rate adaption is described in more detail below.

It is important to note that the access attributes used by the calling party do not have to match the access attributes used by the called party. For example, a user with a μ-law telephone can talk to a user with an A-law telephone; it is the network that must perform the appropriate conversion. As another example, one packet-mode user might use a B-channel while the user at the other end of the virtual circuit might handle packet traffic over the D-channel. Access to the local exchange at one side of the connection is independent of the access to the LE at the other side.

3.2.4 General Attributes and Supplementary Services

General attributes, shown in Table 3.5, are used to further specify characteristics of an individual bearer service, such as supplementary services, quality of service, interworking, and other operational and commercial aspects of the service. Most of the general attributes have been left for further study, to be published in the 1992 recommendations. Progress was made in the 1985-1988 study period, however, on supplementary services. Some of the supplementary services have been defined in the 1988 recommendations, while others will be defined in subsequent versions.

Supplementary services are defined in the I.250-series recommendations and seven general categories of these services have been described so far. Supplementary services allow the network to provide a service to the user above and beyond the mere transport of bits. These services are based upon information already known to the network, such as the address of the calling party, and do not involve any conversion or modification of user-supplied data by the network. Therefore, supplementary services are not considered a value-added service nor do they provide end-to-end communication. Users can tailor their network access based upon information already known to the network and independent of data supplied by the other end user.

TABLE 3.5   **Bearer Service General Attributes**

Attribute	Possible values of attributes			
General attributes				
10. Supplementary services provided	Number Identification	Call Offering	Call Completion	Multiparty
	Community of Interest	Charging	Additional Information Transfer	
11. Quality of service	Under Study			
12. Interworking possibilities				
13. Operational and commercial aspects				

The supplementary services identified by the CCITT and described in Recommendation I.250 are briefly described in the following paragraphs.

Number Identification supplementary services are services based upon the presentation of the calling party's ISDN number to the called party. These services include:

- *Direct Dialing In (DDI):* Allows a user to call another user on an ISDN-compatible PBX or private network without operator assistance

- *Multiple Subscriber Number (MSN):* Allows multiple ISDN numbers to be assigned to a single ISDN interface (e.g., different telephone numbers all terminating at the same residence)

- *Calling Line Identification Presentation (CLIP):* Displays the calling party's ISDN number to the called party (also called automatic number identification, or ANI)

- *Calling Line Identification Restriction (CLIR):* Allows a calling party to restrict the display of the calling ISDN number to the called party

- *Connected Line Identification Presentation (COLP):* Provides the calling party with the ISDN number of the party to whom the caller is actually connected

- *Connected Line Identification Restriction (COLR):* Allows the connected party to restrict the display of its ISDN number to the calling party

- *Malicious Call Identification and Sub-Addressing:* Identified as possible supplementary services but are not yet part of CCITT recommendations

Call Offering supplementary services are those affecting the connection and routing of calls. These services include:

- *Call Transfer:* Allows a user to transfer an established call to a third party

- *Call Forwarding Busy (CFB):* Allows a user to have the network automatically forward incoming calls to another number when this user's line is busy

- *Call Forwarding No Reply (CFNR):* Allows a user to have the network automatically forward incoming calls to another number if there is no answer on this user's line

- *Call Forwarding Unconditional (CFU):* Allows a user to have the network automatically forward all incoming calls to another number

- *Line Hunting:*   Allows incoming calls to a given ISDN number to be automatically distributed over a group of interfaces (also called automatic call distribution, or ACD)

- *Call Deflection:*   Identified as a possible supplementary service but is not yet a part of CCITT recommendations

Call Completion supplementary services are those affecting the completion of incoming call setup. These services include:

- *Call Waiting:*   Allows a user to be notified of an incoming call even when there is no information channel available (e.g., a second incoming call when the only B-channel is in use). The user can either accept, reject, or ignore the incoming call.

- *Call Hold:*   Allows a user to interrupt communications on an existing call and then subsequently reestablish the connection.

- *Completion of Calls to Busy Subscribers:*   Identified as a possible supplementary service but is not yet a part of CCITT recommendations.

Multiparty supplementary services allow communications between more than a single pair of users. These services include:

- *Conference Calling:*   Allows multiple users to simultaneously communicate with each other.

- *Three-Party Service:*   Allows a user to place an active call on hold and place a new call to a third party. The user can then switch back and forth between the two calls, join the calls together to form a three-way conversation, or split a three-way conversation back to two separate calls.

Community of Interest supplementary services allow the definition of "private" networks within the public ISDN. These services include:

- *Closed User Group (CUG):*   Allows users to form private groups, where access in and out is restricted. A user may belong to more than one CUG. Members of a CUG may communicate with each other but not necessarily with users outside of the group. Some members of the CUG may be able to call users outside of the group and/or receive calls from users outside of the group.

- *Private Numbering Plan:*   Identified as a possible supplementary service, but is not yet a part of CCITT recommendations.

Charging supplementary services provide information about current network charges and allow charges for ISDN calls to be directed to a user other than the calling party. These services include:

- *Advice of Charge:* Allows the paying party to be informed of usage-based charges related to this call. This service may be provided at call setup time, during the call, and/or at the end of the call.
- *Credit Card Calling and Reverse Charging:* Identified as possible supplementary services but are not yet a part of CCITT recommendations.

Additional Information Transfer supplementary services allow information to be transferred between users in addition to the basic call. This type of service includes:

- *User-to-User Signaling (UUS):* Allows a limited amount of information (data) transfer across the signaling channel associated with a given ISDN call

The availability and definition of supplementary services will increase over the next several years, since these will bring new capabilities to the ISDN customer.

The service that can be offered from a single ISDN C.O. is limited unless that C.O. can communicate with other ISDN central offices. A network signaling system, then, must be in place to provide this interoffice communication. The ISDN supplementary services will take advantage of the capabilities of the network signaling system.

Chapter 7 describes Signaling System No. 7 (SS7), the signaling network that will connect ISDN switching offices. SS7 will also be able to provide many new types of services. SS7, however, is not directly accessible by most users; thus its services are not directly accessible either. It is the ISDN supplementary service definitions and procedures, then, that will allow ISDN customers to take advantage of the capabilities of the signaling network.

3.2.5 Teleservices

Teleservices are value-added services (VAS) that may be provided in addition to the bearer services described above. Teleservices are described in the I.240-series recommendations. What really separates teleservices from bearer services are the higher-layer, end-to-end functions (OSI layers 4 through 7). A teleservice may be offered to a user by another user of the network or by the network itself. The higher-layer attributes include:

- Type of user information, including speech, sound, text (teletex), Group 4 facsimile, mixed-mode text facsimile, videotex, video, and interactive text (telex)

- Layer 4 protocol, including CCITT and ISO transport layer protocols

- Layer 5 protocol, including CCITT and ISO session layer protocols

- Layer 6 protocol, including CCITT and ISO presentation layer protocols, such as document interchange protocols, resolution and graphics mode, and encryption scheme

- Layer 7 protocol, including CCITT and ISO application layer protocols, such as Message Handling Systems (MHS) and directory services (CCITT X.400- and X.500-series recommendations)

3.3   OTHER ISDN SERVICES

3.3.1   Rate Adaption

B-channels operate at 64 kbps, but user equipment does not always generate data at that rate. For example, a personal computer in an office may not be able to operate at speeds greater than 9600 bps. If a user is transmitting 9600 bps of data over a 64-kbps channel, how does the network know which 9600 bits are actual data and which 54,400 bits are garbage? The I.460-series recommendations describe standard *rate adaption* algorithms that may be used by a terminal adaptor to place bit streams operating at any common transmission rate onto a 64-kbps B-channel.

CCITT Recommendation I.460 describes general principles of rate adaption and multiplexing to support existing user-network interfaces. Recommendation X.30 (I.461) describes the support of X.21 and X.21 *bis* data terminal equipment on an ISDN. Recommendations X.21 and X.21 *bis* describe the physical interface to synchronous public data networks and are also the physical layer protocols for X.25.

Recommendation X.31 (I.462) describes support of X.25 DTEs on an ISDN. The rate adaption scheme described in this recommendation may be used for circuit- or packet-mode applications and uses the same multiplexing and error detection and correction procedures as X.25.

Recommendation V.110 (I.463) describes the support of synchronous or asynchronous terminals on an ISDN. Rate adaption is performed in 1 to 3 steps, depending upon the input rate (Fig. 3.3). Rate adaption stage 0 (RA0) accepts asynchronous transmissions at rates between 50 and 19,200 bps and converts the bit stream to one of the synchronous rates shown by inserting additional bits. Synchronous bit streams are adapted by rate adaption stage 1 (RA1) to 8, 16, or 32

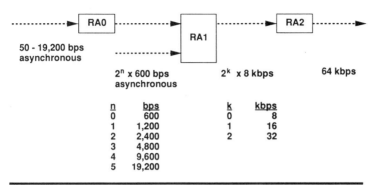

Figure 3.3 Recommendation V.110 (I.463) rate adaption stages.

kbps which are, in turn, converted to 64-kbps bit streams by RA2. Recommendation V.110 is intended for circuit-mode applications only and is popular in Europe and Japan.

Recommendation V.120 (I.465) describes rate adaption and statistical multiplexing for asynchronous transmission at rates up to 19.2 kbps and HDLC-based synchronous and bit transparent data streams at rates up to 56 kbps. V.120 is based upon the HDLC protocol and uses a standard bit-oriented protocol frame format (Fig. 3.4).

The fields in a V.120 frame, and their function, include:

- The Flag bit pattern (01111110) is used to delimit the start and end of the frame.

- The Address field provides a logical link identifier and gives V.120 the capability to multiplex several users' low-speed bit streams on a single 64-kbps channel.

- The Control field identifies the type of frame and may carry sequence information.

- The Information field carries the Header and User Data. The Header contains miscellaneous information, including the indication of errors, the control state for the physical interface, and an in-

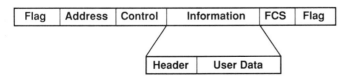

Figure 3.4 Recommendation V.120 (I.465) rate adaption frame format.

dication of how to reassemble the user's messages. The User Data contains the user's bit stream.

■ The Frame Check Sequence (FCS) contains information for the bit error detection algorithm.

V.120 uses the same bit error detection and correction procedures as HDLC, including error correction by retransmitting erroneous frames. *Flag stuffing,* or the insertion of Flag bit patterns in the bit stream, is used to accommodate idle time on the line. A simple layer 3 protocol based upon Recommendation Q.931 (I.451) is used to establish the user-network connection and to identify the protocol and the bit rate.

Recommendation V.120 is intended for circuit-mode applications. This algorithm is popular in the United States and is the subject of ANSI standard T1.406.

3.3.2 Packet-mode Services

One of the most important ISDN services will be to provide packet data transfer using, in all likelihood, the CCITT Recommendation X.25 protocol. Packet switching is supported today on packet switched public data networks (PSPDNs). How, then, will X.25 and today's PSPDNs fit into an ISDN?

Data terminal equipment supporting Recommendation X.25 cannot directly access the ISDN since X.25 protocols are not compatible with ISDN protocols. A terminal adaptor (TA) that can serve a dual role, however, can be connected to the DTE. First, the TA uses X.25 protocols and appears to the DTE like X.25 data circuit-terminating equipment (DCE). Second, the TA uses ISDN protocols and appears to the network as an ISDN terminal (TE1). Recommendation X.31 (I.462) defines the operation of a TA that will allow an X.25 DTE to communicate with an ISDN.

There are two ways in which an ISDN can support a PSPDN. In particular, the PSPDN may be part of the ISDN or the ISDN may be used to provide a connection from the user to a PSPDN that is totally separate from the ISDN. Recommendation X.31 also describes support of X.25 packet-mode devices by an ISDN and defines these two cases, or scenarios.

X.31 Case A describes *access to PSPDN services,* or what used to be called the minimum service integration scenario. Packet switched calls are passed transparently through the exchange termination (ET) component of the local exchange to an ISDN access unit (AU) port (Fig. 3.5). In essence, the user's X.25 DTE uses the ISDN to access the PSPDN's X.25 DCE; access to another DTE is across the PSPDN using X.25 virtual call procedures. As shown, the ISDN can provide a

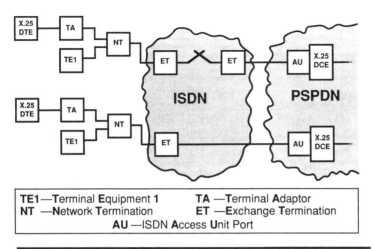

TE1—Terminal Equipment 1   TA —Terminal Adaptor
NT —Network Termination   ET —Exchange Termination
AU —ISDN Access Unit Port

Figure 3.5   Recommendation X.31 Case A (access to PSPDN services) packet-mode service.

switched connection between two ETs to access the AU or the ET can be directly connected to the AU. In this scenario, the D-channel is reserved for user-network signaling only and cannot be used for packet-mode service; users may obtain packet-mode transfer only on a B-channel. Packet mode is not available on the D-channel because the D-channel terminates at the local exchange and the LE cannot handle data packets.

X.31 Case B describes *access to the ISDN virtual circuit service,* or what used to be called the maximum service integration scenario. In Case B, packet service is provided over an ISDN virtual circuit (Fig. 3.6). The PSPDN may still be a separate network, but the packet handling (PH) function is part of the ISDN; thus, the local exchange appears to the user (X.25 DTE) as a network node (X.25 DCE). Internally, CCITT Recommendation X.75 or some other internetworking protocol might be used to interconnect the ISDN packet handler to the PSPDN or to another ISDN packet handler. In the Case B model, two DTEs obtain a virtual circuit service across the ISDN. Since the packet network is within the ISDN, packet service can be provided on either the B- or D-channel. Most major switch manufacturers in North America are basing their equipment on the Case B scenario.

3.3.3 Broadband Services

As mentioned in Chap. 2, broadband ISDN (B-ISDN) services are those that require speeds greater than that which can be delivered from a single primary rate interface (1.536 or 1.920 Mbps) trunk.

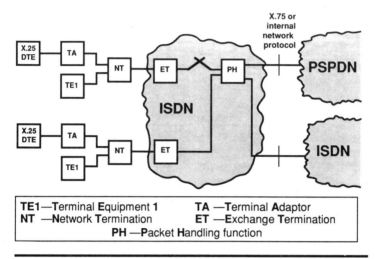

Figure 3.6 Recommendation X.31 Case B (access to the ISDN Virtual circuit service) packet-mode service.

B-ISDN services have not yet been fully defined by CCITT recommendations, although Recommendation I.121 describes general broadband aspects of ISDN. Potential B-ISDN applications include video telephony, video and document retrieval services, extended quality television (EQTV), and high-definition television (HDTV).

B-ISDN services can be broadly categorized as either communications or distribution services. *Communications services* include all of the current telephone network services, plus conversational, messaging, and retrieval services. *Conversational services* provide two-way, real-time, end-to-end information transfer between two users; possible applications include broadband videoconferencing, multilingual television, high-speed LAN or computer-to-computer data transfer, high-resolution imaging, and high-speed facsimile. *Message services* offer user-to-user communication via mailboxes, such as voice, video, and document mail services. *Retrieval services* allow users to obtain information stored in databases, such as videotex or video, still images, documents, and data.

Distribution services may or may not operate under control of the user. *Distribution services without user control,* or pure broadcast services, provide a continuous flow of information from some central source, where the user cannot control the start and stop of the information being broadcast; examples would include high-quality and pay-per-view television, high-speed data such as financial and weather reporting services, and document distribution. *Distribution services with user control* are similar, except users can access individual parts of the transmission and control what they see and in what order, namely, broadcast videography, such as an online newspaper service.

3.4 SAMPLE SCENARIOS

The table of ISDN bearer service attributes seems to allow incredible flexibility in the request for services. Remember that an ISDN device signals the network to set up a call by specifying an attribute profile for the desired service. There are, in fact, thousands of possible combinations of the listed attributes although not all possible combinations make sense. What will all of these options do to the cost of ISDN terminal equipment?

Note that while the network switch must be able to recognize all legal (and allowed) attribute combinations, an individual ISDN device can only support a limited set of those attributes. For example, an ISDN telephone and X.25 DTE might use the following attribute profiles (see Tables 3.3 and 3.4):

Attribute	Telephone	X.25 DTE
1	Circuit mode	Packet mode
2	64 kbps	(Packet throughput FFS)
3	Speech	UDI
4	8-kHz integrity	Service data unit integrity
5	Demand	Demand
6	Bidirectional symmetric	Bidirectional symmetric
7	Point to point	Point to point
8	B-channel	B-channel
9	I-series (D-channel)	I-series (D-channel)
	G.711 (B-channel)	LAPB/PLP (B-channel)
		Rate adaption class

While ISDN terminal equipment must know how to set up calls, the user does not have to keep track of this information and, in fact, would probably never be aware of these options. All of this information can be stored in read-only memory (ROM) within the device since most ISDN devices will have only a single attribute profile associated with them (possibly with one or two options).

Consider an ISDN telephone. Some ISDN telephones will probably have an external or internal switch setting so that either the μ-law or A-law companding schemes may be selected, thus allowing international sales of the same piece of equipment. The ISDN telephone, then, is actually a relatively simple device since it only generates a small subset of all possible attributes. While an ISDN C.O. switch will be somewhat more complex than today's switches, ISDN terminal equipment should (eventually) not be prohibitively expensive.

3.4.1   Bearer Service Categories

The statement was made above that not all combinations of bearer service attributes make sense. The CCITT has, in fact, defined bearer service categories to identify some of those combinations that are particularly meaningful.

Information transfer attributes 1 through 4 are called *dominant attributes* and are used to identify a particular bearer service category. Current ISDN recommendations have identified eight circuit-mode and three packet-mode bearer service categories.

The circuit-mode bearer service categories are:

- *64-kbps unrestricted, 8-kHz integrity:* Supports UDI transfer to support various user applications including speech, 3.1-kHz audio, multiple subrate information streams multiplexed onto a single 64-kbps channel, or transparent access to an X.25 PSPDN.

- *64-kbps, 8-kHz integrity, speech information transfer:* Intended to support human speech.

- *64-kbps, 8-kHz integrity, 3.1-kHz audio information transfer:* This service category corresponds to the service currently offered by an analog telephone network. It provides for the transfer of speech or 3.1-kHz audio information, such as voiceband data via modem or Group 1, 2, or 3 facsimile.

- *Alternate speech and 64-kbps unrestricted, 8-kHz integrity*: Provides the alternate transfer of either speech or 64-kbps UDI within the same call. This service category is provided to support multiple capability terminals.

- *2-× 64-kbps unrestricted, 8-kHz integrity:* Provides UDI transfer over two B-channels.

- *384-kbps unrestricted, 8-kHz integrity:* Provides UDI transfer over an H_0-channel.

- *1536-kbps unrestricted, 8-kHz integrity:* Provides UDI transfer over an H_{11}-channel.

- *1920-kbps unrestricted, 8-kHz integrity:* Provides UDI transfer over an H_{12}-channel.

The packet-mode bearer service categories are:

- *Virtual call and permanent virtual circuit:* Provides for transfer of UDI in user packets over a virtual circuit on a B- or D-channel.

- *Connectionless packet-mode bearer service:* Provides for connectionless (datagram) transfer of UDI in user packets on a B- or D-channel; this service is FFS.

- *User signaling bearer service:*   Allows user-to-user signaling packets; this service is FFS.

3.4.2   Final Comments

The importance of distinguishing between information transfer attributes and access attributes should be clear. For example, use of μ-law companding (attribute 9) is of importance only between the ISDN telephone and the local exchange. The network itself does not really care; it is only switching bits. Furthermore, a different companding scheme could be used at the remote side; this should not cause either user a problem nor will either user even be aware of this fact.

The reader should keep in mind that service requests are sent in signaling messages on the D-channel. This is always the case. If the service request asks for a B- or H-channel, the actual user-to-user communication will be granted on the requested channel.

ISDN devices must also know how to recognize the incoming calls that they can handle. This is not as complex as it might appear at first. Suppose that a given residence has a computer, two ISDN telephones, an ISDN television, and an ISDN coffee pot on its BRI connection to the LE. When an incoming telephone call comes in, the LE will broadcast a signaling message on the D-channel to all devices at the residence indicating the attributes of the incoming call. Only the telephones should recognize that they can act on this call and they will ring; all other devices will ignore the call and take no action. If the incoming call had attributes consistent with a data application, only the computer would attempt to make a connection; the telephones would remain silent.

4

ISDN Physical Layer Protocols

To fully appreciate the ISDN user-network interface, it is important to understand the protocols that are used across the interface. Protocols are nothing more than the set of rules that expedite communication. Just as people follow rules for diplomacy, religion, and the practice of medicine, so must ISDN devices use protocols as well.

This chapter will briefly describe the ISDN protocol architecture, as well as the physical layer (OSI layer 1) protocols for the basic and primary rate interfaces. The broadband ISDN protocol architecture and frame structure will also be described.

4.1 ISDN PROTOCOL ARCHITECTURE

The ISDN protocols for the D-channel are roughly equivalent to the lower three layers of the OSI Reference Model (the chained layers). Since these protocols describe only the user-network interface and no user-to-user communications, there are no D-channel counterparts for the OSI end-to-end layers. The three layers of D-channel protocol are:

- *Layer 1:* Describes the physical connection between terminal equipment (TE) and the network termination (NT), including the connector, line coding scheme, framing, and electrical characteristics. The physical connection is synchronous, serial, and full duplex; it may be point to point (PRI or BRI) or point to multipoint (BRI only). The D- and B-channels share the physical line using time division multiplexing. The layer 1 protocol is discussed in this chapter.

- *Layer 2:* Describes the procedures to ensure error-free communication over the physical link and defines the logical connection between the user and the network. The protocol also provides rules for multiplexing multiple TEs on a single physical channel (multipoint) in the BRI. The layer 2 protocol, LAPD, is discussed in Chap. 5.

- *Layer 3:* Defines the user-network interface and signaling messages used to request services from the network. The layer 3 protocol is discussed in Chap. 6.

The peer-to-peer interaction between the three protocol layers is consistent with the OSI model. Layer 3 signaling messages are carried in the Information field of layer 2 frames, which are transmitted across the layer 1 physical link.

Before discussing the protocol layers in any detail, it is critical to pinpoint the place where each protocol layer has relevance. The CCITT ISDN protocols describe the D-channel user-network interface at the S and T reference points (Fig. 4.1). Different layers of protocol see these reference points differently.

The ISDN layer 1 protocol defines the physical connection between ISDN terminal equipment (TE1 or TA) and network termination equipment (NT2 or NT1). As discussed earlier, CCITT ISDN recommendations do not describe the physical connection between the NT1 and local exchange because the transmission line is considered internal to the network. In any case, communication across the local loop (U reference point) is a physical layer issue only.

The ISDN layer 2 and 3 protocols define the logical link and signaling protocol, respectively, between ISDN terminal equipment (TE1 or TA), customer-premises switching equipment (NT2), and the C.O. switch (LE). The NT1 provides only a layer 1 service; thus, layers 2 and 3 are transparent to it.

It is important to emphasize that the CCITT ISDN protocols are specified only across the S and T reference points and only on the D-channel. The user may choose any protocol(s) for the bearer services and teleservices on the B-channel. The B- and D-channels share the same physical layer standard since B- and D-channels are time division multiplexed on the same physical line (Fig. 4.2).

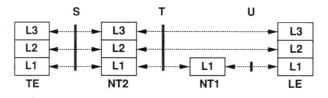

Figure 4.1 Protocol reference points and architecture for the ISDN D-channel.

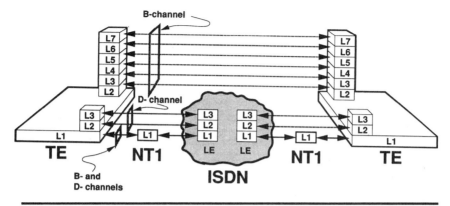

Figure 4.2   Relationship of B- and D-channel protocol architectures.

To support the idea of signaling and user information as separate data paths, the CCITT has introduced the concept of the *control plane* (or C-plane) and the *user plane* (U-plane). Protocols within the C-plane are for the transfer of information for the control of user connections and/or network resources, such as call establishment, call termination, changing service characteristics during the call, and requesting supplementary services. Protocols within the U-plane are for the transfer of information between user applications, such as digitized voice and video, and user data. Information in the U-plane may be carried between users transparently by the network or may be manipulated (e.g., A-law to μ-law PCM conversion).

4.2 THE BASIC RATE INTERFACE

4.2.1 CCITT Recommendation I.430 (S/T Reference Point)

The basic rate interface layer 1 protocol is specified in CCITT Recommendation I.430. Recommendation I.430 defines ISDN communication between terminal equipment and network termination equipment across the S/T reference point.

The BRI comprises two B-channels and one D-channel (2B + D), although it can be configured as 1B + D or as a single D-channel only.

Basic rate access may use a point-to-point or point-to-multipoint configuration. In a point-to-point physical configuration, the network termination (i.e., NT1 or NT2) and terminal equipment (i.e., TE1 or TA) can be up to 3300 feet (ft) (1 km) apart (Fig. 4.3).

There are two point-to-multipoint options. In the short passive bus option, up to eight TEs can be connected to a single NT on a bus up to 500 ft (150 meters) in length; the TEs and NT may be anywhere

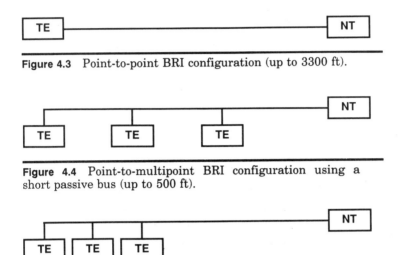

Figure 4.3 Point-to-point BRI configuration (up to 3300 ft).

Figure 4.4 Point-to-multipoint BRI configuration using a short passive bus (up to 500 ft).

Figure 4.5 Point-to-multipoint BRI configuration using an extended passive bus (up to 3300 ft).

on the bus (Fig. 4.4). In the extended passive bus option, multiple TEs are grouped together at one end of a bus, up to 3300 ft from the NT (Fig. 4.5).

The physical connection between the TE and NT requires at least two wire pairs; one pair for each direction of transmission. These are shown as the transmit and receive loops, respectively, attached to power source/sink 1 in Fig. 4.6.

In today's analog telephone sets, power to ring the bell, store the last number dialed, and light the light-emitting diodes (LEDs) is provided by the central office. This is the reason that telephones continue to operate when there is a power failure (unless the C.O. itself is damaged). Under ideal circumstances, the C.O. can provide about 370 milliwatts (mW) of power, while telephones draw a little over 150 mW.

The complexity of the NT1, TEs, and TAs is significantly greater than today's telephone devices. For example, all ISDN TAs and TEs will have some internal memory identifying its address and bearer service attribute profile and supporting the ISDN protocols. ISDN devices, then, will need to draw more power than most of today's equipment. With today's technology, an NT1 would require approximately 400 mW of power and terminal equipment would need at least 200 mW, well more than can be supplied by the C.O. Even if the central office could supply the additional power, the ISDN local loop will be a

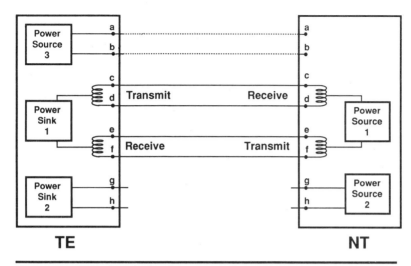

Figure 4.6 BRI electrical reference configuration.

digital transmission facility, meaning that ac power cannot be supplied over the same line. Furthermore, power cannot be supplied by the C.O. over optical fiber, a future direction for local loop installations in many areas.

The issue of the power source for terminal equipment is one of the most controversial surrounding the BRI. An ISDN device may draw power from several sources:

- Power source 1—*phantom power* supplied on the transmit and receive data pairs
- Power source 2—alternative power supplied on an additional wire pair from
- A local ac or dc power supply

In North America, the operating telephone companies will not supply power for CPE. In this environment, the NT1 may be plugged directly into an ac or dc power source in the home or office. NT1 products in North America will typically use an extra wire pair for power distribution to the TEs and TAs. In Europe, the operating company is responsible for delivering dc power to the NT1 which will, in turn, supply phantom power to the terminal equipment over the data pairs.

The BRI specification provides connector positions and an optional wire pair for power distribution from the NT to the TEs (power source/sink 2 in Fig. 4.6). Using this additional pair, the NT can distribute power to TEs on the line; this also provides a mechanism so

TABLE 4.1   I.430 Connector Pinout

Pin No.	Function		Polarity	Required?
	TE	NT		
1	Power source 3	Power sink 3	+	No
2	Power source 3	Power sink 3	-	No
3	Transmit	Receive	+	Yes
4	Receive	Transmit	+	Yes
5	Receive	Transmit	-	Yes
6	Transmit	Receive	-	Yes
7	Power sink 2	Power source 2	-	No
8	Power sink 2	Power source 2	+	No

that a single battery-backup capability in a house can support all ISDN devices, obviating the need for a battery in every piece of ISDN equipment. Power source 3 (in Fig. 4.6) may be used for power transfer in TE-TE interconnections; the use of this pair is not subject to CCITT recommendations.

The physical connector for the BRI will be an 8-pin subminiature modular plug and jack (RJ-45), based on Draft ISO Standard 8877. The pin assignments are shown in Table 4.1.

The line coding used on the BRI is called pseudo-ternary signaling (Fig. 4.7). With pseudo-ternary signaling, a 0 bit is represented by a line signal of approximately 750 millivolts (mV) that alternates between positive and negative polarity; a 1 bit is represented by the absence of line voltage. Since the polarity of the 0 bit signals alternate, this signaling scheme is dc balanced; that is, there is no net dc current on the line over a period of time. This allows longer physical lines, easier inductive and capacitive coupling, and reduces problems associated with static electricity.

Two 0-bit pulses in a row with the same polarity form a *code violation.* Code violations are not errors. Instead, they are an important part of the BRI signaling scheme since they are used to provide transmission synchronization. Since a single code violation defeats dc balancing, all code violations appear in pairs on the BRI.

Transmissions on the BRI are organized into blocks of bits called *I.430 frames,* each containing 48 bits. Figure 4.8 shows the I.430 frame format, as well as the possible pseudo-ternary signal levels for

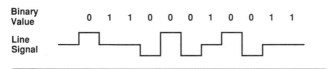

Figure 4.7   Pseudo-ternary signaling example.

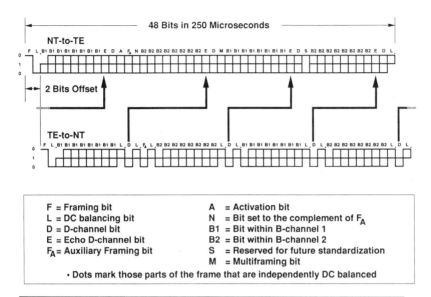

Figure 4.8   I.430 transmission frame.

each bit (i.e., positive, zero, or negative voltage representing a 0, 1, or 0, respectively). Four thousand I.430 frames are transmitted every second (each lasting 250 μs), yielding the BRI bit rate of 192 kbps. Each frame contains 16 bits from each of the two B-channels and 4 bits from the D-channel, yielding data rates of 64 kbps and 16 kbps, respectively. The interleaving scheme of the B- and D-channel bits in one frame on the BRI is:

Channel:	B1	D	B2	D	B1	D	B2	D
Number of bits:	8	1	8	1	8	1	8	1

The start of frames sent from the TE to the NT are offset by two bit times from the beginning of frames sent from the NT to the TE. In this way, the NT drives the timing for all TEs.

Frames sent in the two directions are basically the same, with the notable exception that the NT-to-TE frame carries echoed D-channel bits (E), which merely repeat the bits that were transmitted on the D-channel in the TE-to-NT direction. The E-bits are of particular importance in the point-to-multipoint configuration. Since there may be multiple TEs on the BRI line, some mechanism must be in place to ensure that only a single TE is ever transmitting on the D-channel in the TE-to-NT direction. No such problem exists for the B-channel, since it will be owned by a single TE at a time. There is also no such problem in the NT-to-TE direction of transmission since there is only one NT device.

The E-bits are part of the contention mechanism used by the TEs to ensure that there is only a single transmitter on the D-channel. TEs listen to the E-bits to determine whether they should keep transmitting. All transmitting TEs monitor the E-bits. If an E-bit value is different than the last bit transmitted on the D-channel by this TE, the TE knows that it does not control the D-channel and has to stop transmitting. In this way, collisions may occur on the D-channel, but no data is ever lost. D-channel contention resolution, called *perfect scheduling*, is described in more detail in Chap. 5.

The dc-balance (L) bits are used to ensure that there is no net dc current on the line. A given L-bit is responsible for ensuring dc balancing (i.e., an even number of 1 bits) in the block of bits since the prior L-bit. The L-bit, then, will be 0 if preceded by an odd number of 0s and will be 1 if preceded by an even number of 0s.

The remaining bits in the BRI frame are for physical signaling and timing. In particular, the framing (F) bit is a 0 bit that is a code violation with respect to the last 0 transmitted in the previous frame. In fact, the polarity of this pulse will always be positive. The I.430 coding rules specify that the first 0 bit transmitted after the initial F- and L-bits will be another code violation, thus preserving the integrity of dc balancing.

The 1988 BRI standard defines *multiframes,* a grouping together of 20 I.430 frames. Recommendation I.430 multiframes provide an 800-bps Q-channel in the TE-to-NT direction. The exact use of the Q-channel has not yet been specified and, according to CCITT recommendations, support of multiframing by the NT is not mandatory.

The multiframing (M) and auxiliary framing (F_A) bits are used in the multiframing procedures (Table 4.2). The M-bit (only present in the NT-to-TE direction) is set to 1 in the first frame of each multiframe; it is set to 0 in all other frames.

Each multiframe in the TE-to-NT direction contains four Q-channel bits, designated Q1, Q2, Q3, and Q4. The four Q-channel bits occupy the F_A-bit position in every fifth frame. In those frames not carrying Q-channel information, the F_A-bit is set to 0. In the NT-to-TE direction, the F_A-bit indicates frames in which Q-channel information should appear. Thus, the F_A-bit is set to 1 in every fifth frame and set to 0 in the other frames.

The F_A-bits also serve a function to ensure frame alignment and synchronization. Recall that the first zero following the F-bit and its dc-balance-bit must be a code violation. In the NT-to-TE direction, the N-bit will be set to the logical complement of the F_A-bit; i.e., if $F_A = 1$, $N = 0$, and vice versa. Therefore, either the F_A- or N-bit will

TABLE 4.2   I.430 Multiframing

Frame Number	TE-to-NT	NT-to-TE	
	F_A	F_A	M
1	Q1	1	1
2	0	0	0
3	0	0	0
4	0	0	0
5	0	0	0
6	Q2	1	0
7	0	0	0
8	0	0	0
9	0	0	0
10	0	0	0
11	Q3	1	0
12	0	0	0
13	0	0	0
14	0	0	0
15	0	0	0
16	Q4	1	0
17	0	0	0
18	0	0	0
19	0	0	0
20	0	0	0

be a zero, ensuring that a second code violation occurs within 13 or 14 bit times of the beginning of a frame.

In the TE-to-NT direction, the F_A-bit is set to zero in those frames not carrying Q-channel bits. Therefore, a second code violation will occur within 13 bit times of the beginning of the frame in four out of five frames.

The activation (A) bit is used to indicate that the BRI line is activated and sending real user data; its use is part of the activation procedure of the physical interface, described below. The use of the spare (S) bit is for further study.

Two points should be made about TEs connected to the passive BRI bus in the point-to-multipoint configuration:

- All TEs on the bus follow the same framing rules. This means that if several TEs transmit a 0 bit at the same time on the D-channel, *all* will use the same polarity signal. Sending a 1 bit is the same as an open circuit, or sending 0 volts (V).

- The TEs are attached to the bus in parallel rather than in series; therefore, the total voltage on the bus is *not* the sum of all voltages applied to the bus. A 1-bit value will be detected by the NT only if *all* TEs apply zero voltage; a 0 bit will be detected by the NT if *one or more* TEs apply a voltage. It is not possible for two TEs to apply opposite polarity signals on the bus.

Finally, Recommendation I.430 defines five different signal patterns, called INFO signals, that indicate the state of the physical BRI link. These signal patterns are defined as follows:

- *INFO 0:*   No line signal; may be sent from NT or TE

- *INFO 1:*   A continuous signal at a rate of 192 kbps, repeating the pattern 0 (positive polarity), 0 (negative polarity), and six 1s; sent in the TE-to-NT direction only

- *INFO 2:*   An I.430 frame where the B-, D-, E-, and A-bits are set to 0, and all other bits are set according to the appropriate framing rules; sent in the NT-to-TE direction only

- *INFO 3:*   An I.430 frame with operational data on the B- and D-channels; sent in the TE-to-NT direction only

- *INFO 4:*   An I.430 frame with operational data on the B-, D-, and echoed D-channels, with the A-bit set to 1; sent in the NT-to-TE direction only

These INFO signals are used as part of the TE and NT activation and deactivation procedures. Typically, there will not be any electrical activity across the S/T reference point unless at least one TE is active; this is an INFO 0 signal. The TE activation procedure, in general, is:

1. A TE will send an INFO 1 signal when first connected, when power is applied (or restored), or when frame alignment is lost.

2. The INFO 2 signal from the NT will provide the TE with appropriate frame synchronization since the TE derives timing from the NT's frames.

3. The TE will send the INFO 3 signal to indicate that it has established frame alignment.

4. The NT will respond with the INFO 4 signal to indicate that the BRI is activated and operational.

When power is removed from a TE with a local power supply, the TE will send an INFO 0 signal to indicate this state to the NT.

4.2.2   ANSI T1.601 (U Reference Point)

The CCITT BRI standard describes the physical interface between terminal equipment and network termination equipment. CCITT standards do not address the physical connection across the local loop between network termination equipment (NT1) and the ISDN local exchange, or the U reference point.

For reasons mentioned earlier, ANSI is responsible for the BRI standard for the local loop in the United States, published as ANS T1.601. The ANSI standard will address the U reference point for the BRI to provide the necessary level of service over existing twisted pair without requiring the replacement of all of the nation's local loops.

A "digital" local loop will connect the NT1 and the local exchange. This physical connection is over unloaded twisted pair at distances up to approximately 18 kft. The U reference point supports a serial, synchronous, full-duplex, point-to-point configuration.

The NT1 will provide an eight-position subminiature modular jack and the local loop will terminate at the NT1 side with an eight-position subminiature modular plug. The local loop will be connected to the two middle connectors of the plug; the other six connectors are not used.

One of the main features (and one of the biggest controversies until about 1986) of the U reference point is the method used to provide full-duplex communication over the local loop. The method described in the U reference point standard uses the Echo Canceller with Hybrid (ECH) principle, alluded to in Chap. 1 (Fig. 4.9).

Echo cancellation, in essence, requires that the transmitter insert a negative image of its transmission into its receive circuitry, canceling any returning echo. The hybrid is required to connect the two wire pairs inside the building (I.430 transmit and receive loops) to the local

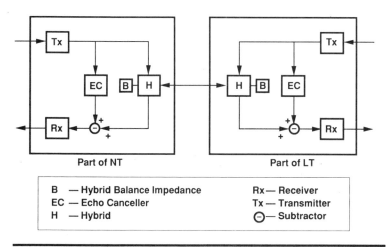

Figure 4.9 Echo Canceller with Hybrid (ECH).

TABLE 4.3 Two Binary, One Quaternary (2B1Q) Signaling Levels

1st bit (polarity)	2nd bit (magnitude)	Quaternary Symbol	Voltage Level
1	0	+3	2.5
1	1	+1	0.833
0	1	-1	-0.833
0	0	-3	-2.5

loop's single pair. Thus, the S/T bus transmit pair feeds both the echo canceller and the output to the local loop; input from the local loop and the output from the echo canceller feed the S/T bus receive pair. The hybrid balance circuitry is necessary to minimize impedance mismatches when converting between the two-wire and four-wire interfaces.

The signaling scheme to be used over the local loop is called two binary, one quaternary (2B1Q). This is a four-level line code, associating a pair of bits with a single quaternary symbol (quat), as shown in Table 4.3. The first bit of each pair represents the sign, or polarity, of the quaternary symbol, while the second bit represents the magnitude.

Although the standard indicates use of a 2.5-V signal for the quat with magnitude 3, a 2.0-V signal level will be allowed until 1992. This compromise came about because network providers are concerned that anything below 2 V might be too low for recognizability, while chip manufacturers are concerned about their ability to reliably and economically meet the ISDN specifications with today's technology.

Because 2B1Q signaling is not dc balanced (Fig. 4.10), the ANSI standard specifies an algorithm to be used to scramble the bit streams to avoid excess dc bias on the transmission line. The U reference point will operate at 160 kbps. Although the BRI operates at 192 kbps across the S/T bus, there are only 144 kbps of user data; none of that data is lost over the local loop. Since 2B1Q signaling associates a pair of bits with a single signal, the signaling rate is 80 kbaud (80,000 signals per second).

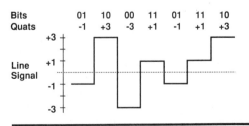

Figure 4.10 Two binary, one quaternary (2B1Q) signaling example.

The basic unit of transmission across the U reference point is a *2B1Q transmission frame* (Fig. 4.11). A transmission frame contains three fields:

- *Synchronization word (SW):*   Used for physical layer synchronization and frame alignment; comprises a specified 9-quat pattern (the equivalent of 18 bits)

- *Data:*   B- and D-channel information; sent in 12 groups, each containing 8 B1 bits, 8 B2 bits, and 2 D bits; comprises 108 quats (216 bits)

- *Overhead:*   Used for network functions, including physical channel maintenance, error detection, and power status indication; comprises 3 quats (6 bits)

Note that the interleaving of B- and D-channel bits across the U reference point is different than it is across the S/T reference point. The B- and D-channel bits are interleaved as follows in the 2B1Q frame:

Channel: B1   B2   D
Number of bits: 8   8   2

While the interleaving schemes are different, this does not cause a problem since the same number of B- and D-channel bits are transmitted during each second. The NT1 is responsible for the conversion between the two different frame formats.

A 2B1Q transmission frame comprises 120 quats (240 bits). Frames are sent every 1.5 ms, or at a rate of 666.666... frames per second. Thus, 8000 2B + D groups are sent every second, maintaining the 64-kbps B-channel rate and 16-kbps D-channel rate.

Transmission across the U reference point is organized into groups of eight 2B1Q frames, called *superframes* (Fig. 4.12). The inverted synchronization word (ISW) signals the first frame of a superframe; it is a 9-quat pattern that is merely the inverse of a normal synchronization word. A superframe organizes the 6 overhead bits of each frame

	SW	12 x (2B+D)	M
FUNCTION	Synchronization Word	Twelve Groups of $2B_8 + D_2$	Overhead
# QUATS	9	108	3
BITS	"18"	216	6

Figure 4.11   2B1Q transmission frame.

Frame
Number

1	ISW	12 x (2B + D)	M_1 - M_6
2	SW	12 x (2B + D)	M_7 - M_{12}
3	SW	12 x (2B + D)	M_{13} - M_{18}
4	SW	12 x (2B + D)	M_{19} - M_{24}
5	SW	12 x (2B + D)	M_{25} - M_{30}
6	SW	12 x (2B + D)	M_{31} - M_{36}
7	SW	12 x (2B + D)	M_{37} - M_{42}
8	SW	12 x (2B + D)	M_{43} - M_{48}

Figure 4.12 2B1Q superframe.

into a block of 48 bits, called the M-channel. The M-channel is a 4-kbps side channel used for maintenance messages, signaling, power status indication, and error detection.

The NT1 derives its timing from the local exchange across the U reference point. That means that the network, in effect, sets the timing for the TEs since the TEs derive their timing from the NT.

4.2.3 BRI Summary

The BRI can be used in two general environments. For the residential and small business customer, the BRI can be used to make the current 3.1-kHz local loop into a 2B + D ISDN channel. BRI access will also be provided to ISDN Centrex customers.

Alternatively, the BRI may be used in a business environment to provide ISDN service from a PBX or ISDN multiplexer to individual offices, where the wire pair can support both a telephone and data terminal, or an integrated voice/data terminal (IVDT).

The BRI can also be used for pair gain. By assigning two different telephone numbers to a BRI line and allocating each B-channel to one of the numbers, a single BRI can provide 1B + D service to two separate offices, dorm rooms, or workstations.

Conversion to the BRI will not be entirely painless for the residential customer. In particular, the telephone wiring inside the subscriber's residence may need to be redone to ensure that two or three wire pairs are running throughout the building. In addition, eight-position modular jacks may be required.

Every subscriber will also need an NT1 to connect the local loop to the in-house ISDN wiring. The NT1 is a relatively complex device compared to today's residential telephone equipment. It must support the electronics for echo cancellation, as well as the I.430 *and* 2B1Q signaling and frame formats. Furthermore, it may contain some sort of power distribution and/or battery backup capability. A brief comparison between CCITT Recommendation I.430 and ANS T1.601 is presented in Table 4.4 to provide a glimpse at the differences between these two standards and at some of the protocol conversion issues for BRI NT1 devices.

4.3 PRIMARY RATE INTERFACE

CCITT Recommendation I.431 defines the physical layer protocol for the primary rate interface. The PRI has a full-duplex, point-to-point, serial, synchronous configuration using two physical channels. Recommendation I.431 provides for both a 1.544- and 2.048-Mbps data

TABLE 4.4 Comparison of the BRI Physical Layer Standards

	CCITT I.430	ANSI T1.601
Reference Point	S or S/T	U
Devices	TE1/TA to NT	NT1 to LE
Distance	3.3 kft (pt-pt) 500 ft (pt-multipt)	18 kft
Physical Configuration	point-to-point or point-to-multipoint serial synchronous full-duplex	point-to-point serial synchronous full-duplex
Bit Rate	192 kbps	160 kbps
User Data Rate	144 kbps	144 kbps
Signaling Scheme	pseudo-ternary	2B1Q
Signaling Rate	192 kbaud	80 kbaud
Maximum Voltage	±750 mV	± 2.5 V
Timing Source	NT	LE
Number of Wire Pairs	2 (Additional 2 pair optional)	1
Full-Duplex Method	One wire pair for each direction	Echo cancellation
Interleaving Scheme*	$B1_8 D_1 B2_8 D_1$ (Twice per frame)	$B1_8 B2_8 D_2$ (12 times/frame)
# Bits/Frame	48	240
# Bits User Data	36	216
# Bits Overhead	12	24
# Frames/Second	4,000	666.666...

* Subscript indicates the number of contiguous bits that are sent on B1, B2, and D-channels

rate. Primary rate electrical and frame formats are based upon CCITT Recommendations G.703 and G.704, respectively.

Unlike the basic rate interface, the PRI will not typically terminate at users' terminal equipment. Instead, the PRI will usually be used as a trunk, connecting a customer's switching equipment (e.g., a PBX or other NT2) to the local exchange.

4.3.1 The 1.544-Mbps interface

The primary rate frame format, signaling, and multiplexing that will be used in North America is based upon the T1 frames discussed earlier (Fig. 4.13). The 1.544-Mbps PRI multiplexes twenty-four 64-kbps channels. One PRI frame contains 1 framing (F) bit plus a single 8-bit sample from each of the 24 channels, for a total of 193 bits per frame. At 8000 frames per second, this yields a total bit rate of 1.544 Mbps, of which 1.536 Mbps is user data.

The first 23 time slots of each PRI frame are assigned to B-channels 1 through 23. The final time slot may be used as either a D-channel (23B+D configurations) or a twenty-fourth B-channel (24B configurations). In the 24B configuration, D-channel signaling must be provided on another PRI across the same user-network interface.

The single framing bit associated with each frame cannot convey very much signaling information to the network. Therefore, 24 frames are grouped together to form a *multiframe* that is similar to the T1 extended superframe format, or ESF (Table 4.5). One multiframe, then, carries a block of 24 framing bits. Six of the framing bits form a pattern called the frame alignment sequence (FAS), used to ensure that the frames are correctly synchronized and that the bits are being correctly interpreted by the receiver. Another 6 framing bits are used to calculate the frame check sequence (FCS) using a 6-bit cyclic redundancy check (CRC) polynomial; the FCS will be used to determine if bit errors are occurring on the line. The remaining 12 bits form a 4-kbps channel that can be used for network maintenance and operation messages.

The 1.544-Mbps PRI will use alternating mark inversion (AMI) signaling. With AMI coding, 0 bits are represented by the absence of voltage on the line and 1 bits are represented by voltage pulses with alternating polarity.

To ensure sufficient *ones density,* or a sufficient number of 1 bits to

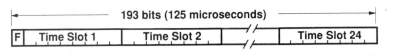

Figure 4.13 PRI frame structure (1.544-Mbps interface).

TABLE 4.5   PRI Multiframe Structure (1.544-Mbps Interface)

Multiframe Frame Number	F-bit Assignment		
	FAS	M	FCS
1	-	m	-
2	-	-	e1
3	-	m	-
4	0	-	-
5	-	m	-
6	-	-	e2
7	-	m	-
8	0	-	-
9	-	m	-
10	-	-	e3
11	-	m	-
12	1	-	-
13	-	m	-
14	-	-	e4
15	-	m	-
16	0	-	-
17	-	m	-
18	-	-	e5
19	-	m	-
20	1	-	-
21	-	m	-
22	-	-	e6
23	-	m	-
24	1	-	-

FAS: Frame Alignment Sequence (001011...)
M: Maintenance channel (For Further Study)
FCS: Frame Check Sequence (For Further Study)

provide timing on the line, a bit could be taken from each octet and set to 1. This bit-robbing procedure was described earlier as restricted digital information (RDI). This approach, however, effectively reduces each channel's bit rate to 56 kbps and is unacceptable when offering 64-kbps "clear channel" service.

Bipolar 8 Zero Substitution (B8ZS) is recommended for use with the 1.544-Mbps PRI to provide the necessary number of 1 bits. With B8ZS, an all-zero octet is replaced by the bit pattern 00011011, where code violations occur in the fourth and seventh bit positions. If the last occurring 1 bit had a positive polarity, an all-zero octet would be replaced with the pattern $000 + -0 - +$; if the previous 1 bit was negative, the all-zero octet would be replaced with $000 - +0 + -$. Since code violations appear in pairs, B8ZS is dc balanced.

4.3.2   The 2.048-Mbps Interface

The 2.048-Mbps primary rate interface is based upon the CEPT E1 carrier, also discussed earlier. The 2.048 PRI multiplexes thirty-two

64-kbps channels. One PRI frame contains 32 time slots, numbered from 0 to 31 (Fig. 4.14). Time slot 0 is reserved for physical layer framing, synchronization, and signaling. Time slots 1 through 15 and 17 through 31 are used for the 30 B-channels, while time slot 16 is reserved for the D-channel. The use of time slot 16 when not used as a D-channel is for further study.

Each frame in the 2.048-Mbps PRI contains a single 8-bit sample from each time slot, yielding 256 bits per frame. At 8000 frames per second, the total data rate is 2.048 Mbps and the user data rate is 1.984 Mbps.

The 2.048-Mbps PRI uses High-Density Bipolar 3 zeroes (HDB3) digital signaling. Like B8ZS, HDB3 is dc balanced and uses code violations to ensure that there are no long runs of zeroes in the transmission.

4.3.3 PRI Support of H-channels

The PRI can allocate H_0- and H_1-channels, in addition to B-channels. H_0-channels have the bandwidth equivalent of six B-channels and can be composed of any six B-channel time slots on the PRI. Table 4.6 lists some suggested time slot assignments for H_0-channel allocation when only H_0-channels are present on the PRI, per Recommendation I.431. The 1.544-Mbps PRI can support three H_0-channels when a D-channel is present or four H_0-channels when the D-channel is absent. The 2.048-Mbps PRI can support five H_0-channels in addition to the D-channel.

An H_{11}-channel uses all 24 time slots of the 1.544-Mbps PRI and an H_{12}-channel uses time slots 1 through 15 and 17 through 31 of the 2.048-Mbps interface. The D-channel is absent with an H_{11}-channel and present with an H_{12}-channel.

The U reference point associated with the PRI is the same that is already used with these higher-speed lines, namely the T1 or E1 user-network interface. In particular, both interfaces achieve full-duplex transmission by using two physical channels between the LE and NT.

4.4   BROADBAND ISDN

One of the main features of ISDN is the ability of the network to support a wide range of services. An important element of this service in-

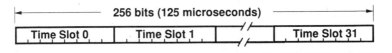

Figure 4.14 PRI frame structure (2.048-Mbps interface).

TABLE 4.6   Examples of Fixed Assignment of Time Slots When Only H_0-Channels are Present on the PRI

	H_0-channel				
	a	b	c	d	e
1.544 Mbps Time slots	1–6	7–12	13–18	19–24	—
2.048 Mbps	1–3 17–19	4–6 20–22	7–9 23–25	10–12 26–28	13–15 29–31
Time slots	1–6	7–12	13–15 17–19	20–25	26–31

tegration is to provide this range of services using a limited set of channel types, access configurations, protocols, and user-network interfaces.

The following sections will briefly describe the broadband ISDN (B-ISDN) transfer modes, protocol architecture, and frame format. Recommendation I.121 describes the broadband aspects of ISDN as currently defined by the CCITT. This recommendation gives an outline of B-ISDN services, channel types, interfaces, and protocols, but many issues still need to be resolved in the 1989–1992 study period.

4.4.1   Synchronous Versus Asynchronous Transfer Mode

The basic rate and primary rate interfaces use a synchronous transmission scheme sometimes called the synchronous transfer mode (STM). In this context, the word *synchronous* refers to the time-dependent nature of the channels within the frames. In the 1.544-Mbps PRI, for example, a framing bit (F) will occur every 193rd bit time, or every 125 μs. The 8 bits following the F-bit are always the B1 channel, the next 8 are always the B2 channel, and so on. No explicit channel identification is provided; channels are known by the time at which they occur.

The BRI and PRI each contain time slots for some number of B- and D-channels. The time slot for a channel is allocated even if there is no activity on the channel.

B-ISDN applications will use high-bandwidth channels. STM frames in the B-ISDN environment could be defined to include some number of B-, D-, H_0-, H_1-, H_2-, and H_4- channels. The potential waste of bandwidth of this method should be obvious; a time slot would be allocated for a channel even if the channel was not active.

Asynchronous transfer mode (ATM) is the recommended solution for implementing B-ISDN. *Asynchronous* in this context also refers to the timing of the channels. ATM is based upon statistical time division multiplexing, where a time slot is allocated for a channel *only if there is activity on the channel.*

The unit of transmission in ATM is called a *cell.* Since the receiver no longer has a way of knowing what channel is being received based upon the time, each cell must contain some type of channel identification.

4.4.2 ATM Protocol Architecture

Figure 4.15 shows the B-ISDN protocol architecture based upon the ATM model. Also shown is an ATM cell.

The B-ISDN protocol architecture is identical to the protocol architecture described earlier, for layer 2 and above. The layer 2 (LAPD) and layer 3 (I.451 Call Control) procedures are the same on the so-called C-plane; these control protocols would be used on the D-channel. Any user protocol(s) may be used in the U-plane on the B- or H-channels.

The OSI layer 1 functions for B-ISDN are handled by three sublayers. The physical media dependent layer provides the interface between the medium being used for transmission and the rest of the protocol stack. The medium choice should always be transparent to the protocol architecture if at all possible; that is, it is not desirable for a higher-layer protocol to be affected by the choice of the physical connection. This sublayer should support optical and electrical media and may support a point-to-multipoint configuration.

The remaining two sublayers are specific to the ATM. The ATM layer is common to all B-ISDN services. Its function is to provide cell transfer capabilities; it builds the ATM cells and puts on the appropriate header information.

The adaption layer supports higher-layer protocols for control and user applications. It also provides support for connections between

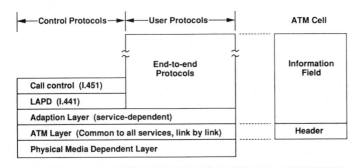

Figure 4.15   Broadband ISDN protocol architecture and ATM cell.

ATM and non-ATM interfaces, such as non-B-ISDN interfaces (e.g., the BRI and PRI) and non-ATM implementations of B-ISDN (e.g., STM). At the transmitting side, the adaption layer is responsible for splitting up large information units (e.g., layer 2 frames) or putting together a collection of small information units (e.g., PCM voice samples) and placing them into the Information field of an ATM cell. At the receiving side, the inverse operations must occur.

4.4.3 ATM cell format

An ATM cell will be of fixed size, comprising two fields, Header and Information (Fig. 4.15). The Header is the responsibility of the ATM layer and is common to all applications. It contains only the information required to transfer the Information field through the ATM network.

The Header has three mandatory functions. First, it identifies the virtual channel so that the receiving side knows to which information connection this cell's Information field belongs. Second, it carries error detection information for the Header. Third, it indicates whether the cell is used or unused. Eventually, the Header may also be defined to carry other information, including error correction information for the Header, cell sequence numbers, terminal identifiers, and/or payload type.

The size of the Header field, according to the 1988 standards, will be in the range of 3 to 8 octets; current activity suggest that a five-octet Header will be used.

The Information field contains application-specific information and is transported transparently by the ATM layer. No processing, including error detection, is performed on the Information field by the ATM layer. The size of the Information field, according to the standard, will be in the range of 32 to 120 octets; 48 octets will probably be the length chosen.

4.4.4 B-ISDN User-Network Interface

B-ISDN user-network interfaces will ultimately be standardized at two bit rates, namely, approximately 150 and 600 Mbps. The overall framing structure of ATM cells is still under study. While several options are under investigation, two generic structures exemplify the choices; one will probably be chosen for the 1992 recommendation.

One possible structure for the interface is the unframed format, where ATM cells are sent, one after another (Fig. 4-16). This structure may or may not contain regularly located framing cells. The other structure under consideration would place ATM cells in the payload portion of an external frame structure (Fig. 4.17). This format might

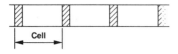

Figure 4.16 Unframed ATM cell format.

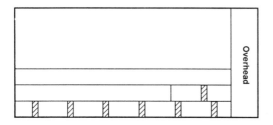

Figure 4.17 ATM cells carried in an external frame format.

allow the mixing of ATM and STM transmissions. In general, the ATM is designed to work with any digital transmission hierarchy.

The high speeds of the B-ISDN interfaces will require a national or international deployment of broadband transmission facilities. Such activity is currently underway. The ANSI standard Synchronous Optical Network (SONET) will define a TDM hierarchy for optical fiber networks. In particular, the SONET hierarchy will provide a multiplexing scheme for rates between 45 Mbps and 2.5 Gbps that will incorporate today's digital TDM hierarchies. SONET, and its companion CCITT recommendations, will pave the way for a robust, worldwide optical fiber infrastructure that will be ideal for B-ISDN implementations. Indeed, the ATM external frame structure (Fig. 4.17) seems to have been designed with SONET in mind. B-ISDN and SONET standards will undoubtedly evolve in parallel.

4.4.5 B-ISDN Channels, Functional Devices, and Reference Points

As noted in Chap. 2, additional H-channels have been proposed for B-ISDN applications. H_2- and H_4-channels were proposed in the 1988 recommendation. H_3-channels, which would operate in the 60- to 70-Mbps range, were not proposed because of limited international interest.

B-ISDN standards will use the same functional device and reference point designations defined in Chap. 2. The notation for devices and protocols with broadband capability, however, will be appended with the letter B. Thus, a B-ISDN terminal will be designated B-TE1 and the B-ISDN T reference point will be designated T_B.

Chapter

5

The D-Channel Data Link Protocol

The primary function of the data link layer according to the OSI Reference Model is to provide an error-free communications link between adjacent devices. The protocol has a number of specific tasks it must perform to realize this goal, including:

- *Framing:* Signal the beginning and end of the transmission and delimit the user data

- *Addressing:* Indicate which device on the line is the transmitter or intended receiver of this frame

- *Sequencing:* Maintain sequential order of transmitted data frames

- *Acknowledgment:* Acknowledge receipt of data frames

- *Time outs:* Handle a situation where a reply does not arrive for a given data frame within a specified time period

- *Error control:* Detect bit errors and out-of-sequence frames

- *Flow control:* Provide a mechanism so that a fast transmitter can be prevented from flooding a receiver with data frames

The ISDN D-channel data link protocol is a bit-oriented protocol called LAPD. LAPD is similar to X.25 Link Access Procedures Balanced (LAPB) and both are subsets of the ISO High-level Data Link Control (HDLC) protocol, although there are significant differences between LAPD and LAPB. It is not the intent of this chapter to provide an exhaustive discussion of the operation and procedures of either protocol. Instead, the highlights and main points of LAPD will be described, along with some comparisons to LAPB.

5.1 LINK ACCESS PROCEDURES ON THE D-CHANNEL (LAPD)

The ISDN data link layer protocol is called the Link Access Procedures on the D-channel (LAPD). This protocol defines the logical connection between the user (TE) and the network (NT or LE) across the S and/or T reference points on the D-channel. It supports serial, synchronous, full-duplex communication across either a point-to-point or point-to-multipoint physical connection.

General principles of LAPD are described in CCITT Recommendation Q.920 (I.440) and operational procedures are described in Recommendation Q.921 (I.441). LAPD is also referred to as the Digital Subscriber Signaling System No. 1 (DSS 1) Data Link Layer.

5.1.1 LAPD Frames

The unit of transmission in LAPD is the frame (Fig. 5.1), comprising the following fields:

- *Flag:* The bit pattern 01111110. The flag signals the beginning and end of the frame.

- *Address:* Identifies the user device (and service) that is sending, or intended to receive, the frame. Always two octets.

- *Control:* Identifies the type of frame and may carry sequence and

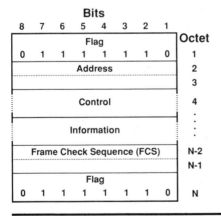

Figure 5.1   LAPD frame format.

acknowledgment numbers. Either one or two octets, depending upon frame type.

- *Information:* Contains level 3 management information or user data or level 2 operations information. Has a variable length but must be octet-aligned; this field is absent in some frames.

- *Frame check sequence (FCS):* Contains the 16-bit remainder from the cyclic redundancy check (CRC) calculation. CRCs are used to detect whether there are bit errors in the frame or not.

It is important to note that bit 1 (the low-order bit) of each octet is transmitted first.

The characteristics of the LAPD protocol that are unique and/or specific to the ISDN environment will be discussed in the following paragraphs.

5.1.2 Transparency and Zero-Bit Insertion

A potential problem with any bit-oriented protocol is the effect of occurrences of the flag bit pattern (01111110) within the frame. That is, if the flag bit pattern actually occurs within the Address, Control, Information, or FCS fields, how does the receiver know to interpret those bits as data rather than as the end-of-frame indicator?

The answer is that the receiver will *not* interpret them correctly. The solution, then, is to make sure that the flag bit pattern never occurs except where the transmitter explicitly wants it, namely, at the beginning and end of a frame. The scheme that ensures that a flag pattern never occurs within a frame is called *zero-bit insertion and removal* (also known as bit stuffing and destuffing).

Zero-bit insertion is quite simple. While the transmitter is sending a frame, it counts the number of contiguous 1 bits. After every fifth contiguous 1 is transmitted, it transmits a 0 bit. Thus, no more than five contiguous 1 bits can ever occur within a frame. For example, if the transmitter wants to send the following bits,

$$0\ 1\ 1\ 1\ 1\ 1\ 1\ 1\ 1\ 1\ 0$$

this bit stream will actually be transmitted ($\underline{0}$ represents an inserted 0 bit):

$$0\ 1\ 1\ 1\ 1\ 1\ \underline{0}\ 1\ 1\ 1\ 1\ \underline{0}\ 0$$

In fact, the number of contiguous 1 bits transmitted is under the control of the transmitter and can be used to signal various events. Exactly six 1 bits (i.e., 01111110) make up a flag. Exactly seven 1 bits indicate an abort signal; the receiver will ignore the aborted frame. Eight or more 1 bits indicate an idle channel.

This zero-bit insertion scheme is slightly different from most bit-oriented protocols, including HDLC and X.25 LAPB. In particular, HDLC/LAPB interprets seven to fourteen 1 bits as an abort signal and 15 or more 1 bits as an idle channel.

5.1.3 The Control Field and LAPD Frame Types

The Control field specifies the type of frame being transmitted. LAPD (and all bit-oriented protocols) define three general types of frame formats, indicated in the Control field (Fig. 5.2):

- *Information (I) frames:* Carries level 2 management information or data from higher layers (including user data). The two-octet Control field contains the sequence number of this I-frame, denoted N(S), and the sequence number of the next expected I-frame from the other station on the link, denoted N(R).

- *Supervisory (S) frames:* Controls the exchange of I-frames. S-frames can indicate acknowledgment, flow control, and receipt of out-of-sequence I-frames. The two-octet Control field also carries the sequence number of the next expected I-frame, N(R). The SS bits specify the type of S-frame.

- *Unnumbered (U) frames:* Controls the status of the logical link and allows exchange of unnumbered data. There is no sequencing associated with U-frames and the Control field is a single octet. These frames are used to initiate and terminate a logical link connection, exchange nonsequenced information, negotiate data link

				Bits					Octet
	8	7	6	5	4	3	2	1	
INFORMATION				N(S)				0	4
				N(R)				P	5
SUPERVISORY	X	X	X	X	S	S	0	1	4
				N(R)				P/F	5
UNNUMBERED	M	M	M	P/F	M	M	1	1	4

N(S)   Sequence number of this I-frame
N(R)   Sequence number of next expected I-frame
S   Supervisory function bit (S-frame type)
M   Modifier function bit (U-frame type)
P/F   Poll/final bit
X   Reserved and set to 0

Figure 5.2 LAPD Control field format.

layer parameters, and indicate certain error conditions. The MMMMM bits specify the type of U-frame.

Table 5.1 lists all I-, S-, and U-frames used in LAPD and briefly describes their function; note that some frame types may only be used as commands, some may only be used as responses, and some may be either. The Poll/Final (P/F) bit (shown in Fig. 5.2) is used for error recovery procedures in a similar fashion as in other bit-oriented protocols.

An ISDN device with no information to send on the D-channel will continuously transmit flags. The exception to this is TEs on a point-to-multipoint BRI, which will send 1 bits in the absence of data. This allows the logical link to become idle, a necessary part of the multipoint D-channel contention resolution scheme (described below).

5.1.4 LAPD Addressing

One of the main features of LAPD is the structure of the Address field (Fig. 5.3) and the ability to multiplex several logical links over the

TABLE 5.1   LAPD Frame Type Summary

Frame Type	Frame Name		C	R	Function
I	I	Information	•		Transfer Layer 3 data
S	RR	Receive Ready	•	•	Acknowledges receipt of previously transmitted I-frames, clears a busy condition signaled by an RNR, and indicates willingness to receive more I-frames
	RNR	Receive Not Ready	•	•	Used for flow control, indicating a temporary inability by the receiver to receive I-frames (a busy condition)
	REJ	Reject	•	•	Requests retransmission of I-frames and clears the RNR busy condition; sent by receiver when an out-of-sequence I-frame is received
U	SABME	Set Asynchronous Balanced Mode Extended	•		Start the logical link for acknowledged information transfer using modulo 128 sequencing (i.e., frames can take on sequence numbers in the range 0 to 127).
	DISC	Disconnect	•		Terminate logical link for acknowledged information transfer
	UI	Unnumbered Information	•		Transfer Layer 3 or link management information using unacknowledged information transfer (i.e., no sequencing numbers)
	UA	Unnumbered Acknowledgement		•	Acknowledges SABME and DISC
	DM	Disconnected Mode		•	Indicates that the logical link has some sort of error and that the station sending the DM cannot continue with information transfer
	FRMR	Frame Reject		•	Reports an error condition that cannot be cleared by the retransmission of an identical frame that caused the error
	XID	Exchange Identification	•	•	Used for automatic data link layer parameter negotiation

C: Command   R: Response

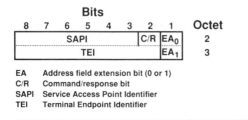

EA   Address field extension bit (0 or 1)
C/R   Command/response bit
SAPI   Service Access Point Identifier
TEI   Terminal Endpoint Identifier

Figure 5.3 LAPD Address field format.

same physical channel. The address, called the Data Link Control Identifier (DLCI), is 13 bits long and comprises two subfields called the Terminal Endpoint Identifier (TEI) and Service Access Point Identifier (SAPI). The TEI and SAPI are described in more detail below.

The command/response (C/R) bit in the Address field is used to differentiate between command and response frames, as defined in Table 5.1. The user side of the logical link will set this bit to 0 for commands and 1 for responses. The network side does the opposite; it sets this bit to 1 for commands and 0 for responses. The C/R bit performs the same function as the Address field in LAPB.

The low-order bit of each octet is called the Address field extension bit. Bit 1 of the first Address octet is set to 0 and bit 1 of the second octet is set to 1, to comply with the HDLC rules for multioctet addresses.

5.1.5 Multiplexing, TEIs, and SAPIs

The BRI allows multiple ISDN terminals to be connected in a point-to-multipoint configuration. Since LAPD provides a point-to-point logical link, there has to be a mechanism in place so that the level 2 protocol multiplexes several logical links.

Figure 5.4 shows the point-to-point connection between two stations. The level 3 entity, or process, in one station is logically connected to its peer level 3 entity in another station. Level 3 messages passed between the stations are carried in the Information field of level 2 (LAPD) frames.

The service access point (SAP) is the conceptual interface between two adjacent protocol layers. Primitives exchanged across a SAP are instructions that allow adjacent protocol layers at one station to exchange information.

The logical connection between the user and the network is, in fact, not quite this simple. Every ISDN TE is capable of supporting more than one level 3 process. One required level 3 service, for example, is the capability to send ISDN signaling messages. Another necessary

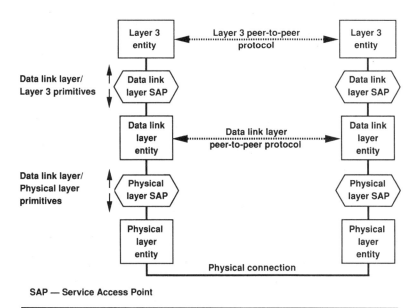

SAP — Service Access Point

Figure 5.4   The data link layer reference model and service access points.

service is the ability to process ISDN Operations, Administration, and Maintenance (OAM) messages. A third process might be the ability to send packet-mode user data. Each of these level 3 processes at the TE must communicate with its peer process in the LE.

Each level 3 process at the TE will have a separate logical link over the D-channel to its peer process in the LE (Fig. 5.5). Each level 3 process is a service that is addressed by a SAPI. Note that several logical links share the single "physical" D-channel. That LAPD can perform this multiplexing function is another unique characteristic of this protocol. (The selection of SAPIs in the figure is not random; the choice of values will be described below.)

The problem of multiplexing several logical links between terminal equipment and the LE is made even more complex by the point-to-multipoint configuration allowed in the BRI (Fig. 5.6). Some of the services available in one TE are the same services available in another TE; thus, the SAPI alone cannot differentiate one logical link from another. The TEs, then, are differentiated from each other by assigning each a TEI. In the figure, TEIs of 93 and 85 are assigned to the two ISDN terminals. Taken together, the SAPI and TEI form a unique address identifying a specific logical link. (The choice of TEIs in this figure is arbitrary; TEI values will also be described below.)

The final complexity with respect to multiple LAPD logical links

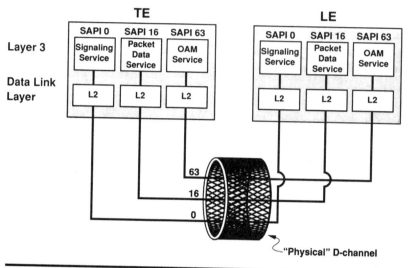

Figure 5.5 Multiple service access points within a TE require multiple LAPD logical connections to the LE.

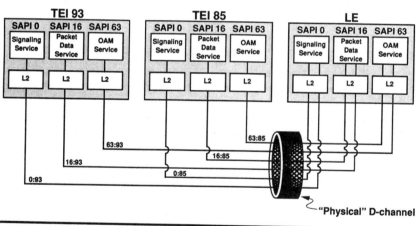

Figure 5.6 Multiple services and multiple TEs require that the LAPD logical links be referred to by their TEI and SAPI.

and multiplexing is the existence of broadcast logical links. The primary purpose of the broadcast logical link is for the local exchange to be able to send a particular frame to every ISDN terminal at an interface that supports a particular service. It may also be used by a TE prior to being assigned a TEI (discussed below). A TEI of 127 is always used for the broadcast logical link.

TABLE 5.2   Service Access Point Identifier (SAPI)
Values

SAPI Value	Related Level 3 Entity
0	Call control procedures
1	Reserved for packet-mode communications using I.451 call control procedures
16	Packet communication using X.25 PLP
32-47	(reserved for national use)
63	OAM, Level 2 management functions
others	(reserved for future standardization)

5.1.6 SAPI Definition

The Service Access Point Identifier is a 6-bit subfield carried in the first octet of the Address field. Although this allows up to 64 SAPI definitions, the CCITT has currently defined only four (Table 5.2). SAPI 0 is used for ISDN call control procedures using messages from the ISDN level 3 protocol, CCITT Recommendation Q.931 (I.451). SAPI 1 is for packet-mode communications using the Q.931 (I.451) protocol, while SAPI 16 is for user packet data conforming to the X.25 level 3 (PLP) procedures. SAPI 63 is used for OAM and level 2 management operations. The remaining values are reserved for future CCITT or national standardization.

It should be noted that not all vendors use all SAPIs as prescribed by the CCITT. For specific implementations and pieces of equipment, a vendor might choose additional values to the four mentioned above and/or might not use all four of these definitions. The reservation of SAPI values for experimental purposes has been left for further study.

5.1.7 TEI Definition and Assignment

The TEI is a 7-bit subfield carried in the second octet of the Address field. This allows the assignment of up to 127 TEIs at a single interface (TEI 127 is reserved for broadcast messages), although this is well more than the number of ISDN terminals that can typically be supported. There are three different classes of TEI (Table 5.3):

- *Nonautomatic TEI assignment user equipment:* Assigned to terminal equipment that is unable to use LAPD procedures to request a TEI from the network. This would include devices where the TEI is programmed into read-only memory (ROM) or where the user selects the TEI using jumpers, thumbwheels, switches, or some other user-selectable option. This approach might be taken to reduce the cost and power requirement of the TE. Even if a TEI is hard wired into the terminal equipment, however, the TEI must be verified and accepted by the local exchange, using LAPD procedures, prior to its use.

- *Automatic TEI assignment user equipment:* Assigned to terminal equipment that is able to use LAPD procedures to automatically request a TEI assignment from the network.

- *Group address (broadcast):* This TEI is used to address all ISDN terminals at an interface. It can also be used temporarily by a TE prior to TEI assignment.

TABLE 5.3   Terminal Endpoint Identifier (TEI) Values

TEI Value	User Type
0-63	Non-automatic TEI assignment user equipment
64-126	Automatic TEI assignment user equipment
127	Group assignment (broadcast) TEI

A TEI is uniquely assigned to one ISDN terminal on a BRI interface. While one TEI may not be assigned to more than one terminal, multiple TEIs may be assigned to a single terminal. Assigning multiple TEIs to one TE may be necessary when the terminal contains more than one level 3 process supporting a given type of service. For example, if a TE supports two applications using an X.25 packet service, both level 3 entities would be assigned a SAPI of 16. These two services represent different user applications, however, so they must somehow be differentiated. One way to accomplish this is to assign two TEIs to the TE so that the two packet services operate on different logical links.

Figure 5.7 shows a LAPD frame exchange demonstrating TEI assignment and the establishment of LAPD logical links:

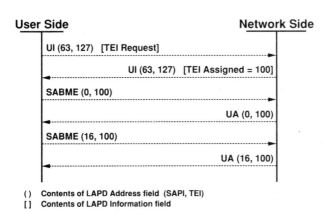

() Contents of LAPD Address field (SAPI, TEI)
[] Contents of LAPD Information field

Figure 5.7   LAPD frame exchange to request TEI assignment and establish logical links.

1. After the TE is physically plugged into the BRI bus, it automatically requests a TEI from the network. This is accomplished by sending an Unnumbered Information (UI) frame, where the contents of the Information field indicate that this is a TEI request. The Address field of the UI contains a SAPI of 63 and a TEI of 127. SAPI 63 indicates that this is an OAM operation and the broadcast TEI is used since this terminal does not yet have a TEI.

2. The network receives the TEI request and responds with a UI frame, where the Information field contains the TEI assignment; in this example, the TE is assigned a TEI value of 100. Note again the use of SAPI 63 and TEI 127 in the UI Address field.

3. The TE now needs to initiate LAPD logical links prior to exchanging any data. In this example, a logical link will first be established to send signaling messages, that is, a logical link for SAPI 0. This process is initiated when the TE sends a Set Asynchronous Balanced Mode Extended (SABME) frame with SAPI 0 and a TEI of 100.

4. The network acknowledges establishment of the logical link by responding with an Unnumbered Acknowledgment (UA) frame for SAPI 0, TEI 100. SAPI 0 (call control) messages may now be exchanged between the user and the network.

5. The TE initiates establishment of a LAPD link for packet-mode data transfer by sending a SABME with SAPI 16, TEI 100.

6. The network responds with a UA to set up the link. SAPI 16 (X.25 packet-mode) data may now be exchanged between the user and the network.

The procedure outlined above is followed by every user device (TE) to obtain an identifier and then to set up a logical link for every level 3 service (or SAPI) that is required.

A 16-bit reference number (Ri), selected at random, is associated with each TEI request. When a TE sees an incoming TEI assignment, it checks to be sure that the reference number in the incoming UI frame matches the reference number that it placed in its TEI request. This procedure provides some protection in case two or more TEs request a TEI simultaneously. The recommendation does not address the situation when two outgoing TEI requests contain the same Ri value.

A LAPD procedure also exists to release a TEI when terminal equipment is being permanently disconnected or if the terminal can detect an imminent power failure about to occur: the logical links are terminated by sending Disconnect (DISC) frames and then the TEI is deassigned using a UI frame.

Current standards do not address the situation where a sudden power failure causes all TEs to "forget" their TEI and crash prior to releasing them. In this case, all of the TEs would ask the network for new TEIs once power was restored, but there is no standard way to have the network erase the old TEIs. Some sort of time-out procedure implemented at the network side is the most common approach to handling this problem.

5.1.8 Contention in the Point-to-Multipoint Configuration

As mentioned earlier, LAPD and the I.430 BRI physical layer implement a contention scheme for the D-channel in the point-to-multipoint configuration. When multiple devices share a communications line (or channel), a problem exists in determining which device is allowed to transmit next.

In LAPD, the problem is further complicated because all logical links are uniquely identified by a SAPI/TEI address and are multiplexed on the "physical" D-channel. Which LAPD logical connection, then, is allowed to be active next?

This problem is similar to that faced by terminals connected to a cluster controller, such as in an IBM BISYNC environment. In BISYNC, a large amount of time and overhead is spent as the controller polls and selects all tributary devices. This overhead is unacceptable in the ISDN environment because of the fast response that is required and the potentially large number of logical links that might be established. In addition, there will probably be only a few logical links active at one time; optimal use of the line dictates that a station be serviced when it is ready and that the idle stations be ignored.

The problem, then, could be solved using a local area network (LAN) medium access control (MAC) approach, since LANs interconnect peer devices (i.e., devices that have equal responsibility to control and access the network). The two most common LAN MAC schemes are contention (used in Ethernet) and distributed polling (used in token passing). These schemes are also unsuitable for the ISDN environment. Contention causes the loss of time slots whenever two stations transmit at the same time, or collide. Furthermore, contention network performance degrades as contending devices (in this case, logical links) are added to the bus. Token passing does not have collisions but does have a minimum time delay associated with the circulation of the token to all stations. This overhead, too, is potentially unacceptable since it limits the performance of the equipment likely to be attached to the BRI.

The ISDN solution is to use a contention scheme called *perfect scheduling*. In this scheme, collisions might occur but no data is ever lost because of a collision. Furthermore, as long as any device has a frame to send, the bus will be used. Thus, this is perfect scheduling from the perspective of the network; there are no wasted or lost time slots, so the network resources are optimally used.

Collisions will not destroy data because of the electronics of the station's passive connection to the bus and the line code used for signaling. Recall that in pseudo-ternary signaling, a 1 bit is represented by the absence of voltage and a 0 bit, by a positive or negative voltage. Recall also that TEs on the BRI transmit continuous 1s when not sending frames on the D-channel; thus, idle TEs apply no voltage to the line.

Finally, recall that the NT echoes back all D-channel bits sent in the TE-to-NT direction. In this way, all TEs can listen to the D-channel while they transmit. If multiple terminals transmit simultaneously on the D-channel, the only way that a 1 bit will be echoed back is if they all transmitted a 1; if any TE transmited a 0, a 0 will be echoed back. The bit echoed back, then, is equivalent to the logical AND function applied to all of the inputs.

All stations monitor the echoed D-channel by comparing the echo to their own transmission. If a TE detects an echoed D-channel bit that is the same as the last bit it transmitted, it continues to transmit. If it detects a bit that is different, it stops its transmission.

There are two more issues involved in the contention scheme. First, what types of transmissions should have priority on the D-channel? Remember that the main purpose of the D-channel is for user-network signaling; it is only because signaling is unlikely to require the full bandwidth of the D-channel that excess bandwidth is allocated to other applications, such as packet-mode user data. Second, how are one or more TEs prevented from monopolizing use of the D-channel?

Frames carrying signaling messages are given priority (priority class 1) over frames carrying nonsignaling messages (priority class 2). Priority class 1 frames have a SAPI of 0; frames with a nonzero SAPI are in priority class 2 (Table 5.4).

To ensure that no TE can dominate the D-channel, a normal and lower priority are defined within each class. The priorities are en-

TABLE 5.4   LAPD Priority Classes and Levels

	Priority Class 1 (SAPI = 0)	Priority Class 2 (SAPI ≠ 0)
Normal	8	10
Lower	9	11

forced by the number of contiguous 1 bits that must be detected by a TE before it can start to transmit, as shown in Table 5.4. After a TE transmits the final flag of a frame, it will let the line become idle (i.e., all 1s). Since all TEs are monitoring the D-channel, they all know when the channel is available for use.

All stations start out in the normal priority level within their class. After detecting the required number of 1 bits, one or more TEs may begin to transmit. Although there may be collisions if more than one TE transmits, only one transmission will be successful.

When a TE successfully transmits a frame, it moves into the lower priority (within that class); i.e., it must wait for a higher number of 1s before it can transmit again. If a station is in the lower priority and detects the number of 1s associated with that priority class, it moves back to the normal priority (and, optionally, transmits). This means that all TEs with signaling messages (SAPI 0) will have access to the D-channel before any TEs with nonsignaling messages. Furthermore, within each priority class, all TEs wanting to transmit will get one opportunity to transmit on the D-channel before any TE gets a second opportunity.

As an example, consider two ISDN terminals that want to transmit a frame containing a signaling (SAPI 0) message. Terminal A has a TEI of 10, while terminal B has a TEI of 17. Initially, both are waiting to detect eight 1 bits before they can transmit. After detecting eight 1 bits on the D-channel, both terminals begin to transmit their frame. Note that the first bit transmitted is a 0 (first bit of the flag), so no other terminals will try to start transmitting.

For several bits, the transmissions of the two terminals will be identical. Both start with a flag bit pattern. Since they are both sending SAPI 0 information, their first Address octet will also be the same (all 0s). The second Address octet will differ since it contains the TEI. In this example, terminal A (TEI 10) will successfully transmit. It will then move into the lower priority and must wait for nine 1 bits prior to a subsequent transmission. Meanwhile, terminal B (TEI 17) detects the collision and ceases its transmission immediately.

Terminal B will successfully transmit at the next opportunity after it detects the next block of eight 1 bits; it, too, will then move to the lower priority.

Since both TEs are in the lower priority, they take no action when they next detect a block of eight 1 bits. After detecting the ninth 1 bit, however, terminals A and B will both move back to the normal priority and begin to transmit their next frame. Terminal A, again, will be successful and will return to the lower priority.

Since terminal B failed in its attempt to transmit and is already back at the normal priority, it only has to detect eight 1 bits before it can transmit again. It will successfully transmit and move back to the lower priority.

This fairness scheme is essential. Without it, those stations with the most low-order 0s in their TEI would be able to dominate the D-channel.

5.2 LAPB AND LAPD

The CCITT recommendations and some ISDN implementations allow the use of the X.25 LAPB protocol on the D-channel. There is no problem distinguishing between the two protocols because their Address fields differ. LAPB has a single octet Address field where the low-order bit is always set to 1; the low-order bit of the first Address octet in LAPD is always 0. Therefore, the network or user can immediately detect which protocol is being used after receiving the first bit following the flag. Table 5.5 summarizes some of the differences between LAPD and LAPB.

Of more significance is the question "Why use LAPB on the D-channel in the first place?" LAPB defines a point-to-point connection between a DTE and DCE, which could certainly be applied to an ISDN

TABLE 5.5   Some of the Differences between LAPB and LAPD

LAPB	LAPD
One octet Address field	Two octet Address field
Two timers (T1 & T3) and one timer parameter (T2)	Four timers (T200, T201, T202, & T203)
Three system parameters (N1, N2, & k)	Four system parameters (N200, N201, N202, & k)
Point-to-point only	Supports point-to-multipoint and statistical multiplexing of several logical links
	Uses UI and XID frames
Modulo 8 (SABM) or 128 (SABME) sequencing	Modulo 128 (SABME) sequencing only
Abort signal is 7-14 contiguous 1 bits	Abort signal is 7 contiguous 1 bits
Idle channel is indicated by 15 or more contiguous 1 bits	Idle channel is indicated by 8 or more contiguous 1 bits
8-bit Address used to differentiate commands from responses	C/R-bit in Address field used to differentiate commands from responses

user and network. The problem is that there is no way to define two LAPB logical links across a single user-network interface the way multiple LAPD links can be defined. Therefore, only a single device may use LAPB across the interface at any given time. If some application is written so that it requires LAPB, that application might be locked out by another application using LAPB at the same time at this interface.

One observes, then, that the use of LAPB for an application in an ISDN device is limited. ISDN devices must support LAPD anyway, for OAM and signaling. The conclusion is that a device connected to an ISDN should not depend on the availability of the X.25 LAPB protocol.

This brings up another issue. X.25 LAPB is used to carry X.25 level 3 (PLP) packets; but how should X.25 level 3 information be carried if the use of the X.25 level 2 protocol is discouraged on the D-channel? Part of the answer is that data from any level 3 protocol, including the X.25 PLP, may be carried in the Information field of LAPD I-frames. How the level 3 protocols are differentiated from each other is discussed in Chap. 6.

The comments made here are not meant to imply that today's X.25 hosts will be obsolete on an ISDN. A terminal adaptor (TA) for an X.25 DTE can easily convert the LAPB frame into an ISDN LAPD frame without affecting the contents of the level 3 information.

6

The D-Channel Layer 3 Protocol[1]

This chapter will provide a broad description of the signaling protocols that are used between a user's terminal and a serving ISDN. The terms *layer 3, user network, basic call control, supplementary services,* and *signaling procedures* as they relate to ISDN will be defined and the explicit use of the ISDN term *user's terminal* will be explained. The structure of the protocols and the message format will also be covered. The procedures for connecting and disconnecting a basic circuit-mode call will be discussed in enough detail to illuminate the user-network signaling process. The access connection and its role in packet-mode calls will be introduced, as will the three techniques for supporting packet services on an ISDN, circuit mode on a B-channel, packet mode on a B-channel, and packet mode on the D-channel.

One of the major additions to the 1988 versions of the CCITT ISDN recommendations concerns supplementary services. The Keypad, Feature Key Management, and Functional protocols for controlling and invoking supplementary services will be described, along with their division into the stimulus and functional categories. The format of these messages and information elements will be discussed, as will the changing user-network interface in the ISDN era.

All of these topics are described in CCITT recommendations. Recommendation Q.930 (I.450) describes general principles of user-network signaling, Recommendation Q.931 (I.451) describes user-

---

[1]Sections 6.1 through 6.4 were written by E. Raymond Hapeman, the chairman of the ANSI T1S1.2 Task Group dealing with ISDN Switching and Signaling Protocols. Ray is a Member of the Technical Staff at Bell Communications Research in Red Bank, NJ.

network messages for basic call control, and Recommendation Q.932 (I.452) describes messages for supplementary services. These protocols form the Digital Subscriber Signaling System No. 1 (DSS 1) Network Layer.

6.1 LAYER 3 USER-NETWORK SIGNALING

This chapter addresses the layer 3 user-network signaling procedures for basic call control and for the control and invocation of supplementary services. That sentence is quite a mouthful; dissecting it will lead to greater understanding.

The term *layer 3* comes from the now-familiar OSI seven-layer model for data communication and networking protocols. Using it in the context of user-network signaling procedures signifies that these protocols provide the functions of an OSI network layer for the call control entities in the user's terminal and in the network. It also signifies that they use the services of a layer 2, or data link layer, protocol (in this case, LAPD). These protocols do not, however, belong to the OSI suite of protocols that is being developed for computer-to-computer communications.

The term *user-network* tells us that these procedures are used across the interface between a user's ISDN terminal and the serving ISDN. To be considered an ISDN terminal, a terminal must be capable of using the procedures outlined in this chapter. It need not, however, be a terminal in the traditional sense of the word; it might be a PBX, concentrator, or, in fact, any other device that has the capabilities needed to terminate the user's side of the ISDN user-network interface. Terminals which cannot use these procedures (such as analog telephones, asynchronous data terminals, and modems) would be connected to a terminal adaptor (TA). In this case, the TA becomes the user's ISDN terminal (for the purposes of this chapter).

It must also be noted that these user-network interface procedures only exist across the local interface between an ISDN user and the serving network. They are not the same ones that are used between the switching nodes in the network (which is Signaling System No. 7) and they do not extend across the network. Information that must be passed along through the network must be read from the ISDN protocol and mapped to the SS7 protocol. If necessary, a reverse mapping is done in the destination ISDN exchange.

The term *basic call control* means that the call will simply be established, maintained, and disconnected. The term implies that a single transmission path is created across the network from one user to another. In basic call control, the path is set up immediately. Also, it is set up directly from the calling party to the intended called party. The CCITT protocols for basic call control are published in Recommendation Q.931 (I.451).

Supplementary services is an ISDN term that encompasses a wide range of features. These features provide additional capabilities so that users can have greater control over how the network handles their transmission paths. For example, call forwarding, call waiting, call transfer, and call hold are a few of the capabilities that are included under the supplementary services umbrella. There is a very important point to be made here: ISDN supplementary services must not be confused with information services or general-purpose computer applications. The CCITT protocols for controlling supplementary services are published in Recommendation Q.932 (I.452).

The final term, *signaling procedures,* means that these procedures are used by the user's terminal and the network to signal back and forth between themselves, to tell each other what they want. Some of the data in a signaling message might be put to other uses or even passed along to the user. Nonetheless, the purpose of these signaling procedures is just that: signaling. These procedures apply to both the basic and primary rate interfaces.

The term *user's terminal* is being used on purpose. The signaling procedures that are employed between a user (which might not even be a human) and the user's terminal are completely outside the scope of this chapter. They are limited only by the ingenuity of manufacturers and the economics of the marketplace. Instructing the terminal to place a call might be as familiar as twisting a numbered fingerwheel or as new as speaking to the instrument. Procedures to announce an incoming call at the terminating end might be a ringing bell or a voice synthesizer that calmly says that a call is waiting to be answered.

6.1.1 The Structure of the Protocols

In analog telephony, users signal their desire to place a call by lifting the telephone receiver from the switchhook. This places an electrical short on the line, allowing current to flow from the central office, out through the user's telephone, and back to the central office, where it passes through the winding of a relay. The relay operates and the network "knows" that the user wants to place a call. The network, in turn, transmits a dial tone to the user as a signal that it is ready to receive further signals (the dial pulses or tones).

ISDN signaling protocols depend upon the exchange of digital messages between the user's terminal and the network. Each message consists of a series of information elements. Information elements, in turn, consist of fields, which are coded with the necessary signaling information.

There are 25 different types of ISDN signaling messages listed in Q.931 and eight more defined in Q.932. Obviously, 33 different messages would be completely inadequate to provide the wide range of services and features that are needed by modern users of telecommunications. The great flexibility of ISDN is achieved by constructing each message so that it conveys the specific information that is needed to support the call or service that is desired at that moment. Even so, each type of message has a specific purpose and its name usually reveals that purpose. For example, there are SETUP, CONNECT, and DISCONNECT messages. How some of them are used will be described in more detail later. A complete list of messages is contained in App. C.

Messages are constructed of a header and a series of information elements. The header, which is required in every message, consists of three parts. They are the Protocol Discriminator to identify the protocol to which the message belongs, a Call Reference Value (CRV) to identify the specific call to which the message applies, and a Message Type to identify the message from among the 33 message types. (The message format is discussed in more detail later in this chapter.)

The information elements follow the header in a prescribed sequence. As with message names, the names of the information elements often reveal their purpose. For example, there are Called party number, Packet-size, and Transit network selection information elements. Some of the information elements (and how they are used in certain cases) are mentioned in the following sections; a complete list and description of information elements is in App. C.

Information elements are constructed of fields. Each field can be coded in a number of different ways so as to contain the necessary information. As with messages and information elements, the names of the fields often reveal the kind of information they contain. For example, the Bearer capability information element contains an Information transfer capability field that identifies the call as speech, digital information, or video and a Transfer-mode field that identifies the call as being circuit mode or packet mode. Interested readers are urged to refer to the appropriate recommendations for a complete description of the fields and how they are coded.

6.2 BASIC CIRCUIT-MODE CALLS

This section describes how a user's terminal and the network signal each other to connect and disconnect a basic circuit-mode call. As described earlier, a basic call is one that is simply established directly from the calling party to the called party, maintained, and disconnected. A circuit-mode call is one in which the entire bearer channel is dedicated to the user for the duration of the call. Its counterpoint is a packet-mode call, in which several users' transmissions (virtual calls) may be multiplexed onto the same channel.

6.2.1 Connecting the Call

The messages exchanged to set up a circuit-mode call are shown in Fig. 6.1 and described below.

The calling party starts the sequence by sending a SETUP message to the network. In the SETUP message, the user sends the network the information that the network needs to connect the call. Some examples of such information are the desired Bearer capability, the identity of the called party, and the B-channel that the user's terminal suggests be used for this call.

Bearer capability is a term that may be new, but it embodies the essence of ISDN; it defines the attributes of the service that the user wants from the network. The discussion in Chap. 3 on bearer services introduced the idea that a call can be packet mode or circuit mode, speech or 3.1-kHz audio, or any of several other options. The fields in the Bearer capability information element identify the user's Bearer service requirements. The Information transfer capability field is a useful example of the concept. This field can contain the code for any one of several different capabilities, including speech, unrestricted digital information (UDI), restricted digital information (RDI), 3.1-kHz audio, 7-kHz audio, or video.

The Bearer capability information element also allows the user to specify the physical interface to be used to provide the requested bearer service. Recall that the North American PRI can be configured

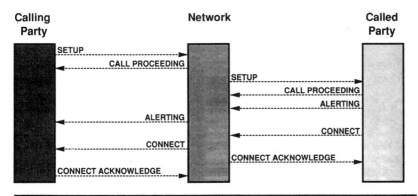

Figure 6.1   Call establishment message exchange.

as 23B + D or 24B channels. In the latter configuration, however, there is no D-channel on which to request services. By design, a D-channel can be used to request bearer services on any B-channel across the user-network interface.

A closer look at the Called party number information element will demonstrate another ISDN feature. This information element has three fields of signaling information: the Type of number, the Numbering plan identification, and the Number digits. The Type of number field can identify the number as an international number, a national number, or a number coming from a numbering plan that is specific to the network. It can even identify the number as an abbreviated number, such as those dialed between Centrex users. The Numbering plan identification field specifies which of several numbering plans the number belongs to: the ISDN telephony number plan described in CCITT Recommendations E.163 and E.164, the data network numbering plan per Recommendation X.121, and the telex numbering plan per Recommendation F.69 are examples. The Number digits field is nothing more than a string of numbers representing the address, coded as International Alphabet No. 5 (IA5) characters. IA5 is nearly identical to the American Standard Code for Information Interchange (ASCII).

The inclusion of the Channel identification information element in a SETUP message points out another ISDN feature. An ISDN user-network interface can have more than one bearer channel. One of them must be chosen for the call that is being connected and both the user's terminal and the network must know which one it is. The actual choice is negotiated by exchanging Channel identification information elements in the messages that are used during the call setup procedures. The network has the final say.

One final point to make about the SETUP message is that the user's terminal can choose to send the called party's address in either of two modes: *enbloc* (complete in a single message) or *overlap* (in a series of messages). If the complete number is sent in a single SETUP message, it is enbloc. On the other hand, if the user's terminal chooses to send the called party number one digit at a time, it is overlap sending. For our example, assume that the enbloc mode is being used.

Upon receipt of the enbloc SETUP message, the network checks to be sure that the contents of the message are valid, that the user is authorized to use the requested Bearer capability, the requested B-channel is available, etc. Satisfied that everything is in order, the network returns a CALL PROCEEDING message to the user to indicate that the call request is valid and that call setup is in progress. The network also activates the B-channel connection and starts setting up the call toward the called party. (We will neither discuss nor diagram the intranetwork signaling that would occur if the called party were served by a different central office switch from the calling party. The user-network signaling procedures are the same regardless of whether or not the two parties are served by the same switch.)

At the terminating end of the call, the network sends a SETUP message to the called party. This SETUP message is not the same one that was sent to the network by the calling party (remember that each interface protocol serves the local interface), but it is put together much the same way and it contains much of the same information. Values that would be different in the terminating and originating SETUP messages would include the call reference value and, possibly, some of the ISDN access attributes.

The Bearer capability information might be particularly important at the terminating end if the called party has more than one terminal connected to the interface. For example, suppose that a voice terminal, a digital data terminal, and a facsimile machine were attached to the line. An incoming call with a Bearer capability information element coded to speech could only be answered by the voice terminal; the others would have to ignore it.

The Calling party number information element might also be included in the terminating SETUP message. If it is, an intriguing possibility arises: we could store a list of our friends' telephone numbers in our ISDN terminal at home and program the terminal not to disturb us during dinner unless the calling party's number were on the list. One significant difference between North American and international implementations of ISDN is that the American National Standard does not support overlap receiving at the terminating end of the call.

In some cases, the called party's first response to the SETUP message is a CALL PROCEEDING message. This is particularly useful if the final destination of the call is a station served by a device that multiplexes calls, such as a PBX. In this case, the PBX would use the CALL PROCEEDING message to inform the network that the call request has been received and is being processed. This is important because the network has some timers running and will take action to correct what it thinks is an error condition if it does not receive a response from the called party before the timers expire.

Usually, the called party's first response to the network is an ALERTING message rather than a CALL PROCEEDING Message. The primary purpose of the ALERTING message is to inform the network that the user's terminal has received the call request and is alerting the user. This action by the called party's terminal equipment is analogous to the action taken by an analog exchange when it rings the called party's telephone and sends ring-back tones to the calling party. In the ISDN case, the ALERTING message is part of the local interface. The network takes steps to inform the originating interface that the called party is being alerted, but this particular ALERTING message does not get sent to the calling party.

After receiving an indication that the called party is being alerted, the network generates an ALERTING message and sends it to the calling party's terminal. Here, as in other cases we have mentioned, ingenuity and the marketplace can probably be counted on to come up with some clever ways to let the calling party know that the called party is being alerted.

When the called party's terminal accepts the call, it sends a CON-NECT message to the network. When the network receives this CON-NECT message, it stops its timers, completes the circuit switched path to the bearer channel, sends a CONNECT ACKNOWLEDGE message to the called party, and initiates procedures to have a CONNECT message sent to the calling party.

At the originating interface, the network sends a CONNECT message to the calling party, thé call is connected, and the two parties can communicate. In the jargon of ISDN, the call is said to now be in the *data transfer phase* (even if it is a voice call).

6.2.2 Disconnecting the Call

As one would expect, disconnecting a call is much easier than setting one up (Fig. 6.2). The procedure starts when one party's terminal sends a DISCONNECT message to the network and disconnects itself from the B-channel. The network returns a RELEASE message to the party that initiated the disconnect and initiates procedures to have a DISCONNECT message sent to the other party. The initiating party's terminal completes the exchange of messages with a RELEASE COM-PLETE message. At this time, the network releases the B-channel.

At the other end of the call, the network sends a DISCONNECT message to the user's terminal. The terminal responds with a RE-

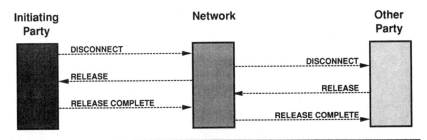

Figure 6.2 Call termination message exchange.

LEASE message. The network releases the B-channel at this interface and sends a RELEASE COMPLETE message to the terminal. At this point, the terminal can also release the B-channel, making all resources available for another call.

It should be noted that the DISCONNECT message has end-to-end significance, while the RELEASE and RELEASE COMPLETE messages have meaning only across the local user-network interfaces.

6.3 BASIC X.25 CALLS

There is a very significant difference between packet switched data calls and other types of ISDN calls: packet switched calls need protocol support during the data transfer phase of the call. Therefore, a procedure which merely provided a circuit-mode connection between two X.25 terminals would be inadequate. Instead, X.25 terminals must have a connection over which they have access to a virtual circuit service from either a packet switched public data network (PSPDN) or the ISDN's own packet handler. The virtual circuit service provides the protocol support that the terminals need for their X.25 call control and data transfer techniques. The task for ISDN, then, is to provide an access connection between the X.25 terminal and its serving virtual circuit service. Once the access connection is in place, the X.25 terminal and the virtual circuit service use X.25 packet layer procedures for the data call. Parameters such as the allowable number of virtual calls or whether or not there are one-way services depend upon the packet handling services offered by the X.25 network, not the access connection capabilities of the ISDN. Readers should take note of the terminology: Q.931 procedures will be used to set up an ISDN access connection and X.25 Packet Layer Protocol (PLP) procedures will be used to set up an X.25 virtual call.

ISDN supports three techniques for setting up access connections. They are:

- "Dial-up" access connections over a B-channel using a basic circuit-mode call to reach a remote packet handler (usually a PSPDN)
- Packet-mode access connections over a B-channel to the ISDN's packet handler
- Packet-mode access connections over the D-channel to the ISDN's packet handler

The paragraphs below will discuss the ISDN procedures to set up and disconnect access connections to be used for X.25 transmissions. The X.25 procedures that are used to establish, maintain, and disconnect the X.25 call are not discussed, as they are outside the scope of this book.

6.3.1 Circuit-Mode Access to Remote Packet Handlers

A circuit-mode access connection is nothing more or less than an ISDN circuit-mode call. Therefore, there is little to be said about the procedures for controlling such an access connection that has not already been said above. The fact that the purpose of the procedure is to create an access connection does, however, restrict some of the options that are available and looking at some of them will illustrate some interesting points about ISDN.

The calling party's intention is to have a bearer channel access connection to a PSPDN. Thus, the called party for the ISDN SETUP message is an access port in the PSPDN, called an access unit (AU) (Fig. 6.3). It seems reasonable that the AU, as both the called party and the called party's terminal, would not normally bother with a CALL PROCEEDING or ALERTING message.

If the AU were to receive an X.25 call setup packet from the PSPDN that was addressed to the ISDN user's terminal and an ISDN access connection did not already exist, the AU would act as the calling party and originate the ISDN SETUP message to create one. Either the user or the AU may initiate an X.25 call over an existing access connection regardless of which party originally set it up.

The Bearer capability information element must specify either UDI or RDI in the Information transfer capability field. It must also specify circuit mode in the Information transfer mode field. This technique uses X.25's data link layer procedures (LAPB) rather than ISDN's (LAPD).

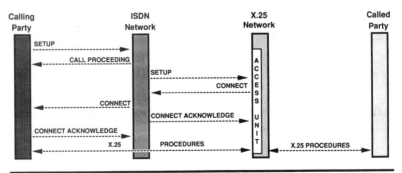

Figure 6.3 Message exchange to establish a circuit-mode access connection to a remote packet handler.

6.3.2 B-Channel Access to the ISDN Virtual Circuit Service

B-channel access to the ISDN packet handler is a technique that users can employ to set up an access connection over a B-channel directly to an X.25 virtual circuit service. The signaling procedures do not impose any restrictions on the location of this packet handler, but it is reasonable to expect that it would normally be local to the ISDN. In any case, that is how it would appear to the user.

The signaling procedures to support this capability are very similar to the ones for the circuit-mode procedure discussed above. There are, however, a few interesting differences. One example is that overlap sending is not allowed. Also, the network does not send a CALL PROCEEDING message; instead, it sends a CONNECT message as soon as it accepts the request for the access connection.

The encodings in the Bearer capability information element reveal some of the other differences. The Information transfer capability field is set to UDI, the Information transfer mode field is set to packet mode, and the Information transfer rate field is set so as to indicate the packet transfer rate.

This technique also uses X.25's data link layer procedures rather than ISDN's.

6.3.3 D-channel Access to the ISDN Virtual Circuit Service

D-channel access to the ISDN virtual circuit service is a second technique which allows users to set up access connections directly to the ISDN's X.25 packet switching capability. To use this technique, the user simply wraps the X.25 packet in a LAPD Information frame, sets the Service Access Point Identifier (SAPI) to 16, and sends the frame to the network over the D-channel. None of the call control messages that are discussed elsewhere in this chapter are used.

6.4 CONTROLLING AND INVOKING SUPPLEMENTARY SERVICES

The terms *control* and *invoke* are used with respect to ISDN's supplementary services because users must do both to get the full benefits of these services.

Users control a supplementary service when they give the network the parameters that the network needs to provide the desired service. The control of supplementary services may or may not be correlated to a call in progress. In fact, control may often be totally unrelated to any specific call. For example, one element in the control of call forwarding is to give the network the number of the ISDN terminal to which calls should be forwarded. This step normally takes place without a call on the line. Note that the fact that a user can control a supplementary service implies that the user has been authorized to use it. The authorization process is not part of the control process that is being discussed here.

To invoke a supplementary service is to start the real-time process that occurs when the network actually performs the requested service. Continuing with the call forwarding example, the service is invoked when a call arrives for the user and is forwarded to another user.

ISDNs support three techniques to control and invoke supplementary services: the Keypad protocol, the Feature Key Management protocol, and the Functional protocol.

The first two techniques are characterized as *stimulus* protocols. Stimulus protocols are those which do not require that the user's terminal have any knowledge of the procedures that are used to control and invoke supplementary services. *Functional* protocols, on the other hand, are protocols which, like the basic call control protocols described above, include specific messages that are generated by the user's terminal to invoke and control specific supplementary services. To use a functional protocol, the user's terminal must know which message to send and how to create it.

These protocols can coexist on the same ISDN switch in a wide variety of combinations. For example, a single user-network interface might use Keypad for one supplementary service, Feature Key Management for a second, and Functional for a third. Or, the switch might support all supplementary services with a single protocol technique. Or, the switch might support all supplementary services with one technique on one customer interface and use a second technique to support the services on another customer interface. The technique(s) to be offered by any individual network is at the option of the network provider.

6.4.1 The Keypad Protocol

The Keypad protocol evokes memories of pushing a pound sign and a couple of numbers to tell the central office to forward all calls. In fact, it was designed with a human user in mind.

To use the protocol, the user's terminal puts a sequence of keypad strokes (0–9, #, *) into the Keypad facility information element of a SETUP or INFORMATION message and sends it to the network. (As expected, the sequence of keypad strokes is usually entered via the terminal's dialing pad by a human user.) The network interprets the sequence of keystrokes and checks to see if the information is complete. If not, the network prompts the user for more information in either or both of two ways: by putting some sort of tone or announcement on the line or by sending an INFORMATION message. The INFORMATION message would normally cause the user's terminal to display a message for the user and/or to generate an audible or visual signal of some sort. After the network has received all of the information that it needs to provide the requested service, it takes the appropriate action (control or invocation).

The specific sequences of keystrokes that are used to control or invoke specific supplementary services have not been standardized. They are a network option, so it is likely that they will differ from location to location.

Note that this protocol meets the definition of stimulus; only the human user and the network need to have any knowledge of the meaning of the sequence of keystrokes.

6.4.2 The Feature Key Management Protocol

The Feature Key Management protocol is the other stimulus protocol that is used to control and invoke supplementary services. In its most simplistic implementation, the human user depresses a *feature key* somewhere on the ISDN terminal, but not on the dialing pad, and the terminal generates a *feature identifier number*. This number identifies the key that was depressed, not the supplementary service procedure that is to take place. The feature identifier number is transmitted to the network and the network looks up what it means.

To use the protocol, the user's terminal puts the feature identifier number into the Feature activation information element of a SETUP or INFORMATION message and sends it to the network. The network interprets the number by looking for its meaning in the user's service profile and checks to see if it has all the information it needs. If not, the network sends an INFORMATION message with an Information request information element to prompt the user for more information. After the network has received all of the information that it needs to provide the service desired by the user, it takes the appropriate action (control or invocation).

The specific feature identifier numbers that are used to control or invoke specific supplementary services have also not been standardized. In fact, the intention is that each feature identifier number might have a different meaning in each user's service profile. As a result, each user might have the same make and model of terminal but a different service profile and, therefore, a different suite of available supplementary services. Or, a user could assign a completely different service to a feature identifier number, thus getting a new service without buying a new terminal. Or, a large number of individual users in a single group (Centrex, for example) might share a service profile.

6.4.3 The Functional Protocol

The Functional protocol is similar to the basic call control protocols in the sense that the user's terminal and the network use a set of defined messages to signal each other for the control and invocation of supplementary services. Terminals that use Functional protocols (unlike those that use stimulus procedures) must know the meaning of the messages they send and receive.

The Functional protocol is divided into two categories of procedures, the separate message approach and the common information element procedure.

The separate message approach uses a distinct message type to signal for each desired function. So far, six messages have been defined for the separate message approach. Three of them are used in the procedures to place a call on hold and the other three are used to retrieve it. To place a call on hold, the user's terminal or the network transmits a HOLD message and gets a HOLD ACKNOWLEDGE message in response. To retrieve the call, a RETRIEVE message is sent and a RETRIEVE ACKNOWLEDGE message is received in return. The other two messages, HOLD REJECT and RETRIEVE REJECT, are used if the requested action cannot be performed for some reason. A serving ISDN can have several calls on hold at the same time; the Call Reference Value in each of these messages identifies the call in question. These six messages are defined in Recommendation Q.932.

The common information element procedure uses a single, common information element (the Facility information element) to signal for supplementary services. The Facility information element may be carried by a FACILITY message, a REGISTER message, or any of the call control messages.

By the end of the CCITT's 1985–1988 Study Period, only the structure and coding of the Facility information element had been defined. None of the procedures to use the information element to control and invoke supplementary services had been developed. One would expect that this subject will be the focus of intense activity during the 1989–1992 Study Period.

Notwithstanding the lack of procedural information, a high-level view of the information element's structure can give some clues as to how it may work. The Facility information element looks more like a message than an information element. It consists of three required fields and a variable number of components. The required fields are:

- A Facility information element identifier to identify this information element

- A Length of facility contents octet to tell the receiving end how long the information element is

- A Service discriminator which, so far, can only be coded to say that the information element is being used in a supplementary service application

It is the components that do the real work of the Facility information element. A component is a structured series of octets that is coded in a way that conveys the necessary signaling information. So far, four different types of components have been suggested: invoke, return result, return error, and reject.

6.5 Q.931 MESSAGE FORMAT

As alluded to in Chap. 5 and earlier in this chapter, ISDN layer 3 messages are carried in the Information field of LAPD Information frames. This section will briefly describe the format of these messages.

Messages are composed of fields called *information elements*. All messages have the same general format and consist of the same generic parts (Fig. 6.4):

- Protocol discriminator

- Call reference value

- Message type

- Other information elements, as required

6.5.1 Protocol Discriminator

Recall that any layer 3 protocol can, theoretically, be used on the ISDN D-channel, although Q.931 is specified for user-network signal-

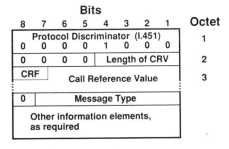

CRF   Call Reference Flag

Figure 6.4 Format of Q.931 (I.451) messages.

ing. In particular, the X.25 Packet Layer Protocol (PLP) will be commonly used on the D-channel for the exchange of X.25 packets.

The first octet of the layer 3 message is the Protocol discriminator information element, indicating the protocol that should be used to interpret the layer 3 transmission. At this time, only two layer 3 protocols are expected to be commonly used over the D-channel, namely, Q.931 and X.25. Table 6.1 lists the values and interpretations of the protocol discriminator. Subsequent discussion in this section assumes use of Q.931 messages.

The reader will observe that a large number of protocol discriminator codings can refer to X.25. This is because X.25 does not have a self-identification procedure such as the one defined for Q.931. Because of the coding rules of X.25 packets, however, bits 5 and 6 of the first octet will never both be zero. Thus, any protocol discriminator octet (i.e., first octet of the layer 3 data unit) with 00 in bits 5 and 6 can refer to any non-X.25 protocol, while all other values in these bit positions may refer to X.25.

6.5.2 Call Reference Value

The Call Reference Value is a number used by the user and the network to refer to an active call. The CRV is assigned at the beginning of a call and remains fixed until the call is terminated (except in the case of call suspension). The CRV has meaning only across a local user-network interface; that is, it has no end-to-end significance. Therefore, there is no reason to assume that the CRV referring to a single call will be the same at the two user-network interfaces. The CRV is analogous to the X.25 logical channel identifier. Both are local references to an end-to-end virtual connection involving two user-network interfaces.

TABLE 6.1   Protocol Discriminator Codings

	BITS 8 7 6 5 4 3 2 1	PURPOSE
through	0 0 0 0 0 0 0 0 0 0 0 0 0 1 1 1	Assigned in I.451; not available for use in the message protocol discriminator.
	0 0 0 0 1 0 0 0	I.451 user-network call control messages.
through	0 0 0 1 0 0 0 0 0 0 1 1 1 1 1 1	Reserved for other Network Layer or Layer 3 protocols, including X.25.
through	0 1 0 0 0 0 0 0 0 1 0 0 1 1 1 1	Reserved for national use.
through	0 1 0 1 0 0 0 0 1 1 1 1 1 1 1 1	Reserved for other Network Layer or Layer 3 protocols, including X.25.
		All other values reserved.

The first octet of the Call reference value information element indicates the number of octets that follow, which contain the actual CRV. To eliminate the possibility that the user and the network will assign the same CRV simultaneously to two different calls, the high-order bit of the call reference value is the Call Reference Flag. This bit is used to identify which end of the logical link originated the call reference; the origination side sets the call reference flag to 0 and the destination side sets the flag to 1. In this way, there can never be a duplicate CRV across a user-network interface.

A special global call reference value is defined with the value of 0. Equipment receiving a message containing the global call reference should interpret the message as pertaining to all current calls at this user-network interface. Use of the global call reference value is similar to the use of logical channel number 0 in X.25.

6.5.3 Message Type

The Message type information element indicates the type of layer 3 message that this transmission represents. All Q.931 and Q.932 messages are described in App. C, along with the appropriate message type value.

6.5.4 Other Information Elements

Unlike many other protocols, particularly the X.25 PLP, Q.931 messages do not have fixed formats. That is, while mandatory and optional information elements follow the Message type information element, there are a number of factors affecting which information elements will actually appear in a given message for a given connection type or application, as suggested in the discussion above.

Information elements are completely self-contained entities. A given message can vary widely in length depending upon which information elements are present, but the message does not contain any indication of the total length. For this reason, the information elements themselves may contain a length indicator. Single-octet information elements are those that comprise only one octet (Fig. 6.5); the information element identifier and contents only occupy one octet. Variable length information elements contain a Length field indicating the number of octets in the contents of the information element (Fig. 6.6). Like messages themselves, variable length information elements can vary widely in length depending upon what information they carry.

Appendix C lists and defines all of the Q.931/Q.932 information el-

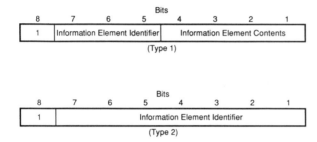

Figure 6.5   Single-octet information element formats.

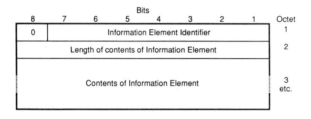

Figure 6.6 Variable length information element format.

ements. Table C.1 indicates which information elements are used with which messages.

6.6   THE HUMAN-NETWORK INTERFACE IN THE ISDN ERA

The user-network interface discussed in this chapter describes the communication between the ISDN user's terminal (e.g., an ISDN telephone) and the network. Before closing the discussion on ISDN user-network signaling, it is important to focus on the interface between the human user and the user's ISDN terminal, although this is not subject to any standardization other than the dictates of the marketplace.

As described earlier, when a person picks up the telephone handset, the telephone equipment closes a circuit and a current is placed on the line (Fig. 6.7). The telephone's off-hook signal results in an audible dial tone coming from the C.O., indicating to the user that it is time to enter (i.e., dial or key) the desired telephone number. As the user enters the number, pulses or dual-tone multifrequency (DTMF) tones are sent to the C.O. and echoed back to the user. The caller periodi-

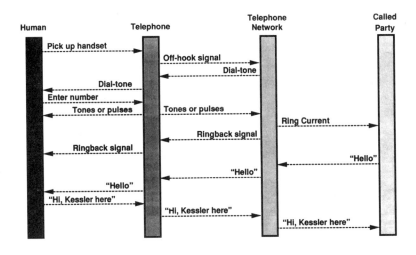

Figure 6.7 Human-telephone and telephone-network interface in today's network.

cally hears a ring signal over the telephone line. Finally, the remote user answers the phone and the two users speak to each other. Note that the network signals for the user (e.g., tones and ringing) and the conversation between the two parties share the same channel.

In the ISDN era, analog tones and signals will no longer travel over the telephone line or through the network; they will be replaced by digital bit streams and network signaling messages. The human-to-telephone interface cannot change too drastically, however. Figure 6.8 expands on the ISDN call setup procedures described earlier to include the interface between the user and an ISDN telephone set. Note how similar the user-telephone interface is before and during the ISDN era but how different the telephone-network interface is. Note also that ISDN signaling is sent on the D-channel whereas the voice conversation occurs on the B-channel.

These user-to-terminal and terminal-to-network interfaces, of course, serve different purposes. Most people trained on today's telephone equipment and today's network will wait for a dial-tone before dialing a telephone number, even in the face of a message on the telephone set telling them to dial and/or flashing lights. Since the telephone network will change, the terminal-network interface must also change. People, however, will not change as quickly; therefore, the human-terminal interface must remain roughly the same (at least for the near future).

It should be noted that not all ISDN equipment will follow the procedures outlined here. For example, some switches and PBXs imme-

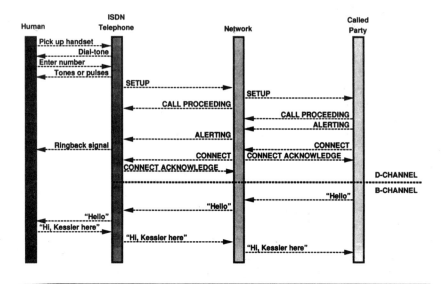

Figure 6.8 Human-telephone and telephone-network interface in the ISDN era.

diately switch over to the B-channel as soon as the telephone goes off-hook. In this case, the telephone-to-switch interface remains basically as it is today. Analog signals, including DTMF tones, dial-tones, ringback signals, etc., are carried over the B-channel, obviating the need for much of the Q.931 messages over the D-channel. These devices allow users to access a wide range of ISDN services but are less expensive than fully digital ISDN terminals.

6.7 ADDRESSING

As mentioned earlier, a major issue for ISDNs is the addressing plan. Network addressing is a familiar concept to all users of a telephone; a telephone number is nothing more than the address of a device attached to the telephone network.

Users of telephones in North America are familiar with the telephone addressing scheme known as the North American Numbering Plan (NANP). NANP addresses currently comprise 10 digits in the following format:

$$N\,0/1\,X\,-\,N\,X\,X\,-\,X\,X\,X\,X$$

where N = a digit from 2 to 9
0/1 = a digit that is either a 0 or 1
X = a digit from 0 to 9

The first three-digit field is the Numbering Plan Area (NPA), more commonly called the area code. The next three digits are the central office code, used to identify the central office within the NPA. The final four digits identify the subscriber line at the central office. The NANP scheme and the hierarchical nature of the switched telephone network are clearly related.

Packet switched networks use a very different numbering plan to identify hosts on the network. CCITT Recommendation X.121 defines the DTE numbering plan for international PSPDN access. X.121 addresses are 14 digits long and have the following format:

$$Z \ CC \ P \ NNNNNNNNNN$$

where Z = zone code
      C = country code
      P = PDN code
      N = network terminal number

The first digit of an X.121 address is called the zone code, used to identify the region on the globe in which the country is located (e.g., North America is zone 3). The next two digits are the country code, used to identify the country within the zone (e.g., the United States has been assigned country codes 10 through 16 within zone 3). The zone and country codes are assigned by the CCITT in Recommendation X.121. The fourth digit in the address is the public data network (PDN) code, assigned by the PSPDN administration in each country. These four digits comprise the Data Network Identification Code (DNIC) that uniquely identifies every PSPDN in the world.

Ten-digit network terminal numbers are assigned by the PSPDN administration to identify DTEs on the network and may have any format. NANP addresses, for example, are often used in North America as network terminal numbers.

The format of an ISDN number is shown in Fig. 6.9 and is described

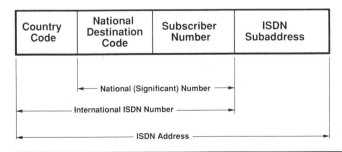

Figure 6.9 Format of an ISDN number (address).

in Recommendation E.164 (I.331). Unlike NANP and X.121 addresses, an ISDN number has a variable length.

The International ISDN Number, which uniquely identifies every ISDN subscriber, may be up to 17 digits long. It comprises two fields, the Country Code and National (Significant) Number, or N(S)N. The country code is used to identify the country and is based upon the international telephony numbering plan of Recommendation E.163. The N(S)N identifies the end user and comprises the National Destination Code and Subscriber Number fields.

Subaddresses provide an additional addressing capability outside of the ISDN numbering plan. They can be used, for example, to provide additional addressing within a private network that is accessed via an ISDN. Subaddresses may be up to 40 digits long.

ISDN addressing issues for subscribers, manufacturers, and service providers are described in the CCITT I.330-series recommendations. Interworking, for example, is defined between ISDNs and networks using other addressing schemes, such as NANP, X.121, and OSI network layer addressing. CCITT Recommendation X.122 specifically deals with numbering plan interworking between PSPDNs and ISDNs or public switched telephone networks (PSTNs).

In 1964, the CCITT recommended that no network administration require subscribers to dial more than 12 digits for international telephone calls. International ISDN numbers, however, will probably be 15 digits or longer. Since ISDN implementations will evolve over time, not all networks will be able to initially handle full ISDN address capability. To facilitate numbering plan interworking between ISDNs and other networks, the CCITT has defined *Time T*. Prior to Time T, no ISDN that interworks with non-ISDN networks will assign an international number longer than 12 digits. After Time T, all ISDNs and PSTNs can make use of full E.164 addresses. Time T is defined as December 31, 1996, at 11:59 pm (coordinated universal time).

Chapter

7

Signaling System No. 7

One of the least understood, yet arguably one of the most critical and exciting, aspects of ISDN is the interoffice network signaling system that must be in place to support the ISDN services. Based upon CCITT recommendations, this signaling network is called Signaling System No. 7 (SS7). ISDN cannot operate using today's signaling network since it is not fast or flexible enough for ISDN applications. SS7 was designed with ISDN in mind.

SS7 will allow the telephone company to offer many new types of telephony services to both business and residential customers. SS7 will carry the calling party's telephone number to the destination C.O., allowing a large set of new services that can be offered based upon the availability of this information to the called party. ISDN supplementary services will allow users to access these new services.

SS7 is a network that allows all network switching offices to communicate with each other. The implementation of SS7 is essential for communication between ISDN local exchanges. Without this interoffice communication, ISDN services could be offered only from individual LEs independently of each other, forming ISDN "islands" rather than a true network.

While ISDN protocols will allow users to access SS7 services, it should be noted that SS7 services could be accessed by other network-dependent protocols. Thus, ISDN needs SS7, but SS7 doesn't necessarily require ISDN.

This chapter will describe network signaling systems, in-band signaling, and clear channel signaling. SS7 will then be presented in more detail. Finally, some of the many possible SS7 and intelligent network services will be presented.

7.1   NETWORK SIGNALING SYSTEMS

The telephone network's signaling system provides a way for switching points to exchange routing and connection control information. An end-to-end connection through the telephone network comprises a series of office-to-office links.

Prior to the 1970s, a telephone call was set up through the network one link at a time, using *in-band* signaling. Network signals shared the same physical channel as the call that was being established and were carried within the same 300- to 3400-Hz voiceband. Trunk channels along the physical route were allocated sequentially; i.e., the path was allocated between the C.O. and class 4 office, then from the class 4 office to the next switching office, and so on. Therefore, even if the final trunk had no available capacity for this call, all of the other network resources had to be allocated before the network knew that the call could not be completed.

7.1.1   Common Channel Signaling

In 1976, common channel signaling (CCS) was introduced into the U.S. telephone network. A CCS network is designed to exchange signaling information between processor-equipped switching offices, using signaling channels that are completely separate from the user's voice channel. This allows network facilities to be quickly allocated, tested, and released. The CCS network can examine all parts of the route of a call to determine if facilities are available; if they are, the signaling network can allocate all of the necessary resources, as well. This allows for fast call setup, minimizes the amount of time wasted on retries, and allows much more efficient routing. With CCS, the average setup time for a toll call is 3 to 7 s, compared to 11 to 15 s before CCS.

CCS networks offer a number of benefits to the user and the network provider. First, long distance bandwidth is conserved since signaling is out of band and signaling for several trunks can be multiplexed on a single signaling channel. Second, costs are kept down since less equipment is needed. In-band signaling requires separate signaling facilities for each user circuit, while a single out-of-band signaling link can support 20 or more user circuits. Third, additional user services can be offered with CCS, such as closed user groups (CUGs), credit card verification, and calling party identification.

The basic principle behind any common channel signaling network is that network signals are carried on a separate channel from the user's voice signals on the interoffice trunks. Thus, the signals are out of band with respect to the user's channel.

7.1.2 CCS Signaling Modes

CCS networks have, in general, two signaling modes. The signaling mode refers to the association between the actual path of signaling messages and the path of the information flow to which the signals refer.

In *associated signaling mode,* signaling messages related to a given information flow between two signaling points (or switching offices) are carried on a signaling trunk directly interconnecting the two signaling points. For example, a network signaling trunk might be provided for each voice trunk group (Fig. 7.1).

Figure 7.1   Associated signaling.

In *nonassociated signaling mode,* the signaling path does not necessarily follow the same physical path as the user trunk groups that it supports (Fig. 7.2). In the example in the figure, the CCS link carrying the signals for the user trunk between switching offices A and C would use the office A-to-B and office B-to-C signaling paths. The A-B and B-C trunks use associated signaling.

A limited case of nonassociated signaling is *quasi-associated signaling,* where all messages relating to a given call will follow the same nonassociated path through the signaling network. If multiple paths between two switching points exist, signal messages could arrive out of sequence using ordinary nonassociated signaling; out-of-sequence arrivals cannot occur in quasi-associated signaling mode.

An extreme case of nonassociated signaling is *disassociated signaling mode,* where the signaling network is totally separate from the user's information network (Fig. 7.3). In this example, the CCS network is essentially a packet switched network carrying only network sig-

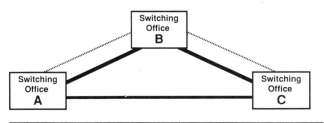

Figure 7.2   Nonassociated (and quasi-associated) signaling.

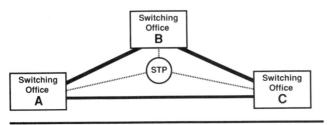

Figure 7.3 Disassociated signaling.

nals and is distinct from the network carrying telephone calls. The signal transfer point (STP) is merely a switching device for network signals.

7.1.3 Common Channel Interoffice Signaling

CCITT's Signaling System No. 6 (SS6) is the international version of the CCS network in common use today around the world. The AT&T version used in the United States is called Common Channel Interoffice Signaling (CCIS).

The introduction of CCIS allowed the telephone companies to offer several new types of services. For example, Inward Wide Area Telecommunications Services (WATS), also called *800 service* or INWATS, allows users to call a number toll-free from anywhere within a predefined area of the country. Basic INWATS service was first made available in the United States in the late 1960s by AT&T and was followed by the introduction of Expanded 800 Service in 1984. Expanded 800 Service uses the CCIS network to provide additional features over and above basic INWATS to give 800 service customers greater flexibility in defining service areas and determining the treatment of incoming calls.

When an 800 number is dialed (e.g., 1-800-CALLGCK), a CCS network can query the network's central 800 database, translate the 800 number to a standard 10-digit telephone number (e.g., 802-555-1010), select the interexchange carrier of choice (if one is needed), determine if a route through the network is available, and, if so, set up the call. The Bell operating companies' nationwide 800 service order changes, updates, and the database itself are maintained in the Service Management System (SMS). The SMS is located in Kansas City, MO, and is administered by Southwestern Bell Telephone. The independent telephone companies, as well as AT&T, MCI, and U.S. Sprint, also maintain databases for 800 service.

Another CCS-based service is Automated Calling Card Service

(ACCS), which offers the customer the ability to charge telephone calls to a number other than that of the originating station without operator assistance. ACCS automates calling card, bill-to-third-party, and collect calls. When a telephone calling card number is entered on the telephone keypad or given to the operator by the user, the calling card information is validated from a central database. The database will then either authorize the call, allowing it to be completed, or deny the call, prompting the user to take appropriate action.

7.1.4 CCS Network Components

Figure 7.4 shows the components of a CCS network. The network switching offices are processor controlled, allowing them to exchange supervisory, address, call progress, and other network signals. A switching office is called an SS7 signaling point (SP). An SP may be a class 5 central office, class 4 toll office, or a tandem office within the ISDN. An SP is sometimes called an SS7 end office or action point.

A signal transfer point (STP) concentrates signaling information from signaling points, switches packets in the CCS network, and provides access to service control points (SCPs). SCPs are databases that store information relevant to customer services, such as calling card validation, automatic number identification (ANI) validation, and 800 number service translation.

Redundancy is an important part of the CCS network since the loss of a single SCP or its associated STP would block thousands of calls. Consider the havoc that was caused when a fire knocked out the Hinsdale, IL, central office on Mother's Day, 1988.

STPs are paired throughout the CCS network and can handle several signaling points in the immediate area; the STP pairs are called *mate STPs*. Each SCP is paired with another, and the two SCPs are in

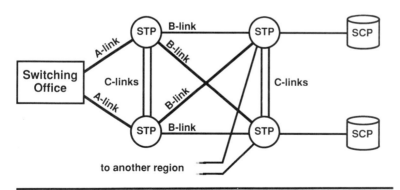

Figure 7.4 Common channel signaling network components.

turn associated with different STPs. If an SCP becomes inaccessible, its mate SCP handles the traffic load; if an STP fails, its mate STP handles the switching.

Access links (A-links) are provided in pairs (or mates), connecting a switching office to each STP of the mated pair. Bridge links (B-links) interconnect STPs in different regions. Cross links (C-links) are used to complete a signal path between mate STPs and may be used if the direct A- or B-links fail.

Redundancy in a CCS network cannot be overemphasized. Redundancy is built into the network to increase the network's reliability without having to depend upon the inherent reliability of each component.

7.1.5 CCITT Signaling System No. 7

Signaling System No. 7 is the standard CCS network for ISDNs, designed to support both voice and nonvoice services. SS7 is optimized for message-oriented signaling, using trunks operating at speeds up to 64 kbps.

The CCIS network in North America is based upon SS6 and will have to be modified prior to the realization of ISDN. There are a number of advantages of SS7 over CCIS/SS6, which are summarized in Table 7.1. CCIS is limited to handling domestic signaling, while SS7 can be used for both domestic and international applications. CCIS signaling links are limited to data rates of 2400 or 4800 bps, while SS7 links can operate at 56 or 64 kbps. Furthermore, the CCIS signaling link

TABLE 7.1 Comparison of CCIS (SS6) and SS7

CHARACTERISTIC	CCIS (SS6)	SS7
Application	Domestic Signaling	Domestic and International Services
Signaling Type	Analog	Digital
Speed	2,400 - 4,800 bps	56 kbps/64 kbps
Link Capacity	2,000 - 4,000 circuits	30,000 circuits
Message Length	180 bits fixed length	<273 octets variable length
Routing	Trunk Group and Destination Office	Destination Office
Architecture	Mixed	Layered
Flexibility	Limited	High

capacity is 2000 to 4000 circuits, while the SS7 link capacity is 30,000 circuits. Finally, CCIS signaling messages are fixed in size to 180 bits; SS7 messages can vary in length, with a domestic (U.S.) maximum size of 273 octets.

Original CCS networks used associated signaling, allocating one end-to-end signaling path to a group of 16 voice trunks. This required that the trunk group and its office assignment be identified prior to the STP being able to route the signaling messages. Furthermore, service interruptions and trunk rearrangements were unavoidable when the network had to be expanded.

Destination routing, on the other hand, allows signaling messages to be dynamically routed through the network based upon the address of the destination end office. Destination routing capability has been added to CCIS and will be the only type of routing strategy used in SS7.

The CCIS protocol structure is highly complex and discussion of it is beyond the scope of this book. The CCIS protocol structure, however, had limited flexibility, making modification and enhancements to network signaling capabilities difficult. The SS7 protocols have a layered architecture (like the OSI model), offering more flexibility for future enhancements. This layered structure means that changes can be made to one layer without affecting the others. It also provides expanded opportunities for adding higher layer services and applications to the signaling network.

SS7 is designed to use either associated or quasi-associated signaling modes. This is because SS7 has no procedures for reordering signaling messages that arrive out of sequence. Associated and quasi-associated signaling guarantee that messages will not get out of order, while nonassociated and disassociated signaling cannot provide this assurance.

7.2 SS7 PROTOCOL OVERVIEW

The SS7 protocol structure has three major components (Fig. 7.5):

- *Message Transfer Part (MTP):* Comprises protocols corresponding to the lower three OSI layers, called the Signaling Data Link, Signaling Link, and Signaling Network Management and Message Handling levels, respectively.

- *Signaling Connection Control Part (SCCP):* Provides some network layer protocol functions, including full OSI addressing capabilities.

- *User and Application Parts:* Provides the end-to-end signaling function for switched voice and nonvoice services in the ISDN. Several different user and/or application parts can operate in parallel (multiplexed) over a single MTP and/or SCCP protocol implementation.

7.2.1 SS7 Message Transfer Part

The Message Transfer Part corresponds to the OSI chained layers and provides a service similar to the X.25 or ISDN D-channel user-network interface.

The MTP level 1 protocol is the Signaling Data Link, corresponding to the OSI physical layer. The signaling system is designed to be used on full-duplex digital links operating at speeds up to 64 kbps; North American implementations will employ 56- or 64-kbps links.

To ensure the appropriate ones density on 1.544-Mbps links, bits are inverted prior to transmission. Since the layer 2 protocol in the MTP is a bit-oriented protocol, zero-bit insertion is used to ensure that no more than six 1 bits will occur in a row. Long runs of 0 bits, however, may occur. By inverting the bits prior to transmitting them, the network is assured that no more than six contiguous 0 bits will occur on the line, thus providing a sufficient number of 1 bits for timing and synchronization.

The MTP level 2 protocol is the Signaling Link, corresponding to the OSI data link layer. MTP level 2 uses a bit-oriented protocol, al-

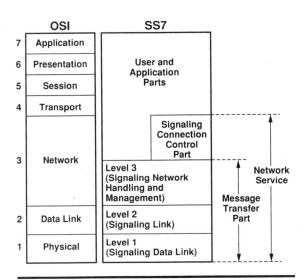

Figure 7.5 Signaling System No. 7 protocol architecture.

though the frame format is different from that of LAPD and LAPB (Fig. 7.6).

As in other bit-oriented protocols, MTP level 2 frames, called *signal units*, begin and end with a flag bit pattern (01111110). Zero-bit insertion and removal (bit stuffing) is used for transparency and the frames contain a 16-bit remainder using a CRC error detection polynomial. The Address field, however, is absent in the MTP level 2 frame; it is not necessary since communication is only over point-to-point links and there is no requirement to differentiate between command and response frames as there is in LAPD and LAPB.

The Backward sequence number is a 7-bit subfield comparable to the N(R) value in the LAPD Control field; it indicates the sequence number of the signal unit being acknowledged. The Forward sequence number is a 7-bit subfield comparable to LAPD's N(S) value and contains the sequence number of this signal unit. The Forward and Backward indicator bits are part of the basic error correction method.

The Length indicator (LI) is a 6-bit value specifying the number of octets following the LI field and preceding the check bits. The value of this field also indicates the type of signal unit being transmitted:

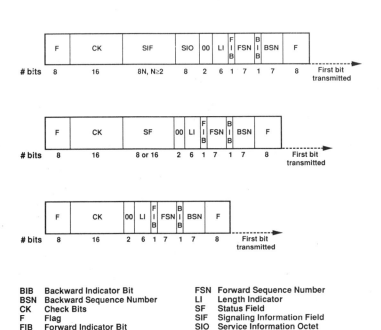

BIB	Backward Indicator Bit	FSN	Forward Sequence Number
BSN	Backward Sequence Number	LI	Length Indicator
CK	Check Bits	SF	Status Field
F	Flag	SIF	Signaling Information Field
FIB	Forward Indicator Bit	SIO	Service Information Octet

Figure 7.6   Format of MTP level 2 signal units: Message Signal Unit (top), Link Status Signal Unit (middle), and Fill-In Signal Unit (bottom).

- An LI value of 0 indicates that the frame is a Fill-In Signal Unit (FISU). This type of frame is sent only when there is no other signal unit to be sent and it contains only acknowledgment information.

- An LI value of 1 or 2 indicates that the frame is a Link Status Signal Unit (LSSU). The one- or two-octet Status Field within this frame is used in conjunction with the link error rate monitor functions.

- An LI value greater than 2 indicates that the frame is a Message Signal Unit (MSU). The first octet after the LI is called the Service information octet, used to associate signaling information with a particular user or application part (see below). The Signaling information field contains higher-layer data from the specified user or application part.

MTP level 2 defines two types of error correction procedures. In *basic error correction,* the procedures are similar to LAPD and other bit-oriented protocols. Frames without bit errors are acknowledged, frames with bit errors are ignored, and out-of-sequence frames are rejected. Frames with errors are corrected using a go-back-n scheme; the bad frame *and all subsequently transmitted frames* are retransmitted. Basic error correction is designed for links with a delay under 15 ms or for nonintercontinental terrestrial links.

Preventive cyclic retransmission uses acknowledgments but no negative responses. Instead, whenever the transmitter has no new frames to send, or when an acknowledgment is overdue, it merely retransmits all unacknowledged frames. Preventive cyclic retransmission is designed for links with a delay greater than 15 ms or for satellite links. Go-back-n transmission is a scheme commonly employed in data link protocols but has a very high overhead on fast links with long delays because of the large number of frames that might require retransmission even if there is only a single bit error.

The MTP level 3 protocol defines the signaling network functions and messages and corresponds to the lower half of the OSI network layer. These functions are divided into three categories:

- *Message discrimination:* Determine if the message is at its destination or has to be relayed to another signal station

- *Message routing:* Determine the next SS7 station to which this message is to be sent

- *Message distribution:* Determine the user or application part (higher layer protocol) to which this message should be delivered if this is the destination station

The MTP level 3 also handles signaling network management functions, including traffic, route, and link management. These functions provide reconfiguration of the signaling network in the case of failures and control traffic in case of congestion. The MTP level 3 functions clearly require communication between signaling points (especially the STPs).

A large part of the signaling network functional specification is concerned with procedures for overcoming link failures and congestion. Procedures are specified for quickly determining when a link has failed, removing it from service, rerouting traffic, and bringing the link back into service after repair. As alluded to earlier, there is an overriding concern for network reliability; the goal is for 99.998 percent availability (i.e., no more than 10 min of downtime per year for any route). This goal is achieved in SS7 by equipment redundancy and the network's dynamic reconfiguration and rerouting capabilities.

7.2.2 SS7 Signaling Connection Control Part

The Signaling Connection Control Part corresponds to the upper half of the OSI network layer.

The MTP level 3 message addresses are limited to a 14-bit signaling point code (SPC), which is insufficient to address higher-layer applications. This limited address space would be roughly equivalent to being able to address a node in a network without being able to address the process or application associated with the node. This limited addressing is adequate for signaling applications since signaling messages carry sufficient information for message distribution.

The addressing is not adequate, however, for nonsignaling applications supported by the signaling network. Each nonsignaling application (e.g., support of ISDN) could be designed as a user part and could provide its own routing and distribution functions. However, this would result in several applications having to implement the same functions, totally contrary to the OSI concepts of layered services and modularity.

To prevent an unnecessary duplication of effort, the SS7 designers have added another layer, the SCCP, that looks to the MTP as just another user part. The combined functions of MTP level 3 and the SCCP permit SS7 to offer full OSI network layer services.

The SCCP can accept signaling point codes (as can the Message Transfer Part) or global titles (e.g., a dialed number) as addresses. The SCCP has access to routing information that allows any of these addresses to be associated with a signaling point code, which the MTP understands. At the destination signaling point, the message is passed to the local SCCP, which is responsible for delivery to the user.

The SCCP defines five classes of service:

0. Basic (unsequenced) connectionless

1. Sequenced connectionless

2. Basic connection oriented

3. Flow control connection oriented

4. Error recovery and flow control connection oriented

7.2.3 SS7 User and Application Parts

The SS7 user and application parts correspond to the higher layers of the OSI model. Each user and application part is complete and independent of the others. They generally communicate directly with the MTP, providing end-to-end signaling service. Several user and/or application parts can operate in parallel over a single MTP or SCCP.

The two user parts originally specified for SS7 were the Telephone User Part (TUP) and the Data User Part (DUP). The TUP specifies the signaling necessary for the control of ordinary telephone communications. It is being actively defined for use outside of North America but will not be supported by North American SS7 networks.

The DUP is designed for circuit-mode data networks and is not intended for ISDN. It has been largely replaced by the ISDN User Part (ISUP). The routine signaling functions of the ISUP are similar to the Telephone User Part, but some of the other features, such as end-to-end signaling (used to modify the characteristics of a call that has already been established) and user-to-user data, will probably communicate with the MTP via the SCCP. The ISDN User Part can support non-ISDN telephone or data networks. The ISUP will be the user part initially supported in North American SS7 implementations.

The Transaction Capabilities Application Part (TCAP) provides a general-purpose, remote operation function. This protocol was originally designed to support queries into databases, such as those supporting telephone credit cards and 800 numbers, although its role is expected to include additional functions. Although the TCAP definition is still evolving, current plans include using the TCAP to carry special billing instructions and customer network control and management information.

The Operations, Maintenance, and Administration Part (OMAP) provides the procedures for network management and supervision from central control points in the CCS network.

7.2.4 SS7 Standards

The SS7 protocols described here are contained in CCITT recommendations. SS7 implementations in the United States will be based upon

ANSI standards, which largely follow their CCITT counterparts. The CCITT recommendations and ANSI standards for SS7 include:

- *SS7 overview:* Recommendation Q.700 (American National Standard T1.110)
- *Message Transfer Part overview:* Rec. Q.701 (ANS T1.111)
- *Signaling data link (MTP Level 1):* Rec. Q.702
- *Signaling link (MTP Level 2):* Rec. Q.703
- *MTP Level 3:* Rec. Q.704
- *Signaling Connection Control Part:* Rec. Q.711–Q.716 (ANS T1.112)
- *Telephone User Part:* Rec. Q.721–Q.725
- *ISDN supplementary services:* Rec. Q.730
- *Data User Part:* Rec. Q.741
- *ISDN User Part:* Rec. Q.761–Q.766 (ANS T1.113)
- *Transactions Capabilities Application Part:* Rec. Q.771–Q.775 (ANS T1.114)
- *Operations, Maintenance, and Administration Part:* Rec. Q.795

7.3 INTELLIGENT NETWORKS AND SS7

A statement was made earlier in this chapter that SS7 networks could offer many useful user services in the absence of an ISDN, whereas ISDNs could not operate in the absence of an SS7 network. This section will describe some of the services available from SS7 and an SS7-based intelligent network.

The SS7 network differs from today's CCIS network in two significant ways. First, an SS7 network will have centralized high-speed databases controlling network call routing and other functions. Second, high-speed data links are used to exchange signals among C.O. switches and between the switches and the databases.

Before discussing SS7 services further, it is necessary to describe the relationship between SS7 and ISDN. An ISDN can be viewed in a narrow sense as a new technology affecting the local loop, permitting transmission of multiple voice and data circuits over a single pair of copper wires. The SS7 common channel signaling network, then, adds new technologies and service capabilities to the central office and interoffice network. Given this view, SS7 services are distinct from the ISDN and these two networks complement each other.

A much broader view is that an ISDN is a total end-to-end digital network, defining and comprising additional user services. From this perspective, SS7 services are merely a subset of the ISDN.

7.3.1 Intelligent Networks

The term and concept of *intelligent network* (IN), also known as the Advanced Intelligent Network (AIN), is undergoing an evolution that will continue into the 1990s. In essence, an IN is one that provides a large set of services to the customer and allows the telephone, data, and signaling networks to easily and quickly incorporate technological advances in both hardware and software. IN definitions will provide an architecture by which a service provider may develop and introduce new communications services. These services are provided from a robust, service-independent set of functions that the IN architecture makes available. The evolution of intelligent networks will closely track the evolution and deployment of SS7.

Early intelligent networks will be implemented in different ways in accordance with specifications produced independently by each of the service providers. These implementations, also known as AIN Release 0, are targeted for 1991.

The first formal phase of the intelligent network, called IN/1 or AIN Release 1, is targeted toward services that can be provided by centralized logic within a switching network (e.g., an SCP within SS7). IN/1 requirements should be released in 1990 and applications should be deployed by 1993.

SS7 goes a long way toward the implementation of IN/1. IN/1 services are primarily voice based and fit well into the current narrowband ISDN standards. IN services require intelligent peripherals, such as ISDN terminals, to provide such functions as voice storage and retrieval, voice code conversion, voice recognition and synthesis, rate adaption, and video code conversion.

The long-term goal is that of Intelligent Network 2 (IN/2), or AIN Release 2. IN/2 is an intelligent network that is totally applications independent and provides a wider range of services than IN/1 by using distributed logic. IN/2 technology and service requirements, however, are relatively far off for a number of reasons. For one thing, new functional elements within the network to support the distributed logic must still be developed. Major advances are required in the capabilities of the signaling network and network control software. Furthermore, intelligent peripherals must be developed to support the new services. IN/2 capabilities may not be fully realized until the late 1990s.

7.3.2 SS7 Network Services

Literally hundreds of new services and capabilities are possible with SS7 and an intelligent network. Out-patient monitoring, opinion polls, electronic mail, voice mail, catalog shopping, video services, telecommuting (commuting to the office via a communications link), meter reading, and information and database services are among the wide range of user services that can be made available from an ISDN C.O. using SS7. Some of the SS7 services that may be made available are described in the paragraphs below, although this is far from an exhaustive list of possibilities (Table 7.2).

INWATS, or 800 service, was described above and is already a widely available service in the United States, offered by a number of common carriers. Not only is it a very attractive service for large and small businesses alike, it is also a big revenue producer for the telephone companies.

INWATS provides a way of allowing people to make a long distance call that will be automatically reverse charged to the 800 subscriber. Since the 800 subscribers pay for the calls, they choose the long distance providers, or interexchange carriers (IEC), rather than the calling parties.

To allow the IECs to compete in the 800 service market and to facilitate access to the appropriate IEC by the local carrier, regulations in the United States mandate that the first three digits after 800 identify the IEC. These three digits, or NXX codes, are assigned by Bellcore. This means that if 800 subscribers change from one long distance carrier to another, they have to change their 800 number, an unacceptable alternative to many companies that have based market-

TABLE 7.2   Sample Network Services Available with SS7

INWATS (800-service)
Network-based automatic call distribution (ACD) service
Enhanced 911 (E911)
Line Information Data Base (LIDB)
Local Yellow Pages with automatic dialing
Private PBX networks
City-wide Centrex service
Private Virtual Network (PVN)

Custom Local Area Signaling Services (CLASS)
    Automatic Number Identification
    Customer-originated Trace
    Selective Call Rejection
    Selective Call Forwarding
    Distinctive Ring
    Automatic Recall
    Automatic Callback
    Important Call Waiting
    Outgoing Calls Barred

ing campaigns around their easy-to-remember 800 number. Furthermore, an 800 subscriber cannot dynamically change the IEC to take advantage of better rates in one geographic region or a lower time-of-day rate.

Shared 800 databases after SS7 is implemented could remove the NXX code restriction. It could allow users to use the most advantageous IEC for a particular call based upon some set of user-defined parameters. While this will be technically feasible in the United States, current regulations prohibit shared 800 databases for this purpose.

Large organizations with INWATS service, such as airline reservation and information systems, often use automatic call distribution (ACD) equipment on their site to route calls to available customer service agents. AT&T's CCIS provided a way that the ACD function can be offered by the network using the Extended 800 Service call distribution feature. Network-based ACD service, in fact, allows dynamic reconfiguration of the call distribution function as the number of lines expands and contracts. Furthermore, the team of people answering the 800 number telephones do not have to be located at the same site; network-based ACD allows the incoming calls to be distributed to many locations in a given area. Other advanced 800 services will include call screening based upon origination number and number translation based upon time of day and/or day of week.

Most people in the United States are familiar with the universal telephone number for police, fire, and emergency medical services, 911. The implementation of 911 service, however, is far from ubiquitous in this country. Emergency services are further complicated by issues such as varying service availability during a given time of day or day of week, lack of familiarity of a dispatcher with another service area, or the unavailability of a local emergency unit at the time of a call. Enhanced 911 (E911), also called Network 911 or 911 Enhanced, allows Public Safety Answering Points (PSAPs) that usually operate autonomously to consolidate their traffic into one location. It can also remove the limitations of interoperability between different local C.O. equipment. In addition, new features are available to the 911 dispatchers. Databases can be created that will automatically switch calls to the correct PSAP based upon some set of parameters (e.g., time of day), aid in the dispatch of emergency personnel, and provide the dispatcher with the calling party's telephone number, address, and other pertinent location information (such as the nearest fire hydrant and any pertinent medical history of the residents).[1]

---

[1]E911 service is available in the absence of SS7, although it is similar to a private network. SS7 will make the E911 offering more economical to the community that it serves and easier to implement by the SS7 service provider.

A Line Information Data Base (LIDB) is a multipurpose database with information about individual customer lines. It can provide capabilities such as an alternate billing service to validate telephone calling cards, screen calls to pay telephones, and authorize third-party billing. It also provides new opportunities for the telephone companies. For example, another database can be used to validate credit and charge cards, such as VISA, Master Card, or American Express, or to provide authorization for check writing purposes. AT&T, in fact, is exploring the idea of allowing some customers to use their long distance calling cards as a general-purpose credit card. This is a potentially lucrative business for AT&T since they have issued nearly 40 million calling cards.

Another possible database service is an online, local Yellow Pages with automatic calling. For example, suppose a customer needs emergency plumbing service on a Sunday morning. A call to the operator, or directly to the database service, can provide the customer with a list of the plumbers who are open, what form of payment they take, and their telephone numbers. With ISDN, this service could presumably be accessed via the ISDN PC or telephone; merely pressing a button on the telephone could dial the selected plumber automatically. This same feature could be used when calling directory information; pressing a key on the telephone would automatically dial the number obtained from the database.

Private networks can also use SS7 services. For example, customers with several PBXs, and tie-lines interconnecting the PBXs, need some sort of signaling system to control their private network. If a standard signaling protocol is used, switches from more than one vendor may be combined in a single network. Some users, such as the U.S. Department of Defense, are already beginning to specify that SS7 internodal signaling capability be available on PBX products for their purchase. This PBX capability is scarce today but should become more widely available over the next few years.

Citywide Centrex is an SS7 service that provides an alternative to private PBX networks. Many firms have employees scattered over several sites. Real estate firms, for example, may have several small offices throughout a community, each with five to ten telephone lines. While the individual offices might not make good candidates for Centrex service, all of the offices taken together might be. Citywide Centrex would allow all of the offices to be tied together and listed under a single number in the telephone directory. Possible additional features include office-to-office calling and programmable call forwarding (e.g., at night or in case one office is closed). This also opens up the opportunity for telecommuting, where several members of a business actually work at home.

Another private network alternative is that of a Private Virtual Network (PVN). The PVN concept is not new, but SS7 makes it feasible for the local exchange carrier to offer the service.

From the customer's point of view, private virtual network circuits are accessed exactly as regular private (leased) lines are. The network, however, does not allocate any dedicated physical resource. Instead, ordinary network trunks are used, with the SS7 signaling and database capabilities monitoring which lines are being used by this "private line" customer. Users, then, have all of the features that they are used to with leased-line service. In addition, they can request special voice and data services on an ad hoc basis to create custom-designed network services. Furthermore, customers can, theoretically, tailor the actual network that will carry their voice and data traffic. For example, PVN customers can specify the IEC to carry their traffic based upon characteristics such as time of day, day of week, and geographic region of call origination to guarantee that they get the best possible rates.

From the LEC's point of view, PVN is attractive since the network services can be reconfigured in software rather than requiring labor-intensive modifications to physical facilities. While some IECs already offer similar service (e.g., AT&T's Software Defined Network), PVNs are a service that can be offered by the LECs·once SS7 is in place.

7.3.3 Custom Local Area Signaling Services

One of the most interesting aspects of SS7 is the new set of customized services that can be brought to the business and residential customer, called Custom Local Area Signaling Services (CLASS). CLASS services differ somewhat from other SS7 services in that the service provision is handled on a call-by-call basis and is based upon data known at the C.O., such as the calling party's telephone number and the status of the called line. Depending upon the vendor and the network provider, there are a myriad of CLASS services that can be made available. Some of the CLASS services that are likely to be seen soon are discussed below.

Calling party identification, also called automatic number identification (ANI), displays the calling party's telephone number and/or directory listing at the called party's telephone set during the ring cycle. This allows the called party to determine whether to answer the call or not. It also provides the customer with the ability to identify and report the source of crank or obscene telephone calls, using a feature called Customer-Originated Trace. Calling party identification is a very important service; not only do many CLASS services require it, but some other SS7 services require it as well, including E911.

Several SS7 services depend upon the user providing a list of telephone numbers to the local exchange so that the network can take appropriate action when an incoming call occurs:

- *Selective call rejection:*   Incoming calls from a calling number *not* on the list will be blocked; the user is not notified of the incoming call and the telephone will not ring.

- *Selective call forwarding:*   Incoming calls from any number on the list will be automatically forwarded to a specified destination station.

- *Distinctive ring:*   Incoming calls from a number on the list cause a special ringing signal to be used.

- *Important call waiting:*   If an incoming call is received from one of the numbers on the list while the customer's line is busy, a special call waiting signal will be sent to the customer.

Automatic recall allows a customer to request that a busy or hard-to-reach telephone number be automatically redialed until the call is completed. Automatic callback allows a customer to automatically return calls to those numbers from which a call was initiated while the customer was busy or otherwise unavailable.

Outgoing calls barred allows users to dynamically program their service to prevent outgoing calls being made to certain numbers. For example, calls to 900 area codes or 976 services could be prohibited.

As an aside, not all CLASS services are free from controversy. ANI, in particular, has raised some very real concerns in the United States about potential abuse or lack of privacy issues. For example, a vendor could collect telephone numbers and develop a mailing list from them, unlisted telephone numbers could become a waste of money, and callers might be deterred from calling certain hot lines (e.g., for AIDS information) for fear of being identified. Indeed, one study suggests that while more than half of the customers might like to purchase ANI service to identify incoming callers, over 85 percent do not want their telephone number displayed when they place calls.

7.3.4   SS7 and ISDN

The intelligent network services described above will be available to the C.O. after SS7 is widely deployed. These services, however, are not directly available to the user without additional user-network procedures. ISDN will provide user access to SS7 services, in addition to its other features.

The availability of CLASS and other SS7 services, then, is a good indicator of the future availability of ISDN in a given area of the country. CLASS services can be made available, at least on a limited basis, as soon as the C.O. switch supports SS7. These services are not being aggressively marketed in many areas in the United States, a reflection of the local telephone companies' lack of widespread SS7 implementation and their desire to market SS7 and ISDN together.

The relationship between SS7 implementation and ISDN availability is obvious. Regardless of how many C.O. switches are upgraded to support SS7 and ISDN, those offices will merely be ISDN islands until there is widespread support of SS7 by local and long distance telephone companies.

The future of ISDN and SS7 requires interswitch connectivity. A number of trials are already underway to test switch interoperability problems caused by the different implementations of ISDN and SS7 on different switches. The first successful ISDN voice/data call between different vendors' switches using SS7 in the United States took place in early 1990. The call was conducted by Bellcore personnel using AT&T 5ESS and NTI DMS-100 switches connected through a Digital Switch Corp. STP using SS7. The success of this event advanced the potential for widespread ISDN deployment by demonstrating that the ISDN islands can be interconnected.

ISDN Communications Services, Applications, and Marketplace

The biggest question regarding ISDN from the perspective of the customer is not necessarily "How can I make it happen?" or "When will it be real?" Instead, it is most likely to be "How can I use it?" This chapter will examine some of the many possible ISDN applications, particularly as they relate to today's voice and data communications strategies and the ISDN marketplace.

8.1 COMPUTER AND COMMUNICATIONS SERVICES

The sections below will present some current computer and communication products and services, their place in a customer's evolution to ISDN, and their future in the ISDN era.

8.1.1 T1 Networks

T1 digital carriers were first deployed within the North American telephone network in 1962 to more efficiently use the trunks between switching offices. During the mid-1970s, the development of microprocessor and chip technology brought the costs of digital carriers down significantly. This, in turn, led to new T1 capabilities for the local loop and the end customer. When first made available to individual customers in 1977, the cost of T1 service was very high. In 1982, AT&T renamed it High-Capacity Terrestrial Digital Service and repriced it to be attractive to customers needing end-to-end digital transmission facilities. Divestiture in 1984 provided additional interest in this service as competition with the U.S. telephone industry dramatically increased. Although T1 facilities were once reserved for the network's internal use, T1 service is now an efficient, cost effective way for business customers to build high-speed private networks.

Figure 8.1 shows a possible candidate for a private T1 network. In this example, a company has two sites, located several hundred miles apart, with a mix of voice and data traffic between them. Leased analog voice lines provide trunking between the two PBXs. Several 56-kbps digital lines connect one computer's front-end processor to high-speed workstations and synchronous terminal cluster controllers. Analog leased lines are used between another host computer and its asynchronous terminals, as well as between facsimile (fax) equipment.

Figure 8.2 shows how these applications might be handled with a T1 network. All user lines at each site attach to a T1 multiplexer and

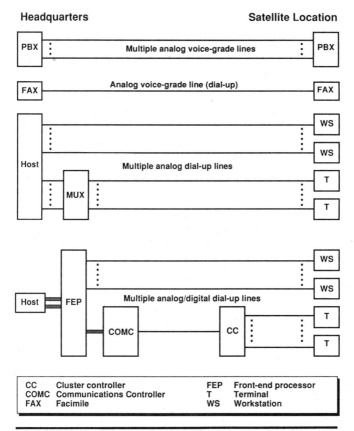

Figure 8.1 Communications between two company sites using traditional telephone company digital and analog, leased and dial-up services.

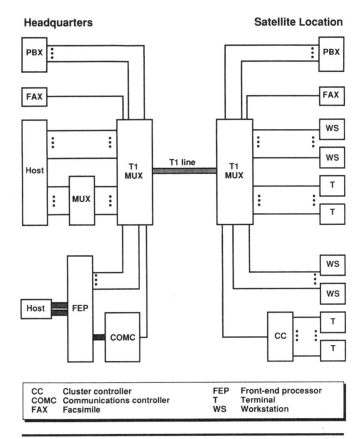

Figure 8.2 Communications between two company sites using a T1 private network.

the two multiplexers are interconnected with a 1.544-Mbps T1 line. Intelligent networks using T1 services are becoming increasingly available as the capabilities of T1 multiplexers increase. Today's T1 multiplexers have many features, including switching, dynamic routing, network management, automatic reconfiguration, and dynamic bandwidth allocation.

The use of T1 technology is justified based upon cost, traffic volume, and the distance between the remote locations. Not all users, then, would be well served by using T1 lines. For example, users with a pure data requirement (as opposed to a mix of voice and data), LANs that do not need to communicate with or through off-site networks, locations that are close together, and low-speed applications would probably not make good use of T1 service. Indeed, these environments might obtain 1- to 3-Mbps private communications using microwave, laser, or infrared technology.

The ISDN primary rate interface provides T1 bandwidth and flexibility, without the cost of the leased T1 line. Users can have a 1.544-Mbps (or 2.048-Mbps) access line between their site and the C.O. and can choose the services they want for each individual access channel. Furthermore, the PRI will support groups of B-channels, providing more than just single 64-kbps channels. These B-channel groups (the H-channels) can be allocated on demand by the user when needed, merely by sending the appropriate call setup messages on the D-channel. T3 lines, operating at 44.736 Mbps, can be replaced with several PRI lines or by B-ISDN trunks.

Today's proliferation of separate analog and digital leased lines will be largely eliminated with an ISDN. As larger bandwidth ISDN channels become available, it will become increasingly convenient and cost effective to use the ISDN services. In the meantime, use of T1 facilities and services places a user on a migratory path to ISDN.

Announcement of Fractional T1 services in early 1989 further demonstrated the relationship between T1 and ISDN. Fractional T1 service allows customers to lease individual 64-kbps channels or groups of channels at significantly lower prices than traditional data or full T1 services.

8.1.2   Private Branch Exchanges

Closely related to the T1 issue is that of private branch exchanges, since PBXs are often interconnected using T1 multiplexers and lines. Computers and communications are becoming increasingly intertwined; communications are not possible without computers and computers that do not communicate are nearly useless in today's business environment. PBXs can be used as data switches to interconnect terminals and hosts. Furthermore, a PBX can connect asynchronous terminals to an X.25 packet assembler/disassembler (PAD), providing asynchronous access to an X.25 network. Optionally, synchronous X.25 devices can be interconnected by a PBX. Again, this type of application puts a customer on a path to ISDN.

A PBX, or private automatic branch exchange (PABX), is a customer-premises switch. In many ways, it is similar to a C.O. switch; it provides local voice and data communications switching capabilities, as well as an interface to other PBXs and other networks (including the public telephone network).

PBXs may have a myriad of device types attached to them (Fig. 8.3). For voice applications, either analog or digital telephone sets can usually be used, although digital sets are typically better suited to use the full capabilities of the PBX. PCs may be directly attached to the PBX or can share the same wire pair as specially equipped telephone sets.

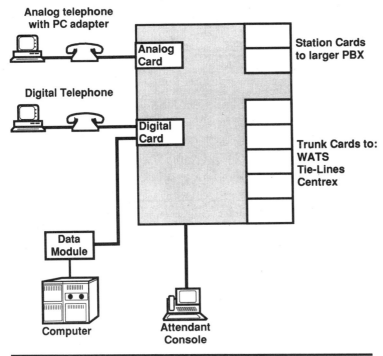

Analog telephone
with PC adapter

Analog
Card

Station Cards
to larger PBX

Digital Telephone

Digital
Card

Trunk Cards to:
WATS
Tie-Lines
Centrex

Data
Module

Computer

Attendant
Console

Figure 8.3   Options for digital PBX applications.

An attendant console, if used, allows an individual to act as an operator, providing a central switchboard function. Data modules allow different types of mainframe computer devices to be attached to the PBX.

A PBX network may become quite large. Small and mid-range PBXs can attach to larger PBXs, allowing a network to be made up of tens of thousands of lines. Some PBXs have a distributed architecture and support remote switching modules; in this way, several buildings in a campus-type setting can each have a local switch.

PBXs today compete with Centrex services, where the same switching functions are provided directly from the central office. This competition will continue in the ISDN era. In an ISDN Centrex environment providing BRI access (Fig. 8.4), user's ISDN terminals (i.e., telephones and PCs) connect to NT1 devices via the four-wire ISDN interface (S/T reference point). The NT1, in turn, is connected to the C.O. over the two-wire BRI interface (U reference point).

In a PBX environment (Fig. 8.5), BRI access is provided to users in much the same way. User's telephones and PCs connect to an integrated services PBX (ISPBX) via the four-wire ISDN interface (S ref-

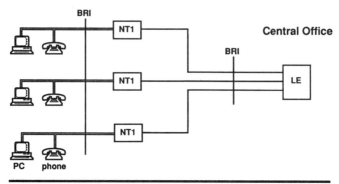

Figure 8.4   ISDN Centrex.

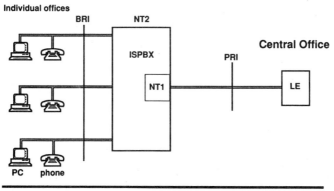

Figure 8.5   Integrated services PBX (ISPBX).

erence point). The ISPBX encompasses both NT1 and NT2 functionality and it, in turn, is connected to the local exchange using PRI access (U reference point for layer 1, T reference point for layers 2 and 3).

Customers wanting the advanced services available with these two technologies have to weigh several factors, including:

- *Capital expense:*   There is the large initial cost of a PBX but no large start-up cost with Centrex.

- *Per-port cost:*   One-time per-port charge with PBX, monthly port charges with Centrex.

- *Salaries and benefits of the local support staff:*   Minimal with Centrex since the LEC manages the Centrex service, while several people may be needed to maintain and manage the PBX.

- *Reconfiguration charges:* There is likely to be a charge from the telephone company whenever there is a move or network reconfiguration on a Centrex service, but reconfiguration costs nothing with a PBX (although there may be a company internal charge and some staff members will be required to actually do the work).

- *Lease versus purchase economic issues:* There are many additional economic issues, such as the cost trade-offs of "leasing" Centrex versus buying a PBX, tax ramifications, capital expenses, etc.

In the ISDN era, these issues will remain largely the same, i.e., buy a PBX for local switching or purchase ISDN Centrex service from the telephone company. While PBXs will still be an attractive communications alternative after ISDN is introduced, growth of PBX sales may well depend upon how attractively priced the LECs make ISDN Centrex service.

Nonproprietary synchronous computer protocols are still not widely supported by most PBXs. The Digital Multiplexed Interface (DMI) standard was proposed to provide this synchronous interface between host computers and PBXs (Fig. 8.6). Originally developed by AT&T, Hewlett-Packard, and Wang Laboratories, DMI has received widespread industry support. The DMI standard for North America will provide 23 user channels and one signaling channel; DMI for Europe will provide 30 user channels, one signaling channel, and one framing channel. The signaling channel will use signaling messages similar to those defined for the ISDN D-channel. All DMI channels operate at 64 kbps and rate adaption algorithms exist for those devices operating at speeds below 64 kbps. The relationship between the DMI standard and the ISDN PRI is unmistakable.

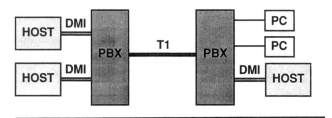

Figure 8.6   Digital multiplexed interface (DMI).

The DMI standard:

- Allows 23 (or 30) terminals to be connected to a host computer over a single twisted-pair
- Reduces the cost of interfacing a computer and PBX

- Provides a PBX-computer interface that is consistent with evolving ISDN standards

- Allows economical, high-speed access of terminals to hosts over a digital PBX network

The DMI standard, then, is one indication of the solid future of PBXs for data transport in the ISDN era. There is a recognition on the part of the ISDN vendors and standards organizations that while the ISDN will do a lot of things for users, some applications (such as local voice and data switching) are still best handled on the customer's site.

8.1.3 Local Area Networks

Over the last several years, most U.S. local telephone companies have started to offer a Central Office Local Area Network (C.O. LAN), or Centrex-based LAN, service. C.O. LANs, like customer premises-based LANs (e.g., Ethernet and token ring), allow data transmission between devices at a local site. The primary differences between a C.O. LAN and a premises-based LAN are the wiring distribution and line speed.

Figure 8.7 shows a typical on-site voice and data network configuration. In this example, local voice service is provided via a PBX. The PBX, in turn, has trunks to the central office for nonlocal telephone calls. PCs, terminals, and hosts are interconnected using a LAN. The LAN medium is typically twisted pair, coaxial cable, or optical fiber. The LAN could have a communications gateway, providing LAN stations access to a wide area data network, such as an X.25 PSPDN.

Figure 8.8 shows a similar customer environment, using Centrex for voice services and C.O. LAN for data services. With Centrex service, each telephone is connected to the C.O. via a pair of wires. With C.O. LAN added to Centrex, no additional wiring is needed for the data devices. The local loop terminates at an integrated voice/data multiplexer (IVDM) on each end. An IVDM assigns a transmit and receive data channel on the local loop using carrier frequencies well above the voiceband, such as 70 and 114 kHz; the voice is kept within the 300- to 3400-Hz passband. A telephone and PC can be attached to the IVDM on the customer side using the standard modular telephone jack (RJ-11) and EIA-232-D interface, respectively. On the network side, the IVDM separates the voice and data traffic and directs it to the appropriate switch. The IVDM on the customer site is CPE and must be purchased by the customer; the IVDM in the C.O. is owned by the telephone company.

The high frequencies used by the IVDM can only be transmitted over unloaded local loops that are less than approximately 18 kft long.

Customer Premises

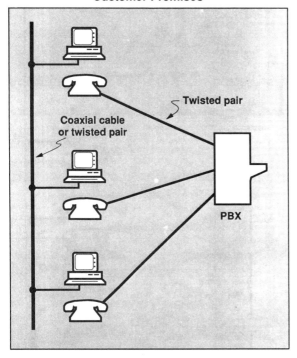

Figure 8.7   Premises-based voice network (PBX) and data network (LAN).

Transmission on C.O. LANs is usually asynchronous and limited to 19.2 kbps.

C.O. LANs provide some advantages over premises-based LANs. Many of the arguments in favor of C.O. LANs are similar to the arguments in favor of Centrex over a PBX. First, the initial cost of a PBX or a LAN might be prohibitively high for some customers, while Centrex and C.O. LAN are charged on a per-line basis. Second, an on-site PBX or LAN requires management staff, power, floor space, and other resources; Centrex and C.O. LAN comes out to the customer site as a set of twisted-pair wires. C.O. LANs, in fact, are usually most economical when sold as an add-on to Centrex service.

From the C.O. LAN customer's perspective, it is the telephone company that must worry about network management issues, wiring, station moves, and network reconfiguration. In a premises-based LAN, the customer is responsible for all of these issues, including providing the appropriate support staff. Furthermore, if the user has two or

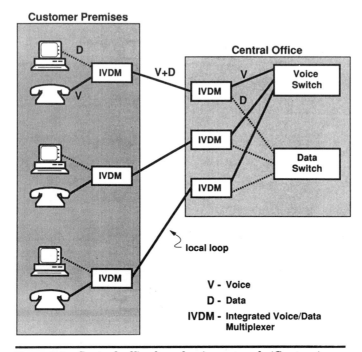

Figure 8.8 Central office-based voice network (Centrex) and data network (C.O. LAN).

more different sites, one premises-based LAN would have to be built at each site and interconnected using leased lines, line-of-sight transmission media (e.g., laser, microwave, or infrared), or some other means. C.O. LANs can easily span more than one building since all wiring is through the C.O. Several LAN surveys have shown that about a quarter of the installed LANs span more than one building and another third (approximately) are on more than a single floor; wiring distribution, then, is a very real issue. If the multiple buildings are in different C.O. serving areas, it is the telephone company's responsibility to interconnect the two central offices (as long as they both offer C.O. LAN service). Finally, premises-based LANs do not currently support voice traffic. Thus, a customer may have two in-house networks for these two applications, along with the attendant staff for both and the associated costs.

C.O. LANs also have some disadvantages compared to premises-based LANs. First, most C.O. LAN service offerings are limited to asynchronous devices. While this limitation is sometimes due to limitations of the data switch in the C.O., it is also often due to the C.O. LAN tariff that was filed and the regulatory environment in the

United States. Some LAN traffic and applications can be accommodated using asynchronous equipment, although there are many synchronous applications that might not be supported, such as BISYNC, X.25, and SNA.

Second, most C.O. LAN lines operate at a maximum of 19.2 kbps. The 19.2-kbps speed of a C.O. LAN cannot always be compared with the higher bus or ring speeds of a premises-based LAN. The Ethernet bus, for example, operates at 10 Mbps with up to 1024 devices sharing time on the bus. A single device gets the bus for a small fraction of time, but no station has any guaranteed bandwidth. The 19.2 kbps on the C.O. LAN is dedicated to a single station; thus, if 1024 terminals were interconnected on a C.O. LAN, they would have an aggregate bit rate of nearly 20 Mbps. If a large number of stations need moderate line speeds, C.O. LANs can provide adequate bandwidth; if the stations need bursts of very high speeds, a premises-based LAN may be needed.

C.O. LANs could fit into a customer's (and network's) evolution to ISDN. Initially, the customer sees that a single twisted pair can carry voice and data, a major point of ISDN. ISDN is, of course, much more than a modification to the local loop, but the first hurdle is getting customers to recognize what the local loop can do. It also eliminates the customer's capital outlay for a premises-based LAN that might be replaced in the near future by ISDN.

After the discussion above, it might seem that premises-based LANs will be obsolete in the ISDN era. No such claim is being made here. The only claim is that ISDN will provide new alternatives to premises-based LANs; consider that ISDN will offer channels operating at 64 kbps and B-ISDN rates will be even higher.

ISDN is designed primarily as a wide area network (WAN) and will not replace customer premises LANs in the foreseeable future. Indeed, LAN interconnectivity is one possible ISDN application. Digital Equipment Corp., for example, has introduced a BRI board to provide MicroVAX LAN servers with access to ISDN.

Many large organizations may have an on-site PBX for ISDN service. The connection from the PBX to the user's terminal equipment will probably be a basic rate interface with either a 1B + D or 2B + D configuration. Using the PBX as a data switch offers a LAN-type service that is on-site and under user control. Again, this approach might be used to replace a premises-based LAN.

8.1.4 Metropolitan Area Networks

Metropolitan area networks (MANs) are conceptually related to LANs. Once thought of only as fast, large, local networks, MANs have evolved their own applications, technologies, and protocols, and the number of MAN implementations will grow rapidly in the 1990s.

MAN standards describe networks that can typically operate at speeds of 100 Mbps, cover a geographic area up to 60 miles (100 km), and support hundreds of devices. Possible MAN applications are very diverse and include LAN interconnection, bulk data transfer, audio and video transmission, terminal-to-host and host-to-host communications, and ordinary voice service.

There are two primary MAN standards currently competing in the marketplace. The first is the Fiber Distributed Data Interface (FDDI), based upon ANSI standards. FDDI has been an emerging technology with standards and products since the late 1980s. It uses optical fiber and a dual-ring topology. It is well-suited to provide a high-speed backbone network for a multibuilding environment or other customer-premises implementation.

The second MAN standard is the Distributed Queue Dual Bus (DQDB). DQDB should be approved as a standard by the Institute of Electrical and Electronics Engineers (IEEE) 802.6 committee in 1990 and forwarded for consideration as an international standard as ISO 8802-6.

DQDB can operate over different types of media, using a dual bus topology. It is also well suited to provide a high-speed public or private network. DQDB products and implementations are expected during the early 1990s and this standard has received enthusiastic support by telephone companies and fiber bypass operators in the United States.

LANs will, in all likelihood, be the dominant on-site data transport mechanism in most corporate environments. MANs, then, take on increasing significance as possible contenders as backbone networks.

MANs fit well in the evolution toward B-ISDN, if not narrowband ISDN. Both FDDI and DQDB operate on optical fiber, and ways of incorporating these strategies into the SONET hierarchy are already under investigation. Several observers, in fact, view MANs as early implementations of B-ISDN.

8.1.5 Packet Switching and X.25

CCITT Recommendation X.25 is the most commonly used protocol for accessing packet switched public data networks (PSPDNs). The user equipment (DTE) typically attaches to the network node (DCE) over a leased line, operating at speeds between 2.4 and 56 kbps. Additional procedures for an X.25 DTE accessing the PSPDN via an ISDN are given in CCITT Recommendation X.32; these additional rules include such issues as security, user and network identification, and encryption.

ISDNs will accommodate X.25 packet transfer, as discussed in

Chap. 3. Recommendation X.31 (I.462) specifically describes support of X.25 DTEs by an ISDN and defines the operation of an X.25-ISDN terminal adaptor.

The ability to continue using in-place X.25 hosts on an ISDN is critical to the success of ISDN since X.25 is so pervasive. Because X.25 protocols are supported on either the D- or B-channel, many dedicated lines for packet switching may be eliminated in an ISDN environment. There will be a requirement for an X.25 TA for ISDN operation and these devices are already being designed and built.

The X.25 TA (Fig. 8.9) will be an additional piece of hardware, much like a modem, that will sit between the local exchange's packet handler and the X.25 host. When sending X.25 data on the D-channel, the TA will merely convert X.25 LAPB frames to LAPD frames; the X.25 PLP packets will remain unaltered. When sending X.25 data on a B-channel, the only X.25-ISDN protocol conversion that must be performed by the TA is at the physical layer.

8.1.6   Frame Relay and Frame Switching

As packet switching is used by more and more customers, packet switched networks must operate at higher and higher speeds to handle the expected increase in traffic volume. This will be particularly true in an ISDN environment, since even more customers will have access to the X.25 network. Today's packet switches have a maximum throughput ranging from about 400 to 8000 packets per second, depending upon switch manufacturer. Packet switches in the future, however, will need even higher throughput rates.

One way to obtain a higher throughput is to build processors that can switch packets faster. Another approach is to use a scheme called *frame relay*. Using X.25 hardware that is currently available, frame relay achieves 5 to 10 times the throughput of existing networks by reducing the amount of processing that is performed at each network node.

X.25 was designed to operate over analog, copper, error-prone circuits. Therefore, both the layer 2 (LAPB) and layer 3 (PLP) protocols

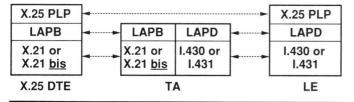

Figure 8.9 Terminal adaptor for ISDN access by an X.25 DTE.

have extensive error-checking procedures. Error rates are expected to drop significantly, however, over ISDN's digital and fiber circuits. While error checking cannot (and should not) be totally eliminated, the extensive internode error-checking procedures associated with X.25 can be greatly reduced, thus improving network throughput. Some studies suggest that the 30 or so X.25 layer 2 and 3 protocol steps performed at every node in a packet network could be reasonably reduced to 6 or so without showing an increase in errors.

The amount of error checking performed within the ISDN can be reduced because of the expected low error rate. The number of errors that will occur, however, will not be zero; therefore error checking must still be performed. The end users (i.e., level 4 though 7 protocols at the hosts) will have to perform some message error and sequence checking, as well as flow control, rather than depending upon the network to perform these tasks. Many current network architectures already have the higher layers handle these tasks anyway.

CCITT Recommendation I.122 defines the basic structure of additional ISDN packet-mode services, including frame relay. Recommendation I.122 does not describe frame relay procedures in detail, although an ANSI frame relay standard is anticipated by 1991.

ISDN frame relay would use an extension to the LAPD protocol, called I.441*. I.441* Core procedures are a subset of I.441* that would be implemented at the user's terminal equipment and within the ISDN itself for the frame relay service. These core procedures provide a minimal subset of LAPD rules to ensure basic link layer operation and correctness of frames. I.441* Core procedures include:

- Frame delimiting and transparency techniques
- Multiplexing/demultiplexing using SAPIs and TEIs
- Ensuring that frames are octet aligned (not including inserted 0 bits)
- Ensuring that frames are neither too long nor too short
- Detection of transmission errors

Note that I.441* Core procedures do *not* include handling of timers, error correction, sequence checking, and many other functions; these are handled by higher-layer protocols. A frame relay switch will merely pass frames bit by bit as they are received. If a bit error is detected, the station will abort the transmission; it is then up to higher layers to detect that a frame is missing.

The frame relay protocol architecture has two possible cases. In frame relay 1 service, I.441* Core procedures are used across the user-network interface (S/T reference point). The end users can use the pro-

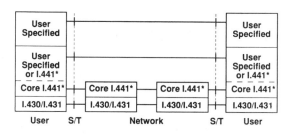

Figure 8.10 Frame relay protocol architecture.

tocols of their choice for the balance of the layer 2 procedures, as well as for the layer 3 procedures (Fig. 8.10). The "upper" layer 2 protocol and layer 3 protocol are transparent to the network. Frame relay 2 service is essentially the same as frame relay 1, except that the upper layer 2 protocol is I.441*.

Recommendation I.122 also describes *frame switching*. At this time, ISDNs provide X.25 support for frame and packet transport. Frame switching will use full I.441* procedures at layer 2 to provide an error-free pathway between ISDN user devices; the users can use any layer 3 protocol, including the X.25 PLP (Fig. 8.11). Unlike packet switching services, the network will provide protocol support only up to layer 2.

Once fully defined, frame relay and frame switching will be available on any ISDN channel in either the BRI or PRI.

8.1.7 Proprietary Network Protocols

Two of the most important proprietary network architectures today are IBM's Systems Network Architecture (SNA) and DEC's Digital Network Architecture (DNA), or DECnet. A question of major concern to customers is the future of SNA and DECnet, and other proprietary architectures, in the ISDN era.

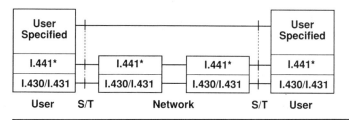

Figure 8.11 Frame switching protocol architecture.

SNA and DECnet have changed significantly since their initial introduction in the 1970s. Both have evolved over the last 10 years to be in closer alignment with the OSI model. In addition, IBM and DEC have both announced support for open network architectures and OSI protocols. Both networks support X.25, allowing host-to-host communication across an X.25 PSPDN. Both support versions of local area networks, allowing for communication across a LAN.

Both architectures will undoubtedly continue to evolve to support ISDN. While there may remain a need for proprietary communications between two hosts that are directly interconnected, ISDN support will become imperative. At the very least, the ISDN can be used to allow the transfer of X.25 packets.

There are a number of ways in which an SNA, DECnet, and other proprietary device can interact with an ISDN. First, the device can implement one, two, or three of the ISDN protocol layers. At level 1, the device can use the circuit-mode service on the B-channel to obtain a connection to another device; any user protocol(s) may be used in this case since B-channel protocols are transparent to the ISDN. The host could support levels 1 and 2, accessing the ISDN via LAPD frames. Optionally, the device could support all three ISDN protocols, exchanging messages across the D-channel.

Another approach, suggested above, is to access the ISDN using the X.25 protocol suite that both DECnet and SNA already support. Finally, new ISDN supplementary services will be defined when ISDNs go beyond offering basic bearer channel services. Digital and IBM will probably define new DECnet and SNA services that will work with the new ISDN services, providing another way for DECnet and SNA to interact with an ISDN. As SNA, DECnet, and other architectures become truly OSI compatible, many of these issues will become moot since OSI protocols will be supported by ISDNs.

The dominant computer vendors have two choices with respect to adopting emerging standards. One option is to embrace the new communications standards and the other is to take a strong proprietary position. In the long run, however, the latter option will probably fail. Users are beginning to demand open systems, OSI protocol support, and the use of standard protocols in a multivendor environment. Furthermore, it is becoming increasingly easier to clone proprietary protocols; thus the economics are less in favor of nonstandard solutions.

8.1.8 What to Do While Waiting for ISDN

ISDN, like any major new technology, will not become generally available overnight nor will it be available in all regions of the country or the world at the same time. The question for a large company might then well be, "Why invest in a piece of an ISDN?" That is, why base a corporate communications network around ISDN at one site while the other sites do not have the same capability? Why not continue to use today's telephony services until ISDNs are implemented throughout the nation?

There are no clear answers to these questions, except to observe that the use and acceptance of ISDN will be a gradual, boot-strapped process; as more customers use ISDN, additional users will want the technology, in turn causing increased availability. Not all users, however, will benefit from an ISDN. Customers who want independent voice and data networks, premises-based LANs, customer-owned network facilities and staff, low-speed networking, and/or very high-speed networking may not be good candidates for initial ISDN offerings.

The prudent customer will probably continue to plan to use traditional telephone network facilities and services for the short term and not place ISDN on a critical path. A strategy that places a customer on a path to ISDN, however, would include the use of C.O.-based services, such as Centrex, and/or ISDN-compatible PBXs.

Customers have many options in these times of evolving network technologies and capabilities. First, users should adopt standards in their networks wherever possible. Second, users should avoid being locked into a single vendor and/or nonstandard communications strategy wherever possible. By adopting standards and multiple vendors, the user has the opportunity to negotiate with several vendors and maintain flexibility for the future. Large users, in particular, can use their size to find out about vendors' future products and services and plan accordingly. Finally, users should never give control of their communications network to a vendor. This final point, by the way, is one of the key advantages to an ISDN solution; ISDN maximizes customer control of the communications resource.

8.2   ISDN APPLICATIONS

The phrase *ISDN applications* can mean different things depending upon the context. All ISDN trials have certain goals, one of which is to test various ISDN applications. Table 8.1 lists some of the common applications being examined in ISDN trials around the world. The applications being investigated by these various trials are oriented more toward *what* the network offers the customers rather than *how* the service should be offered.

8.2.1   Bellcore

Bellcore is writing implementation standards and conformance tests for the regional Bell operating companies' ISDN and SS7 services.

TABLE 8.1   Common ISDN Applications

Voice/data integration	Asynchronous terminal networking
Wide area networking (WAN)	LAN/X.25 gateways
64 kbps facsimile	Elimination of coaxial cable
Wiring simplification	PC networking
Private network interconnection	Enhanced call management
PRI-PBX interface	Computer-PBX interface
Telecommuting (work at home)	Security
Systems monitoring	Integrated voice/data/image
X.25 packet switching on B- and	terminal equipment
D-channels	Office automation
High-speed circuit switching	Network analysis
Videotex	PC-to-FAX
SS7 services	Incoming call management
User-controlled ISDN services	Switched T1 service
Wideband (>64 kbps) services	Video conferencing
Circuit switched data	Modem pooling
Electronic directory	Electronic mail
Database access and sharing	Network reliability
PC-to-PC screen sharing	

They are also defining and testing several new network services, including:

- *Anywhere Call Pickup:* Allows subscribers to answer their telephone regardless of their location, even from a pay telephone.

- *Call Waiting Deluxe:* Warns a user if an incoming call arrives when the user is already using the line; if the second call is not answered within some specified amount of time, the caller will automatically be asked to leave a voice mail message.

- *Who's Calling:* Audibly announces the caller's identity when the telephone is answered, using a computer-generated voice.

- *Personal Mailbox:* Provides all members in a household or business with their own personal voice-message mailboxes.

8.2.2   North American ISDN Users' Forum

In mid-1988, the North American ISDN Users' Forum (NIUF) was formed by the National Institute of Standards and Technology (NIST; formerly the National Bureau of Standards, or NBS). The NIUF, comprising groups representing both implementors and users, was intended to give users a greater role in the development of ISDN and ISDN applications, as well as to provide carriers and implementors with an idea of what applications are most important to users. The NIUF comprises two separate bodies to meet this goal, the ISDN Users' Workshop (IUW) and the ISDN Implementors' Workshop (IIW). A European counterpart to the NIUF will probably be formed by 1991.

Standard ISDN applications address both the services offered by ISDNs and the protocols and implementation of those services. Standard applications are desirable, for example, to allow one vendors' device to access services from another vendor's equipment.

Implementations need to be agreed to because the CCITT standards leave ambiguities. For example, there is a large amount of freedom in how to use the B- and D-channels. Implementation agreements would specify such items as what channel to use for certain applications (B-, D-, or H-), the type of transport mechanism (circuit or packet mode), special messages that might need to be added to a protocol, and the setting of relevant network timers. The NIST-sponsored activity is intended to provide ease of interoperability in what will be a multivendor environment.

One ISDN capability that is of great interest to the NIUF is Incoming Calling Line Identification (ICLID), also known as Automatic Number Identification (ANI) and Calling Line Identification Presentation (CLIP). Several NIUF applications have already been approved using ICLID, including:

- *Sales information management:* Sales representatives call an 800 number to gain access to a central database for the purpose of entering new orders and checking on the status of outstanding orders. Their calling telephone numbers are provided automatically to a sales representative database. Based on the profile identified by the calling numbers, the representatives will be automatically set up for interactive terminal, touch-tone/voice response, or voice conversation sessions. In the case of the voice conversation session, the ICLID information can be used to route the call to an appropriate sales manager who can display the sales representative's information.

- *Customer service call handling (or Incoming call management):* When a customer calls the Customer Service Department, the calling telephone number can be used to access information in a customer database so that customer account information can be automatically displayed to the customer service agent. If the call has to be transferred to another agent for some reason, both the caller's voice channel and information display can be transferred to the new station. This application could be expanded to display a caller's records in other environments, such as in a bank, insurance company, travel agency, accounting firm, credit agency, medical facility, or E911 dispatch center.

- *Telemarketing:* During very busy periods of the day, telemarketing departments may become flooded with more calls than they can handle. Today's Automatic Call Distribution (ACD) systems typically queue incoming calls, but customers must wait on hold until an agent is available. With ISDN, the called number, calling number, date, and time could be automatically recorded for every incoming call. If customers have to wait for more than a few seconds, they can be given the option of waiting for the next available agent or of hanging up and being called back as soon as possible. If the caller chooses to hang up, the information is stored in the Automatic Callback database. When available, an agent can automatically return the call. This application could be expanded to other environments, such as operators at a charity telethon, poison control center, emergency hotline, or service bureau.

- *On-demand video marketing and follow-up:* A customer can dial a special ISDN number to receive information about some product. The information may be in the form of an image, voice plus data, or slow-scan video under control of the customer. The caller's number can be stored in a database and a sales agent can make a follow-up telephone call to the customer.

Other applications selected for initial standardization by the NIUF include:

- *Universal financial system access:* Intended to allow protocol conversion and gateways necessary to allow users of a multivendor network to access financial databases.

- *Point-of-sale terminals:* A point-of-sale (POS) terminal is a combination cash register and computer. As customers make purchases, the POS terminal can keep track of what is being purchased and automatically notify the inventory software of diminishing supplies of certain products. It can also access a credit card validation database to accept or reject a customer's credit card.

- *Encryption:* Security within the public network is a concern to government agencies, the military, and many businesses. Security features include user authentication and security/encryption key distribution. Another issue is maintaining secure communications when one user is on the ISDN and the other user is not.

- *Addressing:* An arrangement that will allow ISDN users to call one 10-digit number for data, voice, and image transmission.

- *Engineering workstation interface to ISDN:* This application would provide a standard engineering workstation interface to ISDN facilities, supporting such requirements as graphic inquiry and interactive engineering design. Initial application plans include interfaces for Apollo, DEC, Hewlett-Packard, IBM, and SUN workstations and graphic terminals.

There are, quite literally, hundreds of other potential applications for ISDN. Some of the other applications being investigated and defined by the NIUF and other organizations include:

- *Wide area networking (WAN):* The ISDN will provide voice and data WAN capability for organizations that are geographically disperse. It can also provide remote access to the organization's private networks, such as an X.25 packet network or a LAN.

- *PC-to-PC screen sharing and desktop conferencing:* Allows PC screen images to be shared by several users in a "conference call" environment. Different users can alter the screen image so that other users' attention can be directed to a portion of the screen. It may use both B-channels, or the B- and D-channel, for simultaneous voice conversations and screen sharing.

- *Asynchronous protocol conversion to SNA/SDLC:* Allows asynchronous terminals to communicate with IBM hosts supporting SNA/SDLC. Access to the host may be via 3174-type controllers using X.25 block-mode PADs or 3725-type front end processors using X.25 and IBM's Network Control Program Packet Switched Interface (NPSI).

- *327x-emulation and coax elimination:* Allows a PC to emulate an IBM 327x terminal and access an IBM host. IBM terminals typically access 3274 controllers using coaxial cable; PCs emulating 327x terminals will access the controller over twisted pair. This not only reduces the cost but makes moving terminals and network reconfiguration much easier.

- *Access to LANs:* Several applications have been proposed where the ISDN access would be available from Ethernet and Manufacturing Automation Protocol (MAP) local area networks. The ISDN could act as a bridge between LANs or as a gateway between the LANs and X.25 packet networks.

- *Fast facsimile:* Group 1 and 2 facsimile equipment uses analog techniques, facilities, and signaling. Group 3 facsimile equipment uses digital encoding and compression techniques, although they contain an internal modem to use analog communications facilities; a G3 fax requires over 10 to 15 s to transmit a page at speeds up to 9600 bps. Group 1, 2, and 3 fax equipment is compatible. Group 4 fax equipment uses digital signaling and compression techniques and will operate over ISDN 64-kbps B-channels. G4 fax will require less than 5 s to transmit a page of a document.

- *Videotex:* A service where users can directly access information databases. Using special, inexpensive hardware, users can make a call over the telephone network to the database, obtaining such information as telephone numbers without going through a directory assistance operator. This type of service could be easily offered to a customer with a PC through an ISDN.

- *Videoconferencing:*   Allows multiple sites to conference together, sharing voice and full-motion video images. One common application might be to offer college or university courses to remote campuses or business locations. The videoconference leader (or lecturer) controls which images the other sites see and can alternate between seeing the other sites; optionally, the leader can allow the other sites to see each other. Voice input from one site can be broadcast out to all other sites.

- *Hotel guest service center:*   Allows guests access to a communications facility that will provide remote guest interaction, streamline registration and check-out procedures, enhance the reservation process, and provide improved customer support.

- *Building security:*   Can provide a mini-911 service for a given customer site. When a person in a building (e.g., a tenant in an office building or guest in a hotel) calls an emergency number, a diagram of the caller's floor is displayed for the emergency operator. The floor plan display pinpoints the caller's location so that the operator can send assistance or can tell the caller which route to take for emergency evacuation. Hazardous materials or other special situations can also be noted on the operator's screen.

- *Electronic Document Interchange (EDI):*   EDI standards, including the ANSI X12-series standards, are making document interchange between different organizations much easier. ISDN can further simplify this application by providing a high-speed public network for document transfers.

One additional thrust in application standards work is to define a standard interface for PCs to an ISDN. Many vendors have already designed plug-in terminal adaptors (i.e., a board in the back of the PC) that act as the basis of a PC-ISDN interface and support many PC applications. Unfortunately, vendors are also creating their own software interfaces for these applications in the absence of standard implementation specifications.

The Hayes AT command set emerged in the 1980s as the industry-standard modem command language. In early 1990, Hayes announced that extensions would be added to the AT command set for ISDN applications; this may well emerge as the industry standard for PC-based ISDN hardware, as well.

Many vendors are defining software interfaces to their ISDN applications software and hardware. These Application Programmer Interfaces (APIs) are high-level language routines, allowing users to write their own ISDN applications using the vendor's hardware and software as a technology platform.

8.2.3   ISDN Applications in the Future

It is difficult to project how the home and business environments will change in the next 10 to 15 years since there are so many social, economic, political, technological, and demographic factors to consider. From a purely communications standpoint, however, it is possible to make a few guesses as to what the future might hold based upon two factors, what users want and where today's technology is headed.

One of the key information breakthroughs that ISDN will bring to both home and office is the ability to support multimedia devices. Since integrated, high-speed voice/data applications can be supported by an ISDN, multimedia terminals can be used.

The importance of this is that people view the world and communicate ideas with more than one medium. A combination of voice, data, text, and images provides the greatest possible means to convey ideas, circumventing even language barriers to some degree.

The introduction of integrated voice/data terminals (IVDTs) and/or ISDN telephone sets on the office desktop is not a new idea. With these devices, it will be possible to obtain all of the services and applications discussed earlier.

The biggest changes might actually occur in the home. The concept of the intelligent home is one that has been around for several decades, even before the evolution of the microprocessor made computer control of a house feasible. ISDN adds the feasibility of easy communications between the home and the outside world.

A control processor could integrate many functions within the home and provide the gateway to communicate with the outside world. Messages can be exchanged between devices within the home. Monitors and sensors can adjust the temperature throughout the house, shut off lights in unoccupied rooms, or notify the occupants or security office of an unauthorized intrusion into the home. Incoming telephone calls could be directed to rooms that are occupied. Speech recognition chips in the control processor could allow verbal programming of house devices; e.g., a person in the home could lock or unlock doors, originate telephone calls, or select a TV station by merely talking to the control processor. A shopping list could be prepared verbally and stored by the control processor for future reference; at an appropriate time, the list could be transmitted to a grocery store with a request for home delivery and an authorization for payment. Personalized educational texts or newspapers can be accessed through informatics networks.

The list of capabilities that can be brought to the office and to the home is nearly endless. The limit, quite literally, is only what can be imagined.

8.2.4 General Comments

Integration of voice and data is an important goal of ISDN. On the
surface, ISDNs provide this integration because voice and data devices communicate with the C.O. via the same twisted pair and receive services from the same network. This is the *physical* integration
of voice and data.

As the applications listed above and in Table 8.1 show, voice/data
integration means much more than physically placing digital voice
and data on the same pair of wires. ISDN voice/data integration can
mean the integration of two types of information streams for a common, single application, or a *logical* integration of voice and data.
Consider how much more productive the customer agent is in the scenario above when a customer's records are displayed on a terminal automatically when the customer calls; consider also the time saved for
both customer and customer service agent. This is true voice/data integration, the use of the two communications technologies for a single
purpose.

ISDN applications can be broadly classified as being *horizontal* or
vertical. Horizontal applications are those that are applicable to a
wide range of industries, including:

- Voice and electronic message centers
- Directory service
- Automatic call distribution
- Order and service desk support
- Conferencing
- Data networking

Vertical applications are those that are particularly applicable to a
specific industry, such as:

- Health care
- Telemarketing
- Hospitality services
- Security and other monitoring services
- Financial institutions
- Educational institutions
- Travel services
- Insurance companies
- Utility companies

As new horizontal applications are devised, users and vendors will find new vertical markets for them. The number of applications are only limited by the intersections in this applications-market matrix.

8.3 ISDN MARKETPLACE

It is difficult to project the market for ISDN; it is a relatively new, untested, and unproven technology that will cost the customers a potentially large sum of money to use. Today's ISDN trials are demonstrating that the technology is stable and that customers like the service, but a question lingers on: "Who will be willing to pay for the service?" As the service becomes more available, costs will come down. Where, then, should initial ISDN efforts be directed?

Several studies have identified different ISDN market segments and their potential for ISDN. Some of this information is discussed below (Table 8.2).

8.3.1 Residential Customers

The residential market actually has two submarkets. The first includes those who use data and telecommunications for household and/or personal purposes. The second includes those who work at

TABLE 8.2   ISDN Market Segments

Customer Market Segment	Definition	Information Requirements	Willingness To Pay
Residential	Mostly single lines	Limited information service needs. Integrated voice/data and associated services are of interest	Low
Small Business	Few employees, ≤4 lines	Limited information service needs. Call management features of interest; data requirements will probably grow	Limited
Medium Business	Single location, >20 employees; multiple locations, <50 employees at each site	Timely information flow very important. Functional integration of voice and data very high.	Moderate to High
Large Business	Several locations, >50 employees at each site	Information management very important, with several application types. Both internal and external networks may be supported.	High
Extremely Large Business	Several locations, >4,000 employees at each site	(same as above)	High, but also a candidate for by-pass

home (telecommuters) or own a business at home. This market comprises a tremendous number of very small users; over 95 percent of U.S. residences have a single telephone line and about half have a cable TV connection.

Most residential customers have a limited need for information services, which has been demonstrated in several home information service trials. This may not be true for the telecommuter or for some small businesses, although many in-home businesses will not differ from the typical residential customer.

Other ISDN applications, however, do have relevance for the residential customers. Meter reading by utility companies, call management functions, security, entertainment (including, but not limited to, video), CLASS, and home finance are a few of the services that would probably be of interest to the residential customer.

A major problem with selling ISDN to residential customers is their willingness to pay for the service. While an often-stated goal for the cost of residential ISDN service is about 1½ times the cost of single-line POTS, someone has to pay for the new inside telephone wiring (if necessary), the NT1, and the ISDN-compatible terminal equipment (i.e., telephones and terminal adaptors). If these costs are borne entirely by the residential customer, ISDN will gain very slow acceptance. Since most customers are reasonably content with today's services from the telephone company, cable TV company, utility meter reading company, and so on, most will not be impressed by the long list of ISDN capabilities.

The business market for ISDN will probably have to grow before the residential market will. Like any new telephony service, most people use the new service at work, realize that they like the service, and then buy that service at home. For example, how many people purchased call waiting and call forwarding from the telephone company before experiencing those services at work or at another residence? This is also in line with an unwillingness to pay; employees at a business do not have to pay for the advanced services before experimenting with them.

8.3.2 Small Business Customers

A small business customer is one with a few employees and less than 25 or so telephone lines. Small businesses have a single location and usually average less than a single telephone line per employee; this is a relatively large market segment.

Most small businesses do not have a large data communications requirement but do have large voice requirements. Their greatest need is to reduce the cost associated with having many lines but to also increase call coverage so as not to miss incoming calls. Call management features, such as call forwarding, automatic callback, and call screening, can be of particular importance in allowing a business to function with limited resources.

With additional services and products available, the data communications needs of a small business can grow. Point-of-sale terminals, for example, can enhance a business's cash and inventory management.

Like the residential customer, most small businesses can not afford to absorb all of the costs associated with installing ISDN, particularly if the gains in sales, service, and/or cash flow cannot be demonstrated.

8.3.3 Medium Business Customers

A medium business is one with more than 25 or so employees at a single site or multiple locations with fewer than 50 employees at each site. This is a moderately sized market segment but an important one since these businesses require data communications and timely flow of information.

The information flow criterion is an important differentiating factor for this market segment. Small businesses have less of a data requirement than a medium-size business. A medium-size business, however, has a higher percentage of its employees directly responsible for profit and loss functions than larger businesses. The timely flow of information is very critical in this market segment.

Typical ISDN applications would include integrated voice/data access to information, PC networking, access to host computers, database queries and updates, data entry, call management, and teleconferencing. ISDN supports all of these applications, with the benefit of eliminating separate access arrangements for each.

Medium-size businesses show a relatively high willingness to pay for ISDN service. Truly integrated voice/data service provides sufficient justification over today's nonintegrated service offerings.

8.3.4 Large Business Customers

Large businesses are those that have several locations, each with more than about 50 employees and several thousand telephone lines. While this represents a relatively low percentage of the total number of businesses, it accounts for a very large percentage of a telephone company's revenue. The primary concern of large businesses is information management directly related to the success of the company.

Information management involves many aspects particular to the multilocation characteristic of the large business. Issues of concern include minimizing costs associated with employee moves and terminal rearrangements, control and management of network resources, ease of use, distance and location transparency, interconnectivity, and high speed.

Large business's information flow needs can be broken down into two types, internal and external. In addition, companies cycle between operating in growth and economically constrained modes.

Internal information flow is both intralocation and intracompany. If a company is in a period of growth, data requirements might include increased data access capabilities, information security, protocol conversion, and coaxial cable elimination. C.O. or premises-based LANs are good candidates for this service; ISDN, too, could provide the interconnection between the diverse equipment. If the company is economically constrained, the need is to increase worker productivity, control costs, and manage resources. While this can be done with premises-based equipment, ISDN or another C.O.-based solution may provide economies of scale: greater reliability, fewer network terminations, C.O. management and staffing, and minimal capital outlay.

External information flow includes interlocation and intercompany communications. Businesses in a growth mode usually have a need for distance transparency. Citywide Centrex, 800 service, distributed communications, and other services that make geographically disperse locations look close together are the types of services that would be needed. Those businesses that are economically constrained generally need to reduce costs by reducing the number of access lines and trunks and using the remaining facilities in a more efficient fashion. These customers can use such ISDN services as integrated voice and data access, calling number display, customer-originated trace, and nuisance call reject.

Large customers are a prime ISDN market because of the many ways in which they can use the ISDN services. Furthermore, large businesses have indicated both a willingness and ability to pay for integrated services.

8.3.5 Extremely Large Business Customers

Extremely large business customers are those with several locations, each having several thousand employees. This market segment is also a small percentage of total customers but a large percentage of revenue. They have the same information needs as the large business customers and make good candidates for ISDN.

Extremely large businesses, however, have sufficient data and telecommunications needs that they have in-house technical staff to support these functions, both to save money and to avoid becoming overdependent on a single vendor. They are usually willing to pay for a service that they want but are also frequently unwilling to wait too long to get the service. While ISDN might be attractive to these customers, local telephone company bypass might also be attractive. Several extremely large customers have announced ISDN plans that include an on-site ISDN switch, connected directly to an interexchange carrier and bypassing the local exchange carrier. This can save a tremendous amount of money for the customer and dramatically affect the revenues of the LEC.

8.3.6 Final Comments

The previous paragraphs have shown that there are several different markets for ISDN and each has its own applications for the service. The sales strategies used to sell ISDN service will undoubtedly differ as well. In fact, these market segments will help sell the service to each other. As customers purchase and use the service, and can demonstrate some tangible advantage (not necessarily economic), other customers will join in.

The Evolution of ISDN Implementations

Some studies estimate that there will be approximately 100,000 ISDN lines in service worldwide in 1990 and that this number is expected to increase to over 4 million by the mid-1990s. The question that constantly surrounds the implementation and growth of ISDN is, "Is the growth of ISDN being driven by ISDN service providers or potential customers?" To a certain extent, the answer is probably "Both."

ISDN standards from the CCITT have been evolving since the early 1980s. The first formal CCITT recommendations were adopted in 1984 and provided the basis for many ISDN trials and pilot offerings throughout the world. The 1988 recommendations are even more complete, defining additional ISDN services to those that have been developed over the last several years and pointing the direction toward future services such as broadband ISDN.

Throughout the 1980s, many ISDN and ISDN-related trials have been performed throughout the world. The trials all had a single overriding goal: to showcase the technology that represents the biggest change ever in both the communications services available to the customer and in how the public views the "telephone company" as a network service provider.

This chapter will briefly examine the evolution of ISDN trials and service offerings in the United States and around the world. This is not an exhaustive list of all such pilots and service offerings but is meant to provide some historical background to today's activity. The first U.S. ISDN tariffs will also be discussed.

9.1 THE ROLE OF ISDN TRIALS

From the perspective of the telephone industry, ISDN is where the future lies. The local loop is the greatest asset of the local exchange carriers, and ISDN provides a way to offer more services over that loop. The voice and data communications markets in North America are growing and will continue to grow, voice at a rate of 3 to 10 percent annually and data at a rate of 15 to 20 percent annually. Since the U.S. divestiture of AT&T, the interexchange carriers (IECs), Bell operating companies (BOCs), and independent telephone companies (ITCs) have been increasingly trying to provide data communications services. Telephone companies throughout most of the rest of the world have been offering data services for much longer periods of time, many dating back to the 1970s with the introduction of public packet switching networks.

ISDN is unusual compared to the more traditional services associated with the telephone industry. ISDNs provide such a myriad of capabilities that nearly any customer can choose some set of useful services. The telephone company provides a digital pipe; the customer chooses how to use that facility. Thus, new network facilities, transmission lines, and customer-premises equipment (CPE) must all be trialed together.

As the telephone companies throughout the world have prepared to offer ISDN service, pilot trials have been performed. Basically, the goals for the telephone companies have been to:

- Test the ISDN market

- Develop ISDN technology, applications, and products

- Be recognized as advanced communications service providers

The trials were also important for customers. The trials needed to show if ISDN can:

- Effectively meet basic data and telecommunications needs

- Redefine the way in which information is managed to achieve business goals

- Provide an economic alternative to today's communication services

9.2 ISDN IN THE UNITED STATES

In November 1972, the CCITT convened a meeting to discuss how studies of digital networks and ISDN should be conducted and how these studies should be coordinated. Eleven administrations offered opinions on the subject: Australia, France, Italy, the Netherlands, Japan, Scandinavia (representing Denmark, Finland, Norway, and Sweden), Spain, Switzerland, the United Kingdom, the United States, and West Germany. Each of the countries considered ISDN to be a long-term study item at that time. Some countries, notably France and Japan, were very enthusiastic about ISDN, viewing it as an important future step. The United States, on the other hand, was one of the least encouraging, indicating that integrated data and telecommunications services should not be based upon a single network with a common signaling system.

While the United States was initially hesitant (if not outright opposed) to the concept of ISDN, it has emerged as a leader in developing ISDN services, applications, products, and standards. The United States has one of the largest networks in the world to convert to ISDN and this conversion has been underway for several years. More than 50 ISDN trials or service implementations already exist in the United States, comprising about 60,000 lines; there are expected to be more than 1 million ISDN lines in the United States by 1992.

For a while, it seemed that every new ISDN announcement in the United States was a new "first": the first trial of ISDN-type service, the first trial of basic rate access, the first trial of primary rate access, the first service offering without a trial, the first paying customer for ISDN service, and so on. The paragraphs below review some of the U.S. ISDN trials and commercial offerings. The activity of the BOCs is described, region by region, followed by the independent telephone companies, the IECs, and private ISDNs.

9.2.1 Ameritech (Illinois Bell, Indiana Bell, Michigan Bell, Ohio Bell, and Wisconsin Telephone)

Ameritech was the first regional Bell operating company (RBOC) to provide ISDN demonstrations in the United States. From mid-1985 to the end of 1986, a Siemens portable ISDN switch was placed in a trailer and used for ISDN shows throughout the Ohio Bell and Wisconsin Telephone service areas. Users who attended the demonstrations were asked to fill out surveys, which were used by Ameritech to determine the reaction to ISDN and to identify potential marketing opportunities.

Ameritech is also the region with one of the first, and probably best-known, U.S. ISDN trials. The McDonald's ISDN Trial in Oak Brook, IL, began on December 16, 1986, with the first simultaneous voice, data, and image telephone call in the United States. The offering serves McDonald's headquarters building, campus (called Hamburger University), and three other McDonald's sites out of the Oak Brook C.O. The trial began with 50 BRI lines at two locations, increasing to over 300 BRI lines at the five sites.

The McDonald's trial involved a large number of participants. On the network side was Illinois Bell Telephone, Ameritech Services, AT&T Network Systems, and Bell Communications Research (Bellcore). Participating customer-premises equipment vendors included AT&T, Fujitsu America, Harris, Hayes Microcomputer Products, NEC America, Telrad, and Wang Laboratories. Many types of CPE were tested, including integrated voice/data terminals (IVDTs), terminal adaptors (TAs), single- and multiple-directory number digital sets, PC-based TAs, an applications processor (providing message desk and directory services), and an attendant console.

The McDonald's trial successfully tested many applications, including file transfer, packet-mode transfer, coaxial (coax) cable elimination, modem pooling, and compressed video. The trial phase of this service ended in 1988 and is now a commercial offering.

Based in large part upon the success of the McDonald's trial, Illinois Bell was the first BOC to file an ISDN tariff. The tariff, for the Ameritech Integrated Digital Service, is described in more detail in Sec. 9.4.1.

Illinois Bell also held a trial using a Northern Telecom, Inc. (NTI), DMS-100 switch and CPE at their Chicago headquarters. This was an internal trial to test business office applications and to gain experience with NTI equipment; no commercial customers are scheduled. Applications included integrated PC and voice transmission over a single twisted pair, modem pooling, coaxial cable elimination, voice mail, facsimile, X.25 gateway, and key equipment replacement.

Other ISDN trials in this region include one conducted by Wisconsin Bell at Alverno College in Milwaukee, using a Siemens EWSD switch, and another conducted by Indiana Bell at the University of Indiana in Bloomington, using an NTI DMS-100. Both trials are testing BRI access in a campus environment.

By the end of 1989, more than half of the metropolitan switching centers in this region were interconnected by digital facilities. Ameritech plans to more than double the number of digital switches in its network and have over 250,000 miles of optical fiber in place by 1992.

9.2.2 Bell Atlantic (Bell of Pennsylvania, Chesapeake and Potomac Telephone, Diamond State Telephone, and New Jersey Bell Telephone)

Like Ameritech, Bell Atlantic used a portable switch to demonstrate ISDN service throughout their service area in 1986. They used an NEC America portable switch linked to an AT&T 1AESS host to demonstrate ISDN to several of their Centrex customers.

One of the major Bell Atlantic ISDN trials started in the fall of 1987 between New Jersey Bell and Bellcore. A Siemens EWSD circuit switch and EDXP packet switch were colocated with an AT&T 1AESS switch in the Red Bank central office to provide BRI service to Bellcore's Navesink Research and Engineering Center. Many vendors' equipment, including a Bellcore-designed ISDN workstation, were tested, resulting in a Centrex ISDN service. This service also provides a facility to test Bellcore's ISDN Network Test System (INTS), as well as continued testing of CPE.

Bell Atlantic started commercial BRI service in 1988 in several areas of the region. A 34,000 line, statewide Centrex service for the Commonwealth of Virginia in Richmond was installed by Chesapeake and Potomac (C&P) of Virginia in early 1988 and supports several hundred ISDN lines. C&P of West Virginia has implemented a 4900-line Centrex at the West Virginia University in Morgantown, where 660 of the lines can support ISDN. C&P of Maryland is providing ISDN service to Johns Hopkins Medical Center in Baltimore and the University of Maryland in College Park. C&P also provides ISDN lines to the Federal National Mortgage Association in Washington, D.C. All of these ISDN services are offered from AT&T 5ESS switches.

Bell of Pennsylvania and the State of Pennsylvania government in Harrisburg are planning a statewide ISDN service, offered from an NTI DMS-100.

In early 1989, the U.S. General Services Administration (GSA) awarded Bell Atlantic a 10-year contract for a private ISDN to interconnect 34 federal agencies. The voice/data network, known as the Washington Interagency Telecommunications Service (WITS), will serve more than 100,000 government employees in the Washington, D.C., area. C&P Telephone Co. will install and operate WITS, which should be in service by 1992.

Bell Atlantic is one of the more aggressive RBOCs in terms of SS7. Bell Atlantic has major SS7 deployments in New Jersey and some deployment in Pennsylvania, Virginia, and West Virginia; 80 percent of the Bell Atlantic central offices, serving over 50 percent of their access lines, should have SS7 by 1991. SS7 on local access switches will support CLASS services in northern New Jersey, the Washington, D.C., metropolitan area, and some locations in Pennsylvania. Database access functions, such as Line Information Data Base (LIDB) and 800 number access, will be implemented when regulations permit. New Jersey Bell started to offer some CLASS services based upon ANI in 1989.

About half of Bell Atlantic's switches had been converted to digital by the end of 1989, and over 300,000 miles of optical fiber cable connected the network's central offices.

9.2.3 BellSouth (South Central Bell and Southern Bell Telephone and Telegraph)

BellSouth is currently very active in providing ISDN; trials officially began in April 1988. They are using three primary switches (AT&T 5ESS, NTI DMS-100, and Siemens EWSD) in three major locations (Alabama, Florida, and Georgia). The main goals of their trials involve architectural and technology issues:

- Interconnection of the 5ESS and DMS-100, tied to an SS7 STP built by Ericsson
- Basic and primary rate access
- Interworking with the Northern Telecom SL-10 packet switch

There are a number of customers involved in the ISDN trials and service offerings in Atlanta including one of the first paying customers for ISDN in the United States that is not in the computer or communications industry, the SunTrust Service Corporation of Georgia. Other customers include AT&T Network Systems Group, Contel Corporation, Hayes Microcomputer Products, and Prime Computer, Inc. These trials will include ISDN loop validation tests, protocol conformance tests, administrative and reporting system evaluation, and testing inter-LATA Centrex, modem pools, and packet and circuit-mode data. A 5ESS switch is being used for this service.

An ISDN facility trial in Boca Raton, FL, uses a Siemens EWSD switch for internal testing by Siemens. This trial includes testing SS7 interoffice signaling capabilities.

South Central Bell's first ISDN customer was the U.S. Army Missile Command (MICOM) at Redstone Arsenal in Huntsville, AL. Announced in mid-1989, MICOM will initially use 25 BRI lines and is expected to grow to 500 lines. Online directory services, voice messaging, and PC-to-PC communications are the primary applications for this installation. It is one of the first steps in the modernization of the U.S. Department of Defense data and telecommunications networks, discussed in Sec. 9.2.10.

BellSouth is another RBOC that is aggressively pursuing SS7. STPs have already been placed in Atlanta and Birmingham, and early support of citywide Centrex service is expected. Plans are already underway to deploy SS7 in all major metropolitan areas in the region and deployment was scheduled for completion in all equal-access tandems by the end of 1988; over 30 percent of their access lines can be served by SS7.

The first SS7 trial linking local and long distance telephone companies involves South Central Bell, Southern Bell, Bellcore, AT&T,

Northern Telecom, and U.S. Sprint; it started in the summer of 1989. NTI DMS-100 and DMS-200 switches in Miami, FL, and Franklin, TN, are using SS7 signaling. Southern Bell is using a Northern Telecom STP, while South Central Bell's STP is a small version of an Ericsson AXE switch. AT&T 3B20 computers act as STPs in their SS7 network.

9.2.4   NYNEX (New England Telephone and New York Telephone)

NYNEX also used a Siemens portable ISDN switch for a mobile demonstration in parts of their service area. In addition to the Siemens equipment, NYNEX is also doing trials with 5ESS and DMS-100 switches.

The first ISDN activities in this region were performed by New England Telephone in the Boston area and by New York Telephone in New York City. One of the goals of the early trials was for the two BOCs to gain first-hand knowledge of the AT&T 5ESS and Siemens EWSD ISDN capabilities and applications. They have also been provided with an ISDN Technology Transfer Package from Bellcore, which comprises the ISDN Network Test System and ISDN CPE-Network Compatibility Test Facility.

The first commercial ISDN service in the region began in 1988 for AT&T Network Systems in North Andover, MA. AT&T has over 1000 ISDN lines as part of a 7-year, 5000-line digital Centrex contract. New York Telephone also started a BRI service to Shearson Lehman Hutton in New York City in 1988, as part of an 8000-line Centrex implementation.

In early 1989, Harvard University in Cambridge announced a 10-year, 22,000 line Centrex contract with New England Telephone (NET). About 5000 of the lines will support BRI service. NET will be responsible for rewiring 175 buildings with over 5000 miles of copper and optical fiber cable; completion is scheduled for 1990.

In 1989, the New York Public Service Commission (PSC) ordered the state's telecommunications service providers to cooperate in the implementation of a statewide ISDN trial. The project will occur in two phases, the first of which will comprise two ISDN links. The first link will between New York City and Jamestown, involving Alltel New York, MCI Communications, New York Telephone, and Northern Telecom; this phase will use NTI DMS-100 and DMS-200 switches. The second ISDN link will be between New York City and Rochester using AT&T 4ESS and 5ESS switches, involving AT&T, New York Telephone, Rochester Telephone, and Teleport Communications. Both links are scheduled for completion in 1991. Phase 2 will be the interconnection of the two links and is scheduled for completion in 1992.

In the PSC's original order, it was made clear that they believe that ISDN has application to business and residential customers alike. In particular, the importance of ISDN to the future of New York City was specifically cited, particularly with respect to its (and, hence, the nation's) place in the worldwide financial market.

9.2.5 Pacific Telesis (Nevada Bell and Pacific Bell)

Pacific Bell's Project Victoria was the first U.S. customer trial of ISDN-like services. Beginning in early 1986, Project Victoria brought a 64-kbps voice channel and five low-speed data channels to a customer site over a single wire pair. This public trial involved 200 customers in the Danville area (near San Francisco). Several banks, utility companies, and information providers also participated.

The main goal of Project Victoria was to see if ISDN services (i.e., voice and data over a single pair) are useful to the residential and small business customer. With a population of over 25 million, and approximately 800,000 small businesses that employ nearly 80 percent of the working population, this market seemed like a natural one to target. Furthermore, the reasoning went, since most very large businesses have already built their own communications networks, ISDN should not be initially targeted at that market.

Project Victoria was successful in the sense that it showed that the *small* customer could use the integrated voice/data ISDN services. Project Victoria's customers, however, did not have to purchase the NT1 or pay the cost of the digital subscriber line, major economic stumbling blocks to selling ISDN to the residential and small business customer. The trial did not test whether ISDN was needed for the large customer or not, but most current studies and service offerings show that they are, indeed, the ideal customer.

Pacific Bell spent over $25 million to develop the multiplexer to provide the ISDN-like service. They interrupted their work in early 1987, however, pending a decision by the Federal Communications Commission (FCC) as to whether the loop termination equipment at the residence would be classified as a multiplexer or CPE. In late 1987, the FCC ruled that the Project Victoria multiplexer was CPE. Since design and development of telecommunications products and CPE is prohibited by the Modification of Final Judgement, Pacific Bell announced that it would not continue work on Project Victoria technology. That decision also caused them to cancel a planned year-long trial in Los Angeles which would have involved more services and customers.

Pacific Bell is also involved in other ISDN activities. In the fall of 1987, they started a series of trials in the San Francisco Bay area involving Lockheed Missiles and Space Corp., AT&T Network Systems, Hayes Microcomputer Products, and Chevron Corporation. These trials used AT&T 1AESS and 5ESS, NTI DMS-100, and NEC NEAX 61E Adjunct switches. Bellcore is also participating, providing protocol verification and performance tests. Primary rate access is being tested between Chevron's NTI Meridian PBX and a DMS-100 central office switch.

The first commercial ISDN sale in the region was between Pacific Bell and the city of Fresno. Fresno's ISDN network will work in conjunction with their existing Centrex network. Pacific Bell is also installing an ISDN for Chevron in San Francisco, using an NTI Meridian SL-100 PBX connected to a DMS-100 switch; both BRI and PRI service will be provided.

In 1989, Pacific Bell filed a public ISDN tariff, described in Sec. 9.4.2.

9.2.6 Southwestern Bell (Southwestern Bell Telephone)

Southwestern Bell Telephone (SWBT) scheduled a three-phase ISDN implementation. The first phase, started in late 1987, involved the implementation of ISDN-capable switches at their Advanced Technology Laboratory in St. Louis: an AT&T 5ESS, Ericsson AXE 10, NTI DMS-100, and Siemens EWSD. These switches were not part of the SWBT network but provided 200 PRI and BRI lines for internal use.

The second phase, scheduled for late 1988, was to interwork the 5ESS, DMS-100, and EWSD switches. The final phase, originally scheduled for 1989, would provide interworking between SWBT's and interexchange carriers' ISDN capabilities, including SS7; these tests will probably not commence until 1991.

SWBT had six customers initiate ISDN commercial service in 1988:

- Tenneco and Shell Oil Co., both in Houston, have about 5000 BRI lines and a 10-year contract with SWBT.

- AT&T Technologies in Oklahoma City is served by 1000 BRI lines.

- 3M Corporation in Austin has 3165 lines to two sites.

- AT&T Network Systems in St. Louis has a 4-year contract for 2300 lines to serve its southwest regional headquarters.

- Rockwell Communication Systems in Richardson, TX, is served by 1200 BRI lines.

The main objectives cited by these customers for using ISDN include:

- Increased call management capabilities
- Flexibility of data communications
- Integrated voice and data to the desktop
- Increased user productivity

The applications being used by the customers include:

- PC-to-PC and PC-to-host communications
- Wide area networking
- Call management: call forwarding, call pickup groups, distinctive ringing, message waiting indication, incoming name/number display
- Electronic directory
- Modem pooling
- Voice messaging
- Screen sharing and file transfers

The first internetworking tests between local and national ISDNs was scheduled for the summer of 1988 at Southwestern Bell. Although SWBT plans to go ahead with testing ISDN links between their own switches, the national ISDN tests will be delayed.

In 1989, Southwestern Bell filed a public ISDN tariff, described in Sec. 9.4.3. Southwestern Bell has installed two SS7 STP/SCP pairs. Their plan to implement an 800 number database by the end of 1988 was interrupted by the FCC.

9.2.7   U.S. West (Mountain Bell, Northwestern Bell, and Pacific Northwest Bell)

U.S. West has a number of ongoing trials and service offerings, most notably in Denver, Minneapolis, Phoenix, and Portland. They plan on being able to offer ISDN in all metropolitan areas in their service area by 1991. Like the other RBOCs, they are using ISDN switches and CPE from a number of vendors.

The first U.S. West trial involved Mountain Bell, Honeywell Information Systems, and the Arizona State Government Transportation and Administration Departments. Many companies are involved in this operation. A DMS-100 switch and Northern Telecom NT1s, TAs, and digital sets are being used. Other CPE is being supplied by Codex,

DEC, Fujitsu America, Harris, Honeywell, Infotron, Motorola, NCR, and Zenith. Applications include integrated voice and data, SNA emulation, high-speed data transport, telemetry, telecommuting, coax elimination, X.25 packet switching on the B- and D-channels, wide area networks (WAN), and PC networking.

Two other early trials involved GTE Communications Systems and Intel Corp., both also in Phoenix. The GTE trial used a GTD-5 EAX switch and GTE Omni PBX to test a PRI connection. Remote switches connected the customer site and the C.O., 12 miles apart, via optical fiber. The Intel trial tested BRI access and the remote switch access to a 5ESS 22 miles away. Both of these demonstrations were featured at the International Switching Symposium held in Phoenix in March 1987 (ISS '87).

U.S. West started two service offerings that were significant because they used analog C.O. switches, supplemented by NEC NEAX 61E Adjunct switches. In November 1987, an ISDN call placed from Minneapolis to Denver became the first to use adjunct switches at both end offices. Customers involved in ISDN trials and services in Minneapolis/St. Paul include 3M Corporation and Control Data Corporation. The ISDN support for 3M will evolve into a joint effort with Southwestern Bell's ISDN service to 3M in Austin in the early 1990s; 3M anticipates use of 20,000 ISDN lines in the Minneapolis/St. Paul area by 1993.

Pacific Northwest Bell (PNB) led a trial from March 1987 to March 1988. Their intention was to identify new service opportunities, identify real costs to the network and to the customer, verify architectural principles, and stimulate network evolution planning. The PNB trial was held in Portland with the U.S. National Bank of Oregon. Expected applications for this trial include digital Centrex voice features, executive call directory, interworking ISDNs via a PSPDN, coax elimination, wide area networking, high-speed facsimile, and SNA packet exchange over the D-channel.

U.S. West is deploying three SS7 STP pairs. An 800 number database is intended to be the first SS7 application, and U.S. West anticipates that 70 percent of its 800 traffic will originate from end offices with SS7 capability by 1995. LIDB services are also anticipated.

9.2.8 Independent Telephone Companies

General Telephone, the largest U.S. independent telephone company, is involved in several ISDN trials. The goals of their trials are not unlike those of the BOCs: portray GTE's leadership role as a service provider, determine the functional performance of the ISDN switching and customer-premises equipment, define ISDN services, and identify the target markets. Their applications include integrated voice and data, coax elimination, LAN access, still-frame image transfer, full-motion compressed video, high-speed facsimile, and circuit- and packet-mode data.

In 1987 and 1988, General Telephone Companies throughout the United States held a series of trials. Their largest trial was in the Tampa area and involved the General Telephone Company (GTC) of Florida, GTE Data Services, and the University of Southern Florida. This trial used an AT&T 5ESS switch, digital telephone sets, and TAs; Fujitsu telephone sets; and NEC and Wang workstations. The intent of the trial was for GTE to determine the functional performance of ISDN switches and CPE, define existing and new ISDN services, and identify the target market.

GTE of California ran a trial in Thousand Oaks and Ontario (both in the Los Angeles area) using a GTE GTD-5 EAX switch. A GTD-5 was also used in the GTE of the Southwest trial at Texas A&M University in College Station. GTE South started a trial in 1988 at Glaxo Inc. in Research Triangle Park, NC, using a DMS-100 switch and a Meridian SL-1 PBX; it was the first trial to simultaneously implement both BRI and PRI access.

United Telecommunications, Inc., comprises the second largest U.S. independent telephone network. In 1987 and 1988, they focused on testing the market for advanced data and telecommunications services, such as C.O. LAN, digital Centrex, SS7, and ISDN. Their SS7 and intelligent network implementation began in 1989.

United has also been conducting trials of ISDN, although their trials have emphasized customer applications more than technology. From August 1987 to April 1988, United Telephone of Florida was a part of an AT&T TriVista study at the Southwest Florida Regional Medical Center in Fort Myers. Their major goals were to study ISDN Centrex applications in a hospital environment, including data storage and retrieval, billing capabilities, and patient information management. Some of the benefits to the medical center were to increase employee productivity, increase revenues, decrease costs, and improve patient relations.

In late 1988, United Telephone of Indiana trialed ISDN Centrex at St. Joseph's College in Rensselaer, another TriVista-type study with AT&T. Carolina Telephone and Telegraph started ISDN service in 1989 to Hardees' headquarters in Rocky Mount, NC, using an NTI DMS-100 switch.

Other independent telephone companies are testing the ISDN waters, as well. In early 1989, Southern New England Telephone (SNET) started a trial with the Travelers Corp. using 12 BRI lines. SNET is also providing BRI service in Connecticut to Pratt & Whitney (East

Hartford), Aetna (Hartford), and the University of Connecticut (Storrs); these three services are offered from a 5ESS switch. Contel of Pennsylvania started an ISDN service to Hershey Foods Corp. in Hershey in late 1988.

Not all trials have concluded with ISDN service. Cincinnati Bell, AT&T, and GE Aircraft Engines participated in a TriVista study in 1988–1989 to demonstrate the applicability of ISDN to a manufacturing environment. GE Aircraft Engines had 80 sites in three main locations; AT&T and Cincinnati Bell proposed a 16,000-line ISDN Centrex provided via an AT&T 5ESS switch and two remote switches.

Although the study team concluded that GE would save nearly $4 million in 7 years, GE declined to start ISDN service. Although GE felt that ISDN was a good idea, they felt that it is too early in the ISDN life cycle to buy the service. They expressed similar concerns as other customers, including some who have purchased ISDN: the lack of stable products, interoperability problems between different vendors' equipment, and the lack of network management tools for large, multisite Centrex ISDN implementations.

Like the RBOCs, the ITCs are implementing SS7 in their end offices. General Telephone started SS7 deployment within its local exchange companies in late 1988 using STPs from AT&T. Eventually, GTE will have four regional STPs; two in California and one each in New England and the midwest. They anticipate that end offices supporting 70 percent of their access lines will have SS7 by 1992 and more than 90 percent by 1995.

United Telecommunications anticipates SS7 deployment in 1989 and is offering CLASS service in New Jersey in conjunction with New Jersey Bell. Cincinnati Bell plans to have SS7 to its end offices by 1990.

9.2.9 Interexchange Carriers

AT&T has been very active with SS7 and ISDN for several years. They have played a major part in many of the LEC's ISDN trials, as described above. They have participated in several TriVista studies: ISDN trials that involved AT&T, a local telephone company, and a telephone company customer. AT&T also conducted PRI and ISDN service studies throughout 1988 with American Transtech, a wholly owned AT&T subsidiary in Jacksonville, and a major supplier of information management services to AT&T and other companies. This trial used an AT&T System 85 PBX directly connected to an AT&T 4ESS switch.

Based in part upon the result of these studies, AT&T became the first U.S. long distance carrier to file an ISDN service tariff in April

1988, described in Sec. 9.4.4. AT&T ISDN service was initially scheduled for availability in 18 metropolitan areas served by 4ESS toll offices, including Atlanta, Baltimore, Chicago, Denver, Los Angeles, New York, Oakland, Phoenix, and Seattle. This list is expected to expand to over 290 offices by the end of 1990.

In July 1988, American Express Travel Related Services Company in Phoenix became AT&T's first PRI customer. They also use a System 85 PBX connected to a 4ESS switch. Other early AT&T PRI customers include First Data Resources (an American Express subsidiary in Omaha), McDonnell Douglas Corp. (St. Louis), WATS Marketing Group (another American Express subsidiary in Omaha), and John Hancock Mutual Life Insurance Co. (Boston).

In mid-1989, the United States Automobile Association (USAA) announced plans to use AT&T's PRI service attached to their NTI Meridian SL-100 PBX, the first user with this cross-vendor application. Initial use will support 2500 customer agents at USAA headquarters in San Antonio. Each USAA regional office is equipped with an InteCom IBX S/80 PBX. In the summer of 1989, tests were scheduled to determine if the S/80 PBXs can attach to AT&T's PRI service.

AT&T's ISDN service is a primary rate interface and provides two main features, called INformation FOrwarding 2 (INFO-2) and Call-by-Call Service Selection. INFO-2, also known as automatic number identification (ANI), passes a caller's 10-digit telephone number to the ISDN customer's premises equipment for identification purposes.

Call-by-Call Service Selection enables a customer to assign channels for a specific purpose on demand rather than requiring that the channels be dedicated to services on a subscription basis. This allows the customer to dictate how the leased channels are used, consistent with the customer's changing calling patterns.

AT&T deployed the first U.S. common channel signaling network when it introduced Common Channel Interoffice Signaling (CCIS), their version of SS6, in 1976. AT&T's deployment of SS7 will follow the availability of the PRI on their 4E ESS tandem and toll switches. Their conversion to SS7 was nearly complete by the end of 1989.

U.S. Sprint will finish converting all of their network switches to support ISDN by early 1990 and will file a PRI tariff soon after the conversion is complete. They will initially offer five ISDN services:

- 56- and 64-kbps circuit switched service
- Access to Telenet for packet switched service
- Dynamic channel allocation
- Automatic number identification
- Virtual private network (VPN) PBX interworking, which will allow several PBXs to share call information across a PVN

Sprint finished full deployment of SS7 throughout its network in late 1988 and has already begun trials of SS7 throughout the United States as a pilot for commercial service, using NTI DMS-250 switches. Their network includes three pairs of STPs and two SCPs (what U.S. Sprint calls Feature Data Bases) and has carried operational traffic since 1987.

MCI has had several delays in getting started with SS7 but will have full SS7 deployment in 1990. MCI has long maintained that they, too, will offer ISDN service. In early 1989, they announced a trial to test the compatibility of their services with NTI Meridian SL-1 and SL-100 PBXs.

MCI will initially offer three ISDN services to users with dedicated access to their network:

- MCI Two-Way Access will allow users to simultaneously carry inbound and outbound traffic over the same channel.

- MCI 800 Enhanced Services Package will provide calling number identification to users.

- MCI Digital Reconfiguration Service will allow users to quickly reconfigure routing and termination of 56-kbps and T1 channels; this will be upgraded to support dynamic reconfiguration.

SS7 will result in faster call setups than is currently possible. The IECs see two major benefits from this: greater customer satisfaction and lower access fees paid to the LECs. In early 1989, BellSouth and Southwestern Bell announced an interregion ISDN trial between St. Louis and Atlanta. This trial will demonstrate compatibility between C.O. switches from different manufacturers and the ability to connect to interexchange carriers. The trial, scheduled for operation in 1992, will also involve MCI and Sprint.

9.2.10   U.S. Department of Defense ISDN Implementation

The U.S. Department of Defense (DoD) is building an international ISDN to serve its military bases throughout the United States, Europe, and Asia. The current Defense Communications System (DCS) comprises the following subsystems:

- *Automatic Voice Network (AUTOVON):* Worldwide DoD telephone network employing leased lines and switches in North America and military-owned switches in Europe and the Pacific.

- *Defense Switched Network (DSN):* Replacement network for the 20-year old AUTOVON; complete implementation due by 1995.

- *Automatic Secure Voice Communications Network (AUTOSECVOCOM) and Defense Satellite Communications System (DSCS):* Special-purpose, secure communications networks.

- *Automatic Digital Network (AUTODIN):* Store-and-forward data network for classified and unclassified data traffic. Transmission is on leased lines in North America and military facilities overseas, operating at 4800 bps.

- *Defense Data Network (DDN):* A packet switched network, intended to replace ARPANET. It should be completely installed by 1992.

With all of these communications subnetworks, it is not surprising that the integrated approach of ISDN is attractive to the military. In 1986, in fact, the DoD formed a committee to lead the transformation of the DCS to an ISDN.

The first step in this evolution will be to convert to all-digital facilities, the goal of the DSN. The ISDN evolution of the DoD has four major components. The first is the Continental U.S. Telephone Modernization Program (CTMP). In 1989, 14 of the DoD's 88 sites were scheduled to be operational with digital switches; all 88 sites should be digital by 1994 (pending funding). AT&T, NTI, and GTE are supplying equipment for the CTMP.

The other three components affect overseas communication. Twenty-eight U.S. Army sites in Korea are being upgraded as part of the Korean Telephone Upgrade, using Northern Telecom DMS-100 switches and SL-100 PBXs. The European Telephone System Upgrade Program affects 170 U.S. military sites in West Germany and other European countries. Siemens KN101 switches are being used for this phase of the upgrade and over 100 switches were operational by the end of 1987. This part of the program is scheduled for completion by 1991. The Japan Telephone Upgrade will involve 12 sites and completion was scheduled for the end of 1988. These three telephone upgrade programs will become part of the DSN.

The military community has adopted many international data communications standards, using fewer of their own special-purpose standards. For ISDN, they will support the BRI and PRI (23B + D but will have 1.544- and 2.048-Mbps compatibility) and SS7. Optical fiber will be used where practical. OSI protocols will also be supported, as defined by the Government OSI Profile (GOSIP).

The DoD has several special application requirements that have been passed to the NIUF, including:

- Security between ISDN and non-ISDN communications

- A two-wire S reference point BRI for use in those environments where ISDN sets will be attached to a PBX but where a four-wire connection is not feasible

- AUTOVON network features on ISDN

9.2.11 Private ISDN Implementations

One of the communications strategies that became viable after AT&T's breakup was for a customer to bypass the local telephone company's switching office. This allowed direct access to the IEC of the customer's choice and reduced the cost of local access. The same technology can be applied to allow customers to build their own ISDNs.

A number of large organizations have built private ISDNs by purchasing an ISDN-capable switch for on-premises use; voice service and point-to-point terminal-PC connections are among the primary motivations for installing these private networks; others are more local control and economy. Private U.S. ISDNs include:

- In July 1988, Duke University in Durham, NC, brought their AT&T 5ESS on-line. That switch supports 14,000 lines, of which 1000 will initially be used for a BRI service.

- The Massachusetts Institute of Technology in Cambridge cut-over a 5ESS switch in late 1988. Over 13,000 lines are supported, including nearly 5000 BRI lines. Applications include standard voice transmission, voice mail, and data communications.

- Lawrence Livermore National Laboratory in Livermore, CA, cut-over a 5ESS switch in late 1989. This switch will eventually provide ISDN BRI service to over 7500 employees at the 1-square-mile laboratory site and a few remote locations in the area. The 17,000-line switch will support 8100 BRI lines, connecting users and approximately 50 host computers. A modem pool of about 350 modems will replace nearly 1000 modems currently in use.

- The University of Arizona in Tucson agreed to purchase a 5ESS switch in the summer of 1988 to support their campuswide network. Their switch, purchased from Mountain Bell, is scheduled to support nearly 15,000 lines, including several hundred BRI lines.

- Motorola is purchasing six Northern Telecom DMS-250 switches and 35 Meridian SL-1 PBXs to form a private voice/data network at sites throughout the United States. A DMS-100 will also be installed at Motorola headquarters in Schaumburg, IL, by Illinois Bell, replacing an AT&T 1AESS. This network will ultimately be upgraded to provide ISDN services.

- Boeing Company in Seattle started their private ISDN in late 1988.

Their network will interconnect several 5ESS switches, purchased from U.S. West Communications.

■ Electronic Data Systems has proposed implementing SS7 in General Motors' private voice/data network. This would be one of the first private SS7 implementations. The GM network has six Meridian SL-100 PBXs and T3 carrier (44.736 Mbps) backbone links. They cite cost savings from reduced call setup and teardown time, as well as more efficient use of existing circuits, as reasons for the proposal.

To use or not to use ISDN frequently becomes an economic issue. To bypass the LEC or not is also an economic issue. It is not surprising, then, that an on-site ISDN switch may be realistic for many organizations.

9.3   ISDN OUTSIDE OF THE UNITED STATES

A major theme of this book is that ISDN is not a technology meant only for the United States or North America. Indeed, it is the first example of a telecommunications network implementation that is based upon international standards as opposed to the standards being based upon a few implementations. A goal of these standards is to have international ISDNs and fewer incompatible communications devices. The paragraphs below will provide a brief summary of some of the international work in ISDN. Again, this discussion is not exhaustive but is meant to exemplify some of the activity that is going on outside of the United States.

The regulatory environment in most countries is very different from that of the United States. Whereas customers in the United States connect to local telephone companies to access the interexchange carrier of their choice, most other countries have a single end-to-end communications carrier. Telephone companies in the United States are regulated by local public utility commissions, as well as by the Federal Communications Commission, resulting in different services being available in different parts of the country at different prices. Most other countries have a government postal, telephone, and telegraph (PTT) authority which regulates these services for the entire country.

9.3.1   Australia

Telecom Australia, the state-owned national telecommunications carrier, has held a number of well-attended user forums to introduce ISDN. These forums are being held for users and the carrier to exchange views on ISDN applications, tariffs, products, and implementation plans. Actual implementation of a commercial ISDN service is expected in 1990.

In the summer of 1988, the Australian government announced that Telecom Australia would no longer have a regulatory responsibility. Telecom Australia and the Overseas Telecommunications Commission (OTC, the state-owned international carrier) retained their monopolies over basic services, including ISDN, but value-added services were opened to full competition. Regulatory tasks now fall to a newly formed, independent body called Austel.

9.3.2 Brazil

Telecommunicacoes Brasileiras (Telebrás) S.A., a state-owned company, was formed in 1972 to coordinate public telecommunications services in Brazil. Telebrás is the holding company of 30 local telephone companies and is responsible for over 95 percent of local telephone service. The Telebrás Research and Development Center (CPqD), established in 1976, represents the vast majority of telecommunications research and development activity in Brazil.

Telebrás research and development activities, in conjunction with many Brazilian industries and universities, have been ongoing since 1975 in areas such as microwave radio transmission, semiconductor lasers, digital switching, digital voice coding, optical fiber, and TDM techniques. This research effort led to the development of the MCP multiplexer product family in the early 1980s: the MCP-30, MCP-120, and MCP-480 multiplex 30, 120, and 480 digital voice channels, respectively, using pulse code modulation and TDM. Digital radio equipment, carrying 480 simultaneous voice conversations and low-bit-rate voice (16 and 32 kbps) and video (2 Mbps), has also been deployed. In all, CPqD interacts with over 50 companies and universities and is involved with over 80 different products.

Telebrás and Empresa Brasileria de Telecomunicacoes S.A., Brazil's long distance carrier, began the process of planning and implementing digital facilities in the network in the early 1980s. In recent years, a huge annual investment has been made to add network users since telephones are available to a relatively small percentage of the population.

ISDN should become commercially available in Brazil in 1992 or 1993. Telebrás is currently planning ISDN trials in Brasília, Belo Horizonte, Rio de Janeiro, and Sao Paulo in 1990. Switch vendors will include Elebra (headquartered in Brazil), L. M. Ericsson Telephone Company (Sweden), NEC Corporation (Japan), PHT Sistemas and Electronicos S.A. (Brazil), and Siemens AG (West Germany), although all switches actually used will be manufactured in Brazil.

9.3.3 Canada

Canada has operated several ISDN trials since the mid-1980s. Initial trials tested echo cancellation to provide full-duplex communication over the local loop, the approach used in the ANSI U reference point standard. Other early trials focused on the network switching systems, SS7, and the local loops. Studies of the customer market for BRI and PRI started in 1987.

The first customer ISDN trials started in 1987 in Ottawa, using a BRI. These early field trials were limited to customers who accessed the network directly through the central office.

In July 1988, Bell Canada announced the first North American customer to receive fully integrated local and long distance public switched network service using PRI access. The site was Telecom Canada headquarters in Ottawa. Telecom Canada is accessing the network through a Meridian SL-1 PBX, which supports about 650 users, providing voice and data communications for digital telephones, IVDTs, and PCs. The PBX connects to the network at a Bell Canada DMS-100 C.O. switch. Telecom Canada users will also be able to interact with users of the ongoing BRI trial at the same central office.

The first ISDN trial between two cities and two carriers in Canada began in 1989 between the cities of Edmonton and Calgary. Both cities are in the province of Alberta and are about 180 miles apart. Edmonton is served by Edmonton Telephones, while Alberta Government Telephones serves the rest of the province.

Bell Canada initiated plans for a trial of an ISDN linking Ottawa, Quebec City, Toronto, and Montreal in 1989. SS7 will also be available in these areas by 1991 and in additional provinces as part of a 5-year upgrade program. Telecom Canada, a consortium of regional carriers, announced plans to test ISDN in 1989.

9.3.4 France

The French telephone network, operated by the state-owned Direction General des Télécommunications (DGT), has been introducing digital facilities since the early 1970s; of the 24 million lines in the network, roughly half are connected to a digital local exchange. DGT is also responsible for one of the largest PSPDNs in the world, Transpac, with more than 40,000 direct customer accesses. In addition, the DGT has been successfully promoting its videotex service, which allows customers to access information services by use of an inexpensive terminal connected to the telephone network; over 3 million of these videotex terminals are currently in use. By 1995, about 92 percent of the customers on the French telephone network should be attached to a digital local exchange and over 90 percent of the exchanges will be capable of ISDN.

French ISDN efforts are aimed at the residential and small business customer; DGT studies show that 87 percent of the country's businesses have five or less employees and 98 percent have less than 50 employees. The RENAN project, launched in 1983, was the first ISDN implementation in that country; Numeris is the ISDN network officially inaugurated on November 29, 1988. The first site to receive ISDN service was the Côtes-du-Nord/St. Brieuc area in western France; these lines were put in place in 1987 and were fully operational in 1988. The service was also expanded to include Paris and its western suburbs in 1988. The addition of other major cities to the network and international ISDN connections began in 1989. The DGT hopes to have ISDN service available throughout the entire country by 1991.

France's ISDN efforts are supplemented by a large number of French firms which are developing ISDN applications in coordination with the French telecommunications authority. Some of the applications being developed, and their intended markets, include:

- Electronic document exchange and retrieval for library applications
- Computer-aided design (CAD) of printed circuit boards and high-speed transfer of data files for manufacturing
- Real estate information transfer, including legal documents, blueprints, maps, and photographs
- Central image storage and retrieval for press agencies
- Information and image storage and retrieval for pharmaceutical companies
- Security applications, such as video surveillance and corporate alarm systems
- Automatic teller machine networking for banks and credit card companies

These applications are very similar to others being developed in other parts of the world, indicating the common need for ISDN applications.

9.3.5 Italy

Italy is currently implementing one of the most comprehensive telephone network modernization programs in Europe, mostly because their existing network is relatively antiquated. The vast majority of residents do not have a telephone; according to the Societa Italiana per L'eservicio delle Telecomunicazioni (STET), the state-owned telephone holding company, the country's telephone density is only about 33 percent, well under the European average of 40 percent.

STET's goal is to offer the same level and quality of network service as the rest of Europe by the year 2000. At this time, about 12 percent of the country's network is digital. This figure will increase to 30 percent by 1992 and 100 percent by the turn of the century. The government also aims to increase the telephone density to be on par with other European countries, targeting a 42 percent density by 1992.

Italian ISDN plans are currently focusing on the BRI and its applications. An ISDN trial was held in Florence in 1984, with an ISDN service offering that started in 1987. Expanded ISDN service followed, with an expected 1000 to 2000 subscribers in seven major cities by 1990.

9.3.6 Japan

Nippon Telegraph and Telephone (NTT) ran their initial ISDN trial from 1984 to 1987 with a service called the Information Network System (INS). INS started with 450 subscribers in three cities and expanded to 50 cities by 1987. Initial plans were to have 200 cities on the network by 1990, with complete national coverage by 1995.

The intent of INS was to demonstrate the ISDN service capabilities. Three channels were offered: a 64-kbps channel for digital telephones, a 16-kbps channel for videotex or facsimile terminals, and an 8-kbps signaling channel. The interface operated at 88 kbps and used time compression multiplexing for full-duplex communication on loops up to 23 kft (7 km) long. This basic rate access is very different from the CCITT BRI definition.

The goal of INS, like that of Pacific Bell's Project Victoria, was to demonstrate ISDN applications and determine if ISDN was useful and marketable. Applications such as video communication, CATV, still-picture communication, facsimile service, multifunction digital telephone service, and data communications proved very popular.

In April 1988, NTT applied to the Ministry of Posts and Telecommunications (MPT) for approval to offer INS-Net 64 service, a true 2B + D basic rate interface per CCITT recommendations. By the summer of 1989, over 1300 BRI lines had been placed in service for applications such as automatic teller machine networking, 64-kbps videotelephones, video conferencing, Group 4 facsimile, and database retrieval service. NTT offered initial INS-Net 64 service in the Nagoya, Osaka, and Tokyo areas, with growth to other major cities beginning in 1989. International ISDN service will be offered by Kokusai Denshin Denwa (KDD) Co., Ltd.

A PRI service offering was initiated in the summer of 1989. In accordance to market demand, NTT will eventually extend the network nationwide by the mid-1990s.

Trials of broadband services have also been conducted since 1984. Video to the home over optical fiber and advanced information services using Captain, a videotex system, are already available in some areas of the country.

9.3.7   United Kingdom

British Telecommunications (BT) engaged in ISDN trials for reasons similar to those of most other telephone companies. BT wanted to:

- Test ISDN standards for user access to the network and network signaling

- Test the architecture and technology of their System X C.O. switch for the provision of voice and data services, as well as for connecting ISDN calls across the network

- Test the operating procedures within BT to support ISDN as a regular service offering

- Provide customers and manufacturers the opportunity to experience advanced data and telecommunications services and see the development of applications that would follow.

British Telecom launched their ISDN pilot service in June 1985 at a System X central office in London. In March 1986, they added the service to a switch in Manchester, shortly followed by a switch in Birmingham. SS7 was used over the digital trunks connecting these offices.

BT's initial ISDN service offered a 1B + D service. By the end of 1987, BT offered 2B + D service from more than 80 central office areas throughout the United Kingdom. Their 2B + D service, however, was not basic rate access as defined by the CCITT. One B-channel operated at 64 kbps, while the second B-channel operated at 8 kbps; the D-channel was used only to map the CCITT Recommendation X.21 in-band signaling into ISDN common channel signaling for call control.

ISDN2, a 2B + D BRI service complying with CCITT Recommendation I.430, is scheduled to begin in 1990 using BT System X (GPT) and System Y (Ericcson) switches. The System X and System Y provide only a 2.048-Mbps PRI rate. This PRI supports an ISDN multiplexer (IMUX) in the central office which, in turn, provides the BRI access. Packet-mode service on the D-channel will not initially be available. ISDN2 service should be in place throughout most of the country by the end of 1991.

Primary rate access is also available in several hundred exchanges throughout the United Kingdom using proprietary protocols. The PRI supports the new integrated services PBX (ISPBX) and offers thirty 64 kbps channels for voice and data. A PRI service based upon CCITT standards is expected by 1993.

BT has been engaged in many international demonstrations of its ISDN service since 1986. In separate demonstrations, they have linked remote switching stages of its System X switch to an exchange in the United Kingdom from Moscow and various sites in the United States. They have also used SS7 to interconnect System X switches with AXE 10 switches.

In late 1985, BT demonstrated a chip set for echo cancellation that they claimed would operate on over 95 percent of the U.S. local loops (after load coils were removed). This demonstration was one of the major reasons that echo cancellation rather than time compression multiplexing was adopted for the ANSI U reference point standard.

9.3.8 West Germany

The Deutsche Bundespost Telekom (West Germany's PTT) committed to ISDN in the early 1980s and began its ISDN pilot in Mannheim (in the Rhein-Neckar region) in 1988. This part of the country has approximately 180 local and 14 long distance exchanges with a traffic capacity of nearly 400 million switched telephone calls. Via Mannheim, this area is connected to a supraregional coaxial cable and radio communications network.

West Germany's first electronic data switching system was placed in the Mannheim office in 1975. Digital carriers were introduced into the long distance network in 1982 and digital switches were introduced in 1985. The Bundepost expects a fully digital switched network by 1990.

Prior to the West German ISDN trials, switches from Standard Elektrik Lorenz AG and Siemens AG were investigated. Additional Siemens switches were installed in Mannheim for the trials and initial ISDN service.

In early 1989, the Bundespost announced commercial ISDN service in eight of the country's largest cities: Berlin, Dusseldorf, Frankfurt, Hamburg, Hannover, Munich, Nuremburg, and Stuttgart. Expansion to over 60 cities is expected in 1990. Nationwide availability is expected by 1993, with 3 million ISDN subscribers anticipated by that time. ISDN connections to the United Kingdom and Italy are expected soon thereafter.

As deployment of narrowband ISDN is well on its way, broadband services are not far behind. Field trials of broadband services began in

Germany in 1986 with the Berlin Communications System Project (BERKOM). Project BERKOM services include video communications, computer integrated manufacturing, and telepublishing.

9.3.9 Other International Activity

ISDN trials and service offerings are not limited to the countries listed above. Many other countries are examining or implementing ISDN and/or SS7, including:

- Israel
- Korea
- New Zealand
- Saudia Arabia
- Sweden

As the European economic community becomes even closer, ISDN activity is sure to spread before and after 1992. As political and economic barriers in Eastern Europe fall, it would also not be surprising to see some ISDN activity expand to that region by the mid-1990s.

International trials are already under way. In 1989, Andersen Consulting placed a call from its Chicago headquarters to its Tokyo office using ISDN services provided by Illinois Bell, AT&T, NTT, and KDD. AT&T, British Telecom, and France Telecom expect international service in parts of Europe in 1990.

9.4 U.S. ISDN TARIFFS

One obvious area of concern in the marketing of ISDN is with respect to the cost of the service. This is of particular importance in the residential marketplace. Some of the U.S. telephone companies believe that it costs 80 to 100 percent more to provide an ISDN service than to provide non-ISDN service. Most customers, particularly residential and small business users, will not pay 100 percent more for a BRI than for POTS; they will merely buy a second telephone line if they need one. One of the goals of many of the LECs is to provide a BRI service at 20 to 50 percent above the current POTS cost. In fact, a BRI service offering costing 1½ times that of POTS has been a stated goal for several years.

Example of tariffs are provided here for information only, as they are subject to change. The significance and stability of ISDN tariffs will increase in the 1990s as more customers pay the tariffed rates rather than special service rates.

9.4.1 Illinois Bell

At the end of March 1988, Illinois Bell became the first BOC to tariff an ISDN interface to the public telephone network. Their BRI service, called the Ameritech Integrated Digital Network, became available in late 1988. The service is initially available in the Chicago and Oak Brook areas; it will spread to other areas as the market demands. Aimed at the business customer, users can buy either circuit switched voice-only services, data-only services, or voice and data services.

To attract customers, Illinois Bell has defined six starter package discounts for first-time users, summarized in Table 9.1. Note that these prices do not include the cost of rewiring the house or business (if necessary) or the cost of the NT1. For large accounts, Illinois Bell will submit ISDN service proposals specifically tailored to the customer's needs.

9.4.2 Pacific Bell

Pacific Bell filed a provisional ISDN tariff in 1989. It comprises three ISDN packages, called Centrex IS. The services include:

TABLE 9.1   Illinois Bell ISDN Starter Package Pricing

	One-time ordering and line connection charges[1]	Monthly[2]
MODEL 1: 10 circuit-switched voice lines	$233.50	$155.00
MODEL 2: 10 voice lines, 5 with packet data	233.50	195.60
MODEL 3: 30 circuit-switched voice lines	643.50	475.00
MODEL 4: 30 circuit-switched voice lines, 8 with circuit-switched data and 8 with packet-switched data	643.50	680.12
MODEL 5: 30 data lines, 10 with circuit-switched data and 20 with packet-switched data	643.50	466.65
MODEL 6: 30 packet-switched data lines	643.50	490.65

NOTE 1: The one-time service ordering charge is $28.50. Line connection charges are $20.50 per line.

NOTE 2: The prices above do not include the monthly per line service transport charge. The charges are $5.58 for downtown Chicago, $9.08 for the Chicago area and some suburban locations (excluding the downtown Chicago area), and $12.58 for the rest of the state.

- *Package A:*   A 1B + D service supporting circuit switched voice on the B-channel; the D-channel may only be used for signaling. The monthly per line cost is $17.50, about the same as a regular voice line.

- *Package B:*   As above but supports packet switched data on the D-channel. The monthly charge is $26 per line.

- *Package C:*   A 2B + D service with a number of possible configurations supporting circuit switched voice or data on the B-channels and packet switched data on the D-channel. The monthly charge is $29.50 per line.

Pacific Bell believes that many customers will initially purchase package A or B as a low-cost entree to ISDN and eventually upgrade to package C.

9.4.3 Southwestern Bell

Southwestern Bell Telephone (SWBT) also filed a tariff to sell ISDN starter packages in 1989. The purpose of their starter packages is to allow customers the opportunity to test integrated voice/data applications and products prior to investing in ISDN services and equipment.

With the SWBT packages, a customer can purchase 8, 16, 24, or 32 BRI lines. There are two options:

- *Starter package 1:*   Circuit-mode voice or data on the B-channels; signaling or packet-mode data on the D-channel. Each line costs $21.50 per month.

- *Starter package 2:*   As above, but it also allows packet-mode data on the B-channels. Each line costs $99 per month, plus a $5.40 per month common line charge.

9.4.4 AT&T

AT&T priced its primary rate interface service as a central office function available under its ACCUNET T1.5 service in April, 1988. Access is provided in 24-channel increments and up to 20 PRI circuits may be supervised with a single 64-kbps D-channel. Since a single D-channel can provide signaling for a number of PRI circuits, a single PRI may be configured to provide 24 B-channels, four H_0-channels, or a single H_{11}-channel. The two main features of AT&T's PRI service are INFO-2 and Call-by-Call Service Selection, described in Sec. 9.2.9.

To use the AT&T PRI service, a customer must have a T1 link from their site to an AT&T PRI-equipped office. In addition, the customer

TABLE 9.2   AT&T ISDN Tariff

Primary Rate Interface	
One-time nonrecurring charge	$3,000
Monthly charge	$400
INFO-2	
One-time service-establishment cost	$250
Cost per number delivered	3¢
Call-by-Call Service Selection	
One-time service-establishment cost	$250
Rearrangement charge	$200
Related Equipment and Service Charge	
System 85 upgrade for PRI interface	up to $50,000
T1 Access to AT&T Point of Presence	
Monthly fixed charge	$300 to $1,200
Monthly per-mile charge	$13 to $40
Installation charge	$400 to $4,000

(This example is based upon 5-8 mile distance; prices
vary based upon location)

must have an AT&T System 85 or Definity 75/85 PBX with a PRI interface. The AT&T tariff is summarized in Table 9.2.

9.5 CONCLUSION

The purpose of this chapter has been to show that ISDN has indeed generated activity all over the world. While trials and services started at different times in different countries, the pace has clearly quickened since 1985 and ISDN service offerings will start to become more of a reality in the 1990s.

As stated, the list presented here is not intended to be exhaustive but merely a broad overview of the evolution of trials and service offerings. This glimpse at the past can suggest the future, however.

The potential of ISDN looks bright, although it is not an immediate solution. Several years ago, ISDN was hailed as the communications strategy that would easily provide all services to all users. ISDN has, in many ways, suffered from its own hype and the high expectations that users had based upon vendors' claims. One of the results of most of the ISDN trials was to show that all of the promises of ISDN technology are real and achievable but not painless or easy. Much of the CPE hardware and software used during the trials were prototype units built specifically for the trials and are still not commercially available. Despite standards, vendor interoperability remains a major issue. While ISDN service from individual C.O.s is available in many areas today, a true nationwide ISDN in the United States is many years away.

One of the recurring themes of the early U.S. ISDN activity has been for the local and interexchange carriers to gain experience with the technology and to educate their personnel and customers. Much of this duplication is due to the lack of a national telecommunications strategy, the multitude of vendors making ISDN switches and CPE, and the fact that there are many very different U.S. telephone companies.

ISDN is being treated with more urgency in some countries outside of the United States for a number of reasons:

- A greater need to upgrade the communications network.

- Lack of competition in the telephone industry makes it easier to adopt a national implementation plan and to use a single vendor's equipment.

- The networks are, for the most part, smaller.

Because of different needs, the U.S. trials have focused more on finding ISDN applications while many non-U.S. trials have focused more on the technology.

9.5.1 Future Directions

Although U.S. ISDN trials have not yet resulted in a national network, they have pointed to future directions. Indeed, because the United States has several separate regional telephone companies, it has experienced in a single country many of the potential problems of interconnecting multinational ISDNs.

First, it is clear that a commitment must be made to SS7. Most U.S. ISDN offerings today are ISDN "islands," where SS7 is primarily being used for CLASS and database services from the local carrier. Eventually, SS7 networks must play an even larger role in call routing and network maintenance to form the backbone of a national, and ultimately international, ISDN. Standards play a very significant role in the deployment of ISDN and SS7; different manufacturers' equipment and different networks can interoperate only if they all comply to the same sets of standards, particularly at network boundaries (including the user-network interface).

Second, network management tools must be developed for the operations, administration, and maintenance of ISDNs. Information is a highly valuable commodity in today's business environment. If customers are to be encouraged to use bigger and better communications networks, new tools will be needed to ensure that the networks can provide the necessary level of service and availability that will be needed for the success of the customer and, in turn, the service provider.

Third, more and more organizations and governments are citing the strategic importance of communications in the international marketplace. Fast, efficient, and accurate information exchange can provide businesses with a competitive advantage. International communications can also foster growth and cooperation between countries, knitting together a closer international community and effectively making the world smaller. If ISDN is a key to this new era of communications, a more rapid deployment is necessary. In turn, the new ISDN applications that are being anticipated will be developed.

To a large degree, the era of national ISDN *trials* is over in the United States and several other countries; ISDN *service* is now the key to the future. The early 1990s, however, will begin a new set of trials for international ISDN communication.

ISDN Products

As ISDN becomes more widely available, more and more ISDN-compatible products are being announced or made available from many vendors. This chapter will briefly describe several products in the following general categories:

- ISDN C.O. switches (LE equipment)
- NT1 devices
- ISDN PBXs and multiplexers (NT2)
- ISDN telephone sets and voice/data terminals (TE1)
- Terminal adaptors (TAs)
- ISDN chip sets
- Protocol analyzers and test equipment

The intent of this chapter is to provide a sampling of the types of products that are available. The information is not meant as an exhaustive survey of the ISDN product market, since that market is constantly changing. In-depth technical information is not provided on most of the products, but enough is provided so that readers get a flavor of how these devices operate. Table 10.1 summarizes the vendors and product types that are mentioned in this chapter; products mentioned here are for illustration only and no endorsement by the author is implied.

10.1 LOCAL EXCHANGE EQUIPMENT

Several vendors manufacture ISDN-compatible switches for the central office, as well as other telephone network switching centers. Some

TABLE 10.1   Summary of Chapter Vendors and Equipment

Companies shown as having more than one location have different headquarters for the divisions responsible for different equipment.

MANUFACTURER	LE	NT1	NT2	TE1	TA	Chip Sets	Test Equip.
Advanced Micro Devices Sunnyvale, CA						•	
AEA Electronics Ltd. Richmond, Ontario							•
Alcatel N.A. Hickory, NC	•		•				
Ando Corp. Sunnyvale, CA							•
AT&T Allentown, PA						•	
Basking Ridge, NJ	•	•		•	•		
Bridgewater, NJ			•				
Atlantic Research Corp. Springfield, VA							•
CXR Telcom Corp. Mountain View, CA							•
DataGraf, Inc. Austin, TX			•				
Digilog Inc. Montgomeryville, PA							•
DSP Technology Corp. Carrollton, TX							•
Ericsson Information Systems Inc. Richardson, TX	•		•				
Frederick Engineering Columbia, MD							•
Fujitsu Business Communications Inc. Anaheim, CA			•				
San Jose, CA				•	•		
Fujitsu GTE Business Systems Inc. Tempe, AZ			•				
GTE Phoenix, AZ	•						
Hard Engineering Huntsville, AL							•
Harris Corp. Camarillo, CA					•		•
Novato, CA			•				
Hayes Microcomputer Products Inc. Atlanta, GA					•		

TABLE 10.1   Summary of Chapter Vendors and Equipment (*Continued*)
Companies shown as having more than one location have different headquarters for the divisions responsible for different equipment.

MANUFACTURER	LE	NT1	NT2	TE1	TA	Chip Sets	Test Equip.
Hewlett-Packard Palo Alto, CA							•
Hitachi America Ltd. Norcross, GA			•				
IBM White Plains, NY					•		
Santa Clara, CA (Rolm)			•	•			
IDACOM Electronics Ltd. Irvine, CA							•
Infotron Cherry Hill, NJ					•		
InteCom Inc. Allen, TX			•				
Intel Corp. Santa Clara, CA						•	
International Computers, Ltd. Stamford, CT				•			
International Data Sciences Lincoln, RI							•
ISDN Telecommunications Co. Sherman Oaks, CA				•			
ITT Secaucus, NJ	•						
Kamputech, Inc. Edison, NJ							•
Mitel Inc. Boca Raton, FL	•		•				
San Jose, CA						•	
National Semiconductor Santa Clara, CA						•	
Navtel Norcross, GA							•
NEC America Melville, NY	•	•	•	•	•		
Network Communications Corp. Minneapolis, MN							•
Newbridge Networks Corp. Herndon, VA			•		•		
Northern Telecom Inc. Research Triangle Park, NC	•						
Richardson, TX		•	•	•	•		

TABLE 10.1   Summary of Chapter Vendors and Equipment (*Continued*)

Companies shown as having more than one location have different headquarters for the divisions responsible for different equipment.

MANUFACTURER	LE	NT1	NT2	TE1	TA	Chip Sets	Test Equip.
OST Inc. Bohemia, NY					•		
Progressive Computing Inc. Oak Brook, IL					•		•
Rockwell International Newport Beach, CA						•	
Siemens Boca Raton, FL	•		•				
Santa Clara, CA						•	•
Tekelec Calabasas, CA							•
Tektronix Mountain View, CA							•
Telebyte Technology Inc. Greenlawn, NY							•
Telecom Analysis Systems Eatontown, NJ							•
Telenex Corp. Mt. Laurel, NJ							•
Teleos Communications Eatontown, NJ			•		•		•
Telrad Melville, NY				•			
TIE/communications Inc. Shelton, CT			•				
Universal Data Systems Huntsville, AL					•		
Vadis, Inc. Richardson, TX				•			
Wandel & Goltermann Research Triangle Park, NC							•
Western Digital Corp. Irvine, CA						•	

of these switches, while intended for the C.O., may also be placed on the customer premises for large private networks.

Recall that the local exchange (LE) functions may be subdivided into two categories, local termination (LT) and exchange termination (ET). The LT function primarily deals with the transmission facility and the termination of the local loop.

The ET functions deal with the switching portion of the LE (Fig. 10.1). First, the ET demultiplexes, or separates, the B- and D-channels. Next, B-channel information is routed to the first stage of

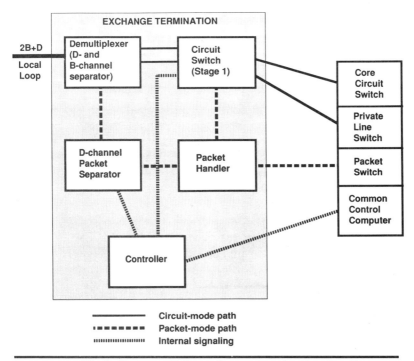

Figure 10.1   Block diagram of the exchange termination function.

the circuit switch and D-channel packets are routed to D-channel packet separation circuitry. The B-channels have access to circuit switching services or the ISDN packet handler. D-channel packets must be examined to determine if they are signaling messages or user data and are handled appropriately. While the figure addresses the basic rate interface specifically, the primary rate interface would be handled in a similar fashion.

As the complexity of ISDN services grows, so must the power of the ET. With the introduction of B-ISDN channels (H_2-channel rates and higher), the equivalent of multiple PRIs must be switched as a single channel. As more packet-mode and/or layer 3 services are adopted, the D-channel packet separation function will also increase in complexity.

The paragraphs below describe three C.O. switches that support ISDN and are in common use in the United States. Although all are different in some subtle and some not-so-subtle ways, they have basic similarities:

- ISDN devices attach to the switch over a digital line and access services with a D-channel plus some number of B- or H-channels. The switch, then, must provide the appropriate interface modules to ISDN CPE.

- At least one D-channel is required for the exchange of ISDN signals.

- Analog telephone sets, in great supply today, can also attach to a special interface in the switch using analog signaling.

- The basic switch architectures are similar. Switching modules perform switching between one interface and another or to trunk lines. Control modules perform overall administration and control functions for all of the other modules. Software is typically modular in design, allowing easy portability, upgrades, and tailoring to specific customer needs.

10.1.1   AT&T 5ESS

In the 1950s, AT&T began to investigate ways to replace their electromechanical switches (step-by-step and crossbar switches) with faster, more economical electronic switches. Electronic switches employ stored program control rather than wired logic, providing easier maintenance and reconfiguration. Faster processing also reduces call setup times.

AT&T has introduced several Electronic Switching Systems (ESS) since the early 1960s, including:

- *1965: No. 1ESS switch:* First electronic local switching office, intended for offices with 10,000 to 65,000 lines.

- *1970: No. 2ESS switch:* Intended for suburban offices with 2000 to 10,000 lines.

- *1976: No. 3ESS switch:* Intended for rural offices serving up to 4500 lines.

- *1976: No. 4ESS switch:* First electronic toll office switch, using time division multiplexing (digital switching) and stored program control. Introduced the 1A processor.

- *1976: No. 1AESS switch:* The 1A processor could be retrofitted to a 1ESS switch, effectively doubling its service capacity. The 1AESS can handle up to 130,000 lines.

This section will focus on AT&T's central office switching system for ISDN, the No. 5ESS. Of the ISDN lines in service today in the United States, over 85 percent terminate at a 5ESS.

The AT&T 5ESS electronic switching system, first put into service in March 1982, has a modular hardware and software design that allows it to be tailored to a specific customer's needs. It uses distributed processing to allow growth of capacity and capability. It is designed to serve a large market; it can be used in metropolitan, suburban, or rural switching offices and can handle up to 100,000 lines. It can replace older switches (e.g., step-by-step, crossbar, and 1ESS switches) or work in a coprocessing environment with other switches (e.g., 1AESS). It can also be used as a premises-based switch in a private network.

The 5ESS hardware architecture has three major components: an Administrative Module, a Communications Module, and one or more Switching Modules (Fig. 10.2).

The Administrative Module (AM) provides the interfaces required to administer, operate, and maintain the switch. The AM uses an AT&T 3B20D dual-processor computer system, which has an expected downtime of less than 2 hours every 40 years. The AM performs call processing functions such as line and trunk group routing determination for the Switching Modules, diagnostic control, some fault recovery, and error detection.

The Communications Module (CM) contains a message switch that transfers call processing and administrative data messages between the other modules. Data packets between modules are transferred through Network Control and Timing links, each of which operates at 32.768 Mbps and contains 256 channels (time slots).

A Switching Module (SM) is an expansion unit for the 5ESS switch. It consists of different types of interface equipment for line and trunk

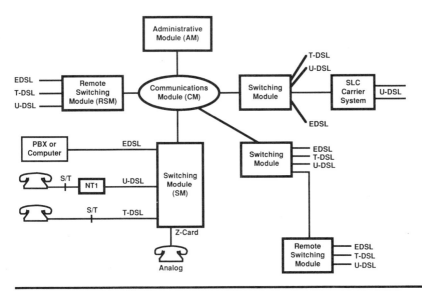

Figure 10.2   AT&T 5ESS hardware architecture.

termination, provides call processing intelligence, and performs the first stage of switching. Switching Modules support analog and digital interface units for lines and trunks via digital subscriber line (DSL) interface modules:

- The T-DSL implements the CCITT BRI across the S/T reference point. It provides a four-wire connection to ISDN sets at distances up to 3300 ft (1 km). This interface is intended for direct connections between the set and the 5ESS switch (or remote switching module).

- The U-DSL is a two-wire interface, representing the U reference point. This interface is to be used if the ISDN station is more than 3300 ft from the switch or if the transmission facility is outside plant. The AT&T BRI specification released in early 1988 for the 5ESS switch is not the same as the ANSI T1.601 standard described earlier in this book, although AT&T is beginning to support the ANSI BRI specification. The line code, frame format, and multiframe format are among the areas of disagreement between the ANSI standard and the AT&T BRI specification. The U-DSL line terminates at the customer side at an NT1.

- The Extended DSL (EDSL) supports the CCITT PRI using a 23B + D or 30B + D format. Like many ISDN switches, the 5ESS supports both the 1.544- and 2.048-Mbps PRI interfaces to provide the vendor with a larger target market. This interface can be used for the connection of a 5ESS switch to an AT&T System 75, System 85, or Definity 75/85 PBX.

Number 5A Remote Switching Modules (RSMs) are used to provide ISDN services to users that are distant from the switch. A digital Subscriber Loop Carrier (SLC) system, the SLC 96, serves to replace or supplement existing cable that can carry up to 96 user channels over a single T1 line.

A Z-card is used for the connection of analog telephones to the switch. The card includes a CODEC and does the appropriate conversion for the ISDN services.

The 5ESS software uses a layered architecture (Fig. 10.3). The kernel of the bare machine is represented by the Command Module, which provides communication and switching between the Administrative and Switching Modules.

The lowest software layer in the 5ESS is the Operating System for Distributed Switching (OSDS) and the UNIX Real-Time Reliable (RTR) operating system. OSDS is implemented in Switching Modules and is specifically designed for switching applications in a distributed environment. UNIX RTR is, in the Administrative Module, a general

Software	Application Software Abstract Switching Machine Data Base Management Operating System
Hardware	Administrative & Switching Modules Command Module

Figure 10.3 AT&T 5ESS layered software architecture.

real-time operating system. OSDS and UNIX RTR interact with the various hardware modules to create a *virtual machine* for the higher functions.

A number of applications use the OSDS and UNIX RTR services. A Data Base Management System (DBMS) supports various databases and distributed management functions for all of the separate processes. The Abstract Switching Machine (ASM) provides a base on which to create application software that is independent of the actual hardware architecture. Application software provides call processing, maintenance, administration, and end-user functions.

Each release of 5ESS software is called a 5E Generic. The 5E4 Generic, released in 1987, was the first version of 5ESS software that supported simultaneous voice and data features, as well as some ISDN functionality. 5E4 software supported voice and data circuit switched applications, as well as B- and D-channel packet-mode service. Interfaces to AT&T's No. 1 Packet Switching System (1PSS) provided customer access to X.25 PSPDNs. Multi-Button Key Services (MBKS) provide single-button access to custom calling features, such as call forwarding, call pick-up, automatic call back on busy, speed calling, conference calling, call hold, and calling identification display. ISDN directory and message services are also supported.

The 5E5 Generic, released in 1989, provided citywide ISDN services, including additional CLASS services and operator facilities. The 5E6 Generic, expected in 1990, will support services for nationwide ISDN. 5E6 will support 2B1Q signaling over the BRI local loop, as well as AT&T's current AMI signaling scheme. On-demand packet-mode service on the B-channel will also be available.

10.1.2 Northern Telecom DMS-100

The Northern Telecom DMS-100 switch family is intended to provide a wide range of telecommunication services. The DMS-100, introduced in 1978, is intended for use in a class 5 office; with appropriate adaptations, it can be used as an equal-access end office. The DMS-200 is intended for switching offices in the toll network, equal-access offices, or access tandem switch applications. The DMS-250 is a toll switch for specialized common carriers requiring tandem switch operation. The DMS-300 is intended for international gateway operations.

The DMS-100 switch family has four functional areas, each comprising a set of modules assigned to accomplish a particular task. The functional areas are:

- *Central Control Complex:* Main processing component for the switch, providing call processing, administrative, and maintenance routines. The Message and Device Controller provides signal buffering and routing between the central processor and peripheral equipment. The Central Processor Unit responds to network conditions and issues appropriate commands to parts of the network. The Program Store Memory stores all program instructions, while the Data Store Memory contains information about ongoing calls and customer information.

- *Network:* Component that actually provides the switching functions of the switch. The Network Module provides a voice path between the originating and terminating Peripheral Modules. The Network Message Controller controls the voice paths by transferring control messages between the Network Module and Peripheral Modules.

- *Peripheral Modules:* Allows connection of devices to the switch, as well as switch-to-switch interconnection. The Line Group Controller (LGC) performs high-level call processing, such as digit analysis and tone control; LGCs control Line Concentrator Modules (LCMs) and remote switching centers. LCMs perform low-level call processing, such as line supervision and digit buffering. A Digital Trunk Controller is a variant of the LGC and can be configured to handle up to 20 DS-1 (1.544 Mbps) trunks and/or CCS network links, such as SS6 and SS7. Trunk Modules provide an interface for analog equipment, providing multiplexing and PCM encoding/decoding for up to 30 analog lines.

- *Maintenance and Administration Module:* This functional area consists of a set of input-output controllers and serves as the interface to local and remote devices to perform system maintenance, testing, and administrative functions. Information from these modules is sent to the Central Control Complex for further action.

Figure 10.4 shows the ISDN basic rate access architecture of the DMS-100. The BRI is implemented using versions of the ISDN Line

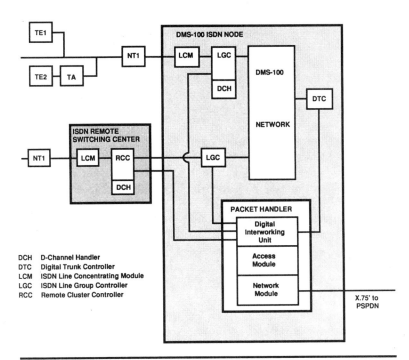

Figure 10.4 Northern Telecom DMS-100 basic rate architecture.

Concentrating Module (ISDN LCM), Line Group Controller (LGC), and D-Channel Handler (DCH).

The DMS-100 supports two types of ISDN line cards. The U Line Card implements the two-wire U reference point basic rate access and the T Line Card implements the four-wire BRI access defined by the CCITT. Like AT&T, Northern Telecom uses a proprietary U reference point standard; support for the ANSI standard is expected soon.

The ISDN Line Concentrating Module accepts a mixture of U and T Line Cards. It provides a number of functions, including traffic concentration and the ability to multiplex four 16-kbps D-channels on a single 64-kbps DS-1 channel.

The Line Group Controller handles ISDN layer 3 signaling. The D-Channel Handler (DCH) Module handles the LAPD functions on frames received on the D-channel. The DCH routes these frames according to their service designation.

ISDN packet-mode services are provided by the packet handler (PH) component of the DMS-100. The PH architecture is based upon the NTI family of DPN 10/15 and DPN 20/50 packet switches.

The DMS-100 Central Control firmware and software performs

those functions necessary for the operation of the switch, such as high-level call control and system maintenance. Peripheral firmware and software perform the repetitive, time consuming tasks such as scanning, control, and maintenance of the telephone interfaces. Like the other switches described here, the software is highly modular so that it can be tailored for specific applications. Software modules accommodate the office class, required features, and supported hardware.

The DMS-100 SuperNode is an extension to the DMS-100 switch family. The SuperNode includes the basic components of a DMS-100 switch but provides the capability of adding processors for specialized applications. These additional processors allow for individual customization of switch capabilities, such as SS7 STP functionality, support for databases (SS7 SCP), and other custom features. ISDN and X.25 protocols can be supported between switches.

10.1.3 Siemens EWSD

The EWSD (Elektronisches Wahl System Digital, or Digital Electronic Switching System) switch, designed by Germany's Siemens AG, is a family of switches that can be customized to a wide range of customer needs and requirements. The EWSD family includes the DE 3, designed as a 7500-line rural exchange; the DE 4, intended as a local or local-transit exchange with up to 30,000 lines; and the DE 5, a 100,000-line exchange combining local, local-transit, and tandem capabilities. EWSD switches may also be used as international gateways and remote switching units. The EWSD architecture is generally similar to the other switches described in this chapter (Fig. 10.5).

The Digital Line Units (DLUs) are the interfaces for direct connection to subscriber loops, remote line units, and remote switching units. The DLU will, for example, convert analog signals into digital form for the ISDN. It will also provide appropriate conversions between the 24-channel, 1.544-Mbps T1 carrier and the EWSD's internal Primary Digital Carrier rate of 2.048 Mbps (32 digital channels at 64 kbps). A Remote DLU is for subscribers who are far away from the switching office and a Channel Bank (CB) is for subscribers accessing the switch over analog facilities.

The Line/Trunk Group (LTG) is a self-contained unit where most of the signaling and call processing functions take place. The LTG forms the interface between the switching network and the DLCs, through channel banks for analog trunks, and directly to digital trunks for PCM transmission lines. The internal Secondary Digital Carrier transmission rate between the LTGs and the Switching Network is 8.192 Mbps (128 64-kbps channels).

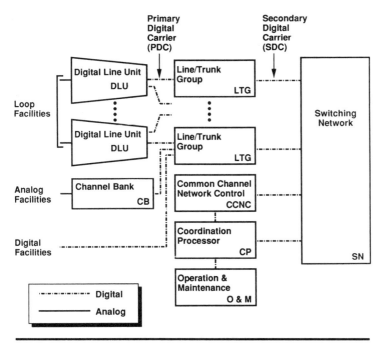

Figure 10.5   Siemens EWSD switching family common hardware architecture.

The Switching Network provides the interconnection between Line/Trunk Groups and the Common Channel Network Control (CCNC); switches messages between the LTG, CCNC, and Coordination Processor (CP); and provides the actual switching functions.

The Coordination Processor is the highest-level processor within the EWSD's distributed processing architecture. The CP controls all major switch processes, call processing functions, operation and maintenance functions, fault detection, and error recovery procedures.

Finally, the Common Channel Network Controller performs common channel signaling operations between switches, using 64-kbps SS7 links.

The EWSD software is modular and organized into three main categories:

- Exchange software provides the programs and data necessary for the switch operation and is distributed in all EWSD hardware processors. Exchange software exists to support all hardware groups, including the Line/Trunk Group, Common Channel Signaling,

Switching Network, Coordination Processor, Message Buffer, and Digital Line Unit.

- Support software provides programs necessary to develop, produce, and maintain Exchange software.

- Operation and Maintenance Communication software allows communication amongst different processors and between processors and a Network Operation and Maintenance Center.

10.1.4 Other ISDN Switches

There are several other C.O. switching systems in use throughout North America and the world that support ISDN, including:

- Alcatel E10-FIVE
- Ericsson AXE 10
- GTE GTD-5 Electronic Automatic Exchange (EAX)
- ITT System 12
- Mitel GX5000 Global Switch
- NEC America NEAX 61E

10.2 NETWORK TERMINATION TYPE 1

Network termination type 1 (NT1) devices provide the physical interface between the transmission line from the local exchange and the customer-premises equipment, including ISDN terminal equipment (TE1) and terminal adaptors. When ISDN PBXs and multiplexers (NT2) are used at the customer site, the NT1 functions will typically be embedded within the NT2 itself.

In the BRI, the NT1 must provide a number of functions, including:

- Conversion between the two-wire local loop and the four-wire S/T bus
- Provide echo cancellation
- Conversion between the I.430 frame format and the 2B1Q frame format
- Conversion between the pseudo ternary and 2B1Q line codes
- Local power distribution (in some cases)

The NT1 has a point-to-point configuration with the LE across the local loop, while up to eight TE1s and TAs may access the NT1 in a point-to-multipoint configuration across the ISDN BRI.

A typical NT1 contains a single six- or eight-position subminiature jack for the termination of the two-wire local loop (U reference point), and one or two eight-position subminiature jacks for the four-wire BRI (S/T reference point) bus. In those NT1s with two BRI connections, there is still only one S/T bus; recall that the NT1 may be anywhere on the short passive bus with respect to the terminal equipment. LEDs on the front of the NT1 can indicate the status ac power, frame synchronization across the U and S/T reference points, and self-test state of the NT1.

An NT1 built by AT&T is shown in Fig. 10.6. This unit is 6.8 in wide by $4\frac{1}{2}$ in deep by $1\frac{1}{4}$ in high, smaller than many modems. It requires a separate ISDN Plug-In Power Unit, which will supply the NT1 and its associated terminal with 10 W of 40-V dc power, per CCITT standards. A rack-mounted NT1 module can hold up to 12 NT1s and requires an ISDN Bulk Power Unit.

Most NT1s available in North America will, in turn, provide power to TEs and TAs across a third wire pair. Some NT1s in other parts of the world may provide some phantom power over the two data pairs.

Other manufacturers also build NT1 devices designed for their particular switches or ISDN CPE. For example, Northern Telecom builds an NT1 for connections to its DMS-100 switch family and the NEC NT-100 is an NT1 device for DSL termination between an NEAX 61E switch and NEC ISDN terminal equipment.

10.3 NETWORK TERMINATION TYPE 2

Network termination type 2 (NT2) is customer-site communications distribution equipment. NT2 can be, for example, a local area network, private branch exchange, or multiplexer. With the introduction of digital PBXs, more and more data is being switched along with voice traffic. In some customer environments, in fact, the PBX doubles as a voice switch and local data switch. LANs, on the other hand, are much less commonly used for the switching of voice; today they are primarily used as data networks. This section will focus on ISDN-compatible PBXs (also called integrated services PBXs, or ISPBX) and ISDN multiplexers.

10.3.1 Private Branch Exchange Products

Most PBX manufacturers that support ISDN today do so using proprietary protocols for PBX-to-PBX signaling, PBX-to-local exchange signaling, and/or supplementary services offerings. Eventually, most manufacturers will modify their protocols to use SS7, Q.931 (I.451), and Q.932 (I.452) for the same reasons that other types of networks have adopted standardization:

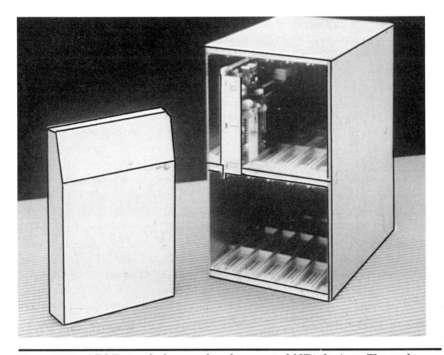

Figure 10.6   AT&T stand-alone and rack-mounted NT1 devices. The rack-mounted module can hold up to 12 NT1s. (*Photograph courtesy of AT&T Network Systems.*)

- To provide greater opportunities to connect their PBX to terminal equipment already owned by the user and to PBXs manufactured by other vendors
- To be cost effective since standard devices may be manufactured in greater quantities at a reduced per-unit cost
- To make it easier to connect their PBX to local exchange equipment built by different manufacturers

Table 10.2 lists some of the manufacturers and models of PBXs that have been announced to support ISDN and/or DMI, including:

- *AT&T Definity 75/85:*   The Definity 75/85 merges together the AT&T System 75 and System 85 products and introduces a common set of applications and hardware. Both Systems 75 and 85 can be upgraded to a Definity 75/85. The Definity 75/85 will have an open ISDN architecture built around CCITT Recommendation

TABLE 10.2   PBX Manufacturers and Models that Support DMI
or CCITT ISDN Interfaces

VENDOR	MODEL	MAXIMUM NUMBER OF LINES	ISDN	DMI
Alcatel	Alcatel One	896	●	
AT&T	System 75	800	●	●
	System 85	100,000	●	●
	Definity 75/85	30,000	●	●
Ericsson Information Systems	MD-110	12,000	●	●
Fujitsu Business Communications	Focus-9600	10,000	●	●
Fujitsu GTE Business Systems	Omni S I	256	●	
	Omni S IV	10,000	●	
Harris	Harris 20-20	1,920	●	●
Hitachi America	HCX 5000 family	25,000	●	
InteCom	IBX S/xx family	16,384	●	
Mitel	SX-2000 ICS	4,000		●
NEC America	NEAX 2400	22,000	●	
Northern Telecom	Meridian SL-1	8,000	●	
	Meridian SL-100	30,000	●	
Rolm Systems	9750 CBX	20,000	●	
Siemens Information Systems	Saturn IIE	600	●	●
	Saturn III	864	●	●
TIE/communications	Morgan	144		●

Q.931 messages and future recommendations for supplementary services. AT&T uses a proprietary PBX-to-PBX network called Distributed Communications System (DCS) but will migrate to support SS7 protocols based upon customer demand. DMI is supported for host-to-PBX communication.

- *NEC NEAX 2400:*   NEC currently uses a proprietary subset of SS7 for inter-PBX signaling but will migrate to full SS7 for greater connectivity to customers and local exchanges.

- *Northern Telecom Meridian SL-1 and SL-100:*   NTI uses a proprietary protocol for internode communications between SL-1s and SL-100s, which they call the Electronic Switched Network (ESN). The ESN message set is sent over one 64-kbps channel on each PRI link. Northern Telecom is a proponent of a common inter-PBX signaling protocol based upon SS7, called the Remote Operation Service Element (ROSE). NTI has developed the ISDN-Applications Protocol (ISDN/AP) software for the SL-1, a communications product for the integration of traditional office automation and voice services with data processing. The ISDN/AP will link the SL-1 to Digital Equipment Corporation's VAX family of computers which will serve as the basis for PBX-to-computer applications. The Meridian 1 PBX, announced in early 1990, will merge the SL-1 and SL-100 product lines; ISDN BRI support is expected in 1991.

■ *Siemens Saturn:*   Corporate Network (CorNet), the Siemens common channel PBX-PBX protocol, uses Q.931 messages for basic call control and a proprietary message set for supplementary services. The CorNet protocol for supplementary services will closely follow evolving CCITT recommendations.

Several C.O. switch manufacturers offer their products directly to customers for customer-premises applications in lieu of traditional PBXs. One result of this is that it broadens their customer base beyond just the operating telephone companies. Several organizations, for example, have purchased AT&T 5ESS switches for on-premises use, and Northern Telecom's Meridian SL-100 PBX is essentially a customer-premises version of their DMS-100 C.O. switch.

10.3.2 ISDN Multiplexers

PBXs are not the only form of customer site distribution equipment that is available. Teleos Communications Inc., for example, makes an ISDN multiplexer called the ISDN Adjunct Processor 6000 (IAP6000) for installation on a customer's premises. On-site TAs and TE1s connect to the IAP6000 using BRI access, just as if it were an ISDN C.O. switch. On the trunk side, the IAP6000 connects to the C.O using a PRI. This device currently works with AT&T 5ESS and Siemens EWSD switches; NTI DMS-100 compatibility is expected.

The Newbridge Networks Corp. 3600 MainStreet multiplexer family represents another form of NT2, supporting both 1.544- and 2.048-Mbps interfaces. The 3600 MainStreet Bandwidth Manager is an integrated voice, data, and image multiplexer. It can provide digital carrier cross-connect functions, terminate T1 or E1 trunks, perform T1-to-E1 conversion, perform μ-law-to-A-law conversion, support 32-kbps ADPCM and other voice compression techniques, and support 2B + D U interfaces. The 3624 MainStreet Intelligent T1 Channel

Bank may be used for point-to-point connections within a private network or for customer access to a public network; it can support a combination of up to 24 analog telephone terminations or 12 BRI terminations. The 3645L MainStreet Networking Multiplexer provides similar capabilities as the 3600 but at higher speeds and capacities (Fig. 10.7).

The B-Link ISDN Statistical Multiplexer (Datagraf, Inc.) is a TE1 emulator for the BRI, providing X.25 packet-mode support on both B- and D-channels. The B-Link appears to a 5ESS switch as an ISDN terminal, using standard CCITT ISDN and X.25 protocols. On the user side, up to 16 asynchronous devices may be attached to the B-Link using the standard PSPDN asynchronous access protocols, namely CCITT Recommendations X.3, X.28, and X.29.

Figure 10.7 Newbridge 3645L MainStreet Networking Multiplexer. (*Photograph courtesy of Newbridge Networks Corporation.*)

The AT&T Model 6500 is a cluster controller for SNA applications. The 6500 will support the PRI, enabling 23 simultaneous dial-up terminal sessions, without the need for individual TAs for each port on the controller.

10.4 TERMINAL EQUIPMENT TYPE 1

As ISDN becomes more widespread, ISDN terminal equipment (TE1) will supply the digital service between the customer and the ISDN C.O. switch. Since TE1s will use standard CCITT-defined interfaces (i.e., the S/T reference point), this will eventually mean that any vendor's equipment can be used on any ISDN. This section will focus on two basic types of TE1, ISDN telephones and ISDN integrated voice/data terminals (IVDTs) and workstations.

10.4.1 ISDN Telephones

As discussed earlier, the interface between the telephone and the network will change in the ISDN era. No longer will the telephone short circuit the line to indicate the off-hook condition nor will the C.O. place a dial tone on the line to signal the user to dial the telephone number. Those, and other, signals will be exchanged digitally in Q.931 messages.

It is equally important to remember that the interface between the human user and the telephone set will not change dramatically in the ISDN era. When people dial a telephone number, they expect some sort of audible feedback, such as tones or pulses. It is disorienting, and often frustrating, to "dial" a telephone number without this feedback. After picking up the handset, most people will wait for a dial tone before they enter the telephone number; they will probably ignore a flashing LED or message on a screen.

Figure 10.8 shows a functional block diagram of a basic ISDN telephone. The input-output (I/O) control circuit addresses the issues described in the paragraph above, that is, the analog human-telephone interface. This block contains the speaker driver for voice and signaling functions, circuitry to interpret keypad input, and a controller for the display. This block might also contain a dual-tone multifrequency (DTMF) circuit to produce feedback tones. The speech circuit and CODEC are responsible for any filtering and analog-digital conversion of the voice signal between the telephone set and the user. The EIA-232-D data interface (optional in many ISDN telephones) provides a serial, asynchronous interface for a data terminal or PC through the ISDN telephone.

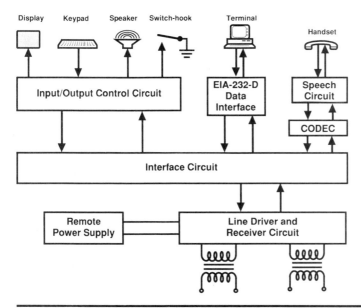

Figure 10.8 Functional block diagram of an ISDN telephone, including an EIA-232-D data interface.

The interface circuit provides the interface between the ISDN protocol set and the telephone functions. It controls the B- and D-channels for voice and/or data applications, handles the Q.931/Q.932 control message interface, implements the LAPD protocol, and provides I.430 BRI framing. The line driver and receiver circuit adjusts the electrical signal levels between the internal circuitry and external lines. A remote power supply will probably be needed to supply the telephone with extra power to drive all of these additional features although, according to CCITT standards, external power could be supplied by the NT1.

A generic ISDN telephone set has the following features:

- *Liquid crystal display (LCD) screen:* A display provides information on the status of outgoing and incoming telephone calls, the telephone number as it is dialed, and appropriate messages, as needed. A second line of the screen can be used to display labels for preprogrammed function keys, called *softkeys.* The softkey labels change as the features and defined commands change during the different phases of the call.

- *Softkeys:* Softkey functions are preprogrammed in the telephone set and support features operating through the ISDN, such as call forward, call waiting, conference call pick-up, call transfer, and make set busy. Other softkey functions support local features that reside within the telephone, such as last number redial, list incoming callers, and speed dialing.

- *User-programmable keys:*   These keys may be programmed by the user to provide any available advanced functions that are not preprogrammed. These keys allow the user to customize the user-network interface.

- *Hold and Release:*   The Hold key places an in-progress call on hold, while the Release key terminates an in-progress call.

- *Speaker volume control.*

An add-user function will probably become a very important telephone feature as ISDN becomes available in the home. Consider what happens when there is an incoming telephone call at a residence. All telephones in the home ring and the first telephone to be picked up will connect to the incoming call. What happens if a second telephone handset is picked up? In the pre-ISDN era, the second telephone is also connected to the call; in the ISDN era, the second user will hear a dial tone and get an outgoing B-channel. There must, then, be a mechanism so that multiple users within the home can talk on the same telephone call; if some feature like this is not available, most residential customers will perceive (correctly) that their level of service has decreased.

Not all ISDN telephones are designed for use over the S/T bus. The AT&T 6500-series Digital Business Sets, for example, are intended to be directly connected to a 5ESS switch over a wire pair employing the U reference point standard; the NT1 is built into the set. These telephones are designed for voice-only applications.

Most ISDN telephones meant for use over the BRI S/T bus are designed to handle simultaneous voice and data and can be equipped with an interface board that allows a data device (e.g., a PC or terminal) to be connected to the telephone set. These data interface boards typically support asynchronous transmission at speeds up to 19.2 kbps or synchronous transmission at speeds up to 56 kbps and provide rate adaption to the 64-kbps B-channel rate. In this way, the entire 2B + D BRI capability may be used; a voice conversation and circuit switched data transfer can occur simultaneously. With a data interface on the telephone set, conversion to ISDN in a user's office requires changing only the telephone set; the existing data terminal can still be used. The EIA-232-D or V.35 interface is typically employed between the terminal and ISDN telephone.

Announced ISDN telephone sets include:

- AT&T 6500-series Digital Business Sets (6504 and 6508)
- AT&T 7500-series ISDN Terminals (7505, 7506, 7507, and 7514) (Fig. 10.9)
- Fujitsu SRS-270D
- NEC America Integrated Services Terminal IST-200
- Northern Telecom Meridian ISDN Digital Telephone (Fig. 10.10)
- ROLMphone 400
- Telrad IDS-287

10.4.2 Integrated Voice/Data Terminals and Workstations

IVDTs are a single-unit TE1 that provide both voice and data capabilities. In some models, the telephone is built into the terminal and the terminal keyboard is used for both voice and data functions (i.e., entering data and entering a telephone number are done from the same keyboard); in other models, an extra keypad for telephony applications is present. The terminal display replaces the telephone's LCD

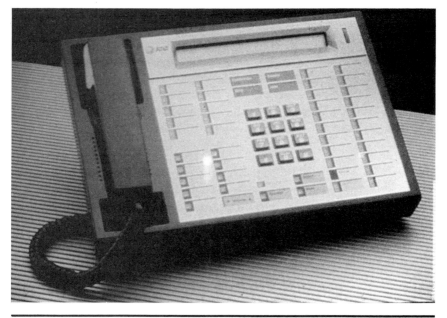

Figure 10.9 AT&T ISDN 7507 Display Terminal. This unit has 31 user-option buttons and supports both voice and data service. (*Photograph courtesy of AT&T Network Systems.*)

Figure 10.10 Northern Telecom Meridian ISDN Digital Telephone. (*Photograph courtesy of Northern Telecom, Inc.*)

display; all voice-related messages appear on the terminal screen. Multiple functions can be supported and displayed at the terminal using multiple screen windows. Prototype ISDN IVDTs include the Fujitsu ISDN Image Station (Fig. 10.11) and NEC America IST-400 and IST-1000 (Fig. 10.12).

Rather than build entirely new equipment, some vendors are designing ISDN workstations around existing PCs and telephones. ISDN interface boards, which are really terminal adaptors (TAs), make the PCs appear as TE1 to the network. The products mentioned below go a step further than a basic TA function, however, in that they actually integrate the voice and data hardware into a single product and provide integrated voice/data applications.

International Computers Limited (ICL) makes three ISDN workstations (Fig. 10.13). Each workstation consists of a PC/AT-compatible microcomputer, telephone, mouse, and BRI interface board (including CODEC). The ICL/ISDN Model 40 and Model 45 are based on an Intel 80286 microprocessor, while the Model 80 is based on the 80386; all run under the OS/2 operating system. Their ISDN Board is compatible with ISDN services supported by the 5ESS, DMS-100, and EWSD switches. The B-channel supports circuit switched voice and data (using V.120 rate adaption), and packet switched data (using X.25).

ICL also has several application software packages for their workstations, including a Phonebook database, voice and data call Telephone Manager, and DeskTop Conferencing, (DTC). The DTC

Figure 10.11   Fujitsu ISDN Image Station. (*Photograph courtesy of Fujitsu ISDN Systems Group.*)

Figure 10.12   NEC America IST-1000 voice/data terminal. (*Photograph courtesy of NEC America, Inc.*)

Figure 10.13 ICL ISDN Workstation and telephone. (*Photograph courtesy of ICL North America.*)

package allow true voice and data conferencing between multiple parties using both B-channels. Screen images may be shared by all users and different colors are used to allow up to eight users to simultaneously draw or point using the mouse. Their Applications Program Interface (API) enables software developers to write additional applications for the ISDN workstation hardware.

ISDN Telecommunications Co. (ITC) offers a Data Voice ISDN PC Card and T1 Megaspeed ISDN PC Card. Both cards fit into a standard IBM PC or compatible. The Data Voice card provides a 2B + D BRI, while the T1 Megaspeed card can be configured for 23B + D or 30B + D PRI. Applications include voice and data communications, voice mail, image transfer, LAN interconnections, electronic mail, and file transfer.

Vadis, Inc., makes an integrated PC desktop system called the PC^2 Series. Their products provide ISDN hardware connectivity and a set of applications, such as Voice Call Manager, Data Call Manager, Electronic Mail, Desktop Calendar, and Automatic Incoming Calling Line Identification Processing for managing incoming calls. The PC^2 series comprises three products. One model is based on the IBM PC AT/XT running DOS V3.2, one on the PS/2 running OS/2 and using the Micro Channel backplane, and one software-only version for non-ISDN users who want the same functionality through a LAN or EIA-232 port. Their products are compatible with the AT&T 5ESS switch and Northern Telecom DMS-100 switch and SL-100 PBX.

10.5   TERMINAL ADAPTORS

Terminal adaptors perform the protocol conversion necessary to attach non-ISDN terminal equipment (TE2) to the ISDN. These devices are, quite expectedly, very important; almost all terminal equipment in use today would be classified as TE2. TAs and ISDN telephones, then, are likely to be the most widely purchased pieces of ISDN equipment in the early days of ISDN availability.

Many manufacturers offer TA equipment, primarily to support analog telephones, asynchronous terminals, BISYNC 3270 terminals, X.25 DTEs, and PCs. TAs are protocol converters; their primary function is to convert the terminal's pre-ISDN protocol(s) for use on the D-channel. Rate adaption may also be performed.

Some examples of available TAs and their features are:

- *AT&T 3270 Data Modules:* Connected to a 5ESS switch, these modules support 3270-type equipment over the BRI; the Model 3270T supports a single IBM 3270-type terminal and the Model 3270C provides up to eight lines to a 3270-type cluster controller.

- *AT&T 7500 Data Module:* Supports asynchronous communication at speeds up to 9600 bps using the RS-232-C (EIA-232-D) interface or synchronous communication at speeds of 56 or 64 kbps using a V.35 interface. This TA is intended for data devices, where simultaneous voice communications is not required (Fig. 10.14).

- *Harris ISDN Terminal Adaptor:* Supports a myriad of non-ISDN equipment, including asynchronous terminals (at speeds up to 19.2 kbps), synchronous terminals (up to 64 kbps), analog telephones, and X.25 DTEs and PADs.

Different configurations provide dual EIA-232-D interfaces for circuit-mode B-channels; dual EIA-232-D interfaces for packet-mode channels; or one voice channel plus an EIA-232-D interface for either circuit-mode B-channel or packet-mode D-channel data.

- *Hayes ISDN PC Card:* Board and software that gives an IBM PC and compatibles full access to ISDN BRI and adapts an analog

Figure 10.14 AT&T ISDN 7500 Data Module. (*Photograph courtesy of AT&T Network Systems.*)

telephone for use on the ISDN. Supports X.25 and HAYES ISDN AT command set for control of data connections. Like many PC-based TAs, this is not a stand-alone product; it is intended to provide a protocol platform for third-party ISDN applications (Fig. 10.15).

- *NEC America TA-100 and TA-300:* Provide a single RS-232-C asynchronous interface for B-channel circuit-mode or D-channel packet-mode data plus either two telephone line interfaces for analog telephones (TA-100, shown in Fig. 10.16) or two RS-232-C interfaces for B-channel circuit-mode data (TA-300).

- *Northern Telecom Personal Computer Terminal Adaptor (PCTA):* A board and software allowing an IBM PC or PC-compatible machine to access the ISDN BRI. Supports B- and D-channel packet-mode data, simultaneous use of the B- and D-channels, X.25, and Northern's ISDN digital telephone-to-PC messaging. Also supports IBM 3270 Emulation.

Other TA vendors and products include:

- Fujitsu SRS-300/400/410 ISDN Terminal Adaptors

Figure 10.15   Hayes ISDN PC Card. (*Reproduced by permission of Hayes Microcomputer Products, Inc.*)

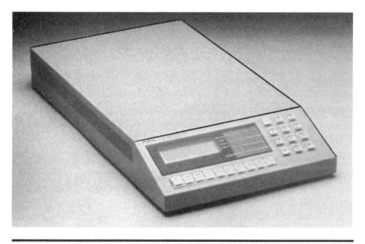

Figure 10.16   NEC TA-100 terminal adaptor. (*Photograph courtesy of NEC America, Inc.*)

- IBM 7820 ISDN Terminal Adapter
- Infotron Passport Terminal Adapter
- Newbridge 1600 MainStreet Terminal Adapters
- OST PC ISDN interface
- Progressive Computing ISDN tel/adapter
- Teleos Communications B100PC
- Universal Data Systems TA100

10.6 ISDN CHIP SETS

Standards are useful in many aspects of life. Not only can they ensure a certain guaranteed level of performance or safety, but they can also open a marketplace to new manufacturers and allow consumers a greater choice of vendors.

Standards actually make it easier and less costly to do business. Packet switching is an example of this. When public packet switched networks were first introduced in the late 1960s and early 1970s, each network used different switches and a different user-network interface. Thus, a manufacturer of packet switching equipment for the customer site could interface only to a few, select networks. Furthermore, a minimal number of these devices could be built since there was limited need for this specialized equipment.

CCITT Recommendation X.25 changed this. A manufacturer could build an X.25 device that would, theoretically, operate with any X.25 PSPDN in the world. Since large numbers of these devices could be built, it made sense to implement the X.25 protocols in chips. This, in turn, further reduced the cost because of the large volume of chips that could be produced. By lowering costs, the X.25 recommendation also helped to increase the PSPDN market.

Widespread deployment of ISDN will also depend upon the availability of low-cost chips implementing the ISDN protocols using very large-scale integration (VLSI) technology. Many such chips are available today, allowing manufacturers to build subscriber line cards for C.O. switches and PBXs, ISDN telephone sets, IVDTs, NT1 devices, and ISDN terminal adaptors for PCs, analog telephones, and other equipment.

Some of the chips and chip sets in common use are described below. Generic names are given, along with general descriptions:

- *Coder-decoder (CODEC):*   Performs voice channel filtering, as well as the analog-to-digital and digital-to-analog PCM conversion. Many such chips allow selection of A-law or μ-law companding; some only support one algorithm or the other. Some have an interface for a DTMF tone generator, used for audio feedback to the user. Applications include use in a digital telephone or on an analog line card.

- *Digital loop (or subscriber line) controller:*   Implements four-wire 2B + D (BRI) S/T reference point, according to CCITT Recommendation I.430. Supports point-to-point or point-to-multipoint physical configurations. Applications include use in NT1, PBX and C.O. switch line cards, TE1, and terminal adaptors.

- *Digital network basic interface circuit:*   Implements two-wire 2B + D

(BRI) U reference point, per the ANSI standard. Most of these chips use echo cancellation, although some use time compression multiplexing (TCM). Applications include use in NT2 or LE line cards.

- *Digital network primary interface circuit:* Provides primary rate access. Some chips allow the selection of a T1 (24 channel) or E1 (32 channel) digital trunk; others are limited to one version or the other. Applications include use in computer, PBX, or LE line cards, or NT1.

- *Data protocol controller:* Implements several versions of bit-oriented protocols, including HDLC (ISO), ADCCP (ANS X3.66), LAPB (X.25), and LAPD (ISDN). Some ISDN-specific protocol controllers support LAPD and Q.931.

- *Loop extender circuits:* Allows connections between devices over lines longer than typically allowed by the standards. These chips can either regenerate the line signal or improve the quality of the signal; either solution may allow longer line lengths.

- *SS7 link controller:* Supports SS7 protocols. Applications include use on SS7 interface boards for NT2 and LE devices.

- *ISDN evaluation kits:* Allows a user to learn about, evaluate, and test a manufacturer's ISDN components. Users can test their own hardware and software ISDN applications, as well as create custom ISDN demonstrations.

ISDN chip sets are built by a number of manufacturers, including:

- Advanced Micro Devices
- AT&T
- Intel
- Mitel Semiconductors
- National Semiconductor
- Rockwell International
- Siemens Semiconductor
- Western Digital

10.7   ISDN TEST EQUIPMENT

Various types of communications test equipment is available to ensure that protocols work correctly and that the medium is carrying bits without errors. The paragraphs below will describe some ISDN-related test equipment.

Protocol analysis and monitoring is essential to track the performance of a network and to ensure that different vendors' equipment will interoperate. A manufacturer of ISDN equipment needs some way of verifying that their implementation is correct, i.e., that it conforms to the appropriate standards. Differences may arise between implementations because of vagueness in the standard and/or different interpretations of the standard.

10.7.1 Media Testing

Analysis and monitoring can take many forms. Break-out boxes can be used to ensure that the physical line is operating correctly. A bit-error rate tester (BERT) or block-error rate tester (BLERT) provides information on the quantity of bit errors and the patterns in which they occur.

One area of real concern with ISDNs is whether the current local loop facilities can merely be deloaded and then used for ISDN applications. This is also an issue with existing in-building wiring, particularly twisted pair. Devices that test the twisted pair are very important, as is equipment that simulates the characteristics of twisted pair for the development of ISDN devices. Test equipment for these purposes include:

- AEA Electronics DLS 100A Wireline Simulator
- Harris biTS-1
- International Data Sciences PRI/T1 tester
- Telebyte Technology Model 451 Wire Line Simulator
- Telecom Analysis Systems (TAS) 2010 Wireband Channel Simulator and TAS 2100 Loop Emulator
- Wandel & Goltermann ISM-1 Signal Balance Ratio Bridge

10.7.2 Protocol Monitoring and Testing

Protocol analyzers monitor the traffic over a line and/or test implementations of a protocol. As a monitor, the protocol analyzer is placed on the line between the two devices to be monitored and passively captures all transmissions on the line for later examination (Fig. 10.17).

Figure 10.18 shows an example of an ISDN protocol monitor display[1] of the transmitted bits, LAPD frames, Q.931 messages, and contents of the B-channels over a BRI:

- The level 1 transmission in the TE-to-NT direction is shown, where each line represents a single I.430 block.
- The D-channel transmission is interpreted as an LAPD frame; since

---

[1]The Strappman 2000 protocol analyzer and the features shown here are for illustration only; this is not a real product.

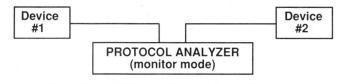

Figure 10.17   Protocol analyzer in monitor mode between two devices.

the entire LAPD frame is not shown on the screen, the '\' character in the I.430 display shows the beginning of the interpreted frame.

- The contents of the two B-channels are displayed in hexadecimal.

Protocol monitors and interpreters can be used to test whether devices are exchanging correct, legal, and appropriate messages.

A protocol analyzer can also be used for protocol conformance testing. Conformance testing is typically done prior to connecting a new device onto a live network, to assess the device's implementation of a protocol. Figure 10.19 shows the physical configuration that might be used for ISDN conformance testing. The device under test (DUT) may

```
                STRAPPMAN 2000 PROTOCOL ANALYZER

Direction: TE ──▶ NT

I.430 BIT STREAM      (Q = Code violation)

Blk.    FL ├ B1 ─┤L   DL  XL  ├ B2 ─┤L   DL ├ B1 ─┤L  DL ├ B2 ─┤L  DL

0050    Q0 Q10000101 \ 00   00  000000001  11 001100010  11 000000001  11
0051    Q0 Q01000000   11   00  000000001  11 010101000  11 000000001  00
0052    Q0 Q10001010   00   00  000000001  00 010100111  00 000000001  00
0053    Q0 Q10101000   00   00  000000001  00 001000000  00 000000001  00
0054    Q0 Q01010100   11   00  000000001  11 001000000  11 000000001  00
0055    Q0 Q10000101   00   00  000000001  00 001100010  11 000000001  11
0056    Q0 Q01000000   00   00  000000001  11 010101000  00 000000001  00
0057    Q0 Q10001010   00   00  000000001  00 010100111  00 000000001  00
0058    Q0 Q10101000   00   00  000000001  00 001000000  11 000000001  00
0059    Q0 Q01010100   00   00  000000001  00 001000000  00 000000001  00

D-CHANNEL      (LAPD)    (\ = Delimiter of LAPD frame shown below)

FRAME TYPE = I      P/F = 0    N(S) = 1   N(R) =     CRC OK
       C/R = 0   SAPI = 00  EI = 99       2

INFO FIELD = I.451 protocol
   Call Reference Length = 1CRV = 5   Flag = 0 (Origination)
   Message Type = RESUME

B1 CHANNEL     (HEX)

42 31 20 54 45 53 54 20 2A 20 42 31 20 54 45 53 54 20 2A 20

B2 CHANNEL     (HEX)

00 00 00 00 00 00 00 00 00 00 00 00 00 00 00 00 00 00 00 00
```

Figure 10.18   Sample display from ISDN protocol analyzer in monitor mode.

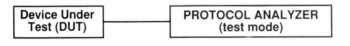

Figure 10.19 Protocol analyzer in test mode.

be an LE switch, PBX, telephone set, or TA; the purpose of the tests is
to assess the DUT's conformance to the standard.

The protocol tester is connected to the DUT. It sends a predetermined set of LAPD frames and/or Q.931 messages and examines the
replies from the DUT to be sure that they are valid responses (Fig.
10.20). The test set in the figure is for Information frame transfer.
Each minitest is preceded by the initialization procedure, defined at
the beginning of each test set. The device under test is a TE; the
tester, then, acts like an NT2 or LE. Q.931 tests would be handled in
a similar fashion.

It is important to realize that the protocol analyzer does not contain
an ISDN protocol implementation itself; it contains only a script of
test frames and messages and the expected responses. Conformance
tests cannot test every possible situation; they attempt to test all legal

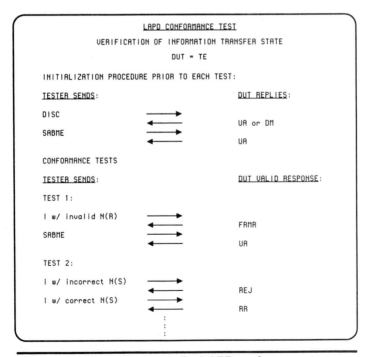

Figure 10.20 Sample portion of a LAPD conformance test.

possibilities and determine if illegal frames, messages, and situations are handled correctly by the DUT.

The protocol analyzer is used very differently as a monitor than as a tester. As a monitor, the device passively monitors the bits on the line and translates them into a format readable by a human. As a tester, the device actively communicates with another device.

Several organizations are involved in creating ISDN conformance tests. ANSI, AT&T, Bellcore, the CCITT, and the National Institute of Standards and Technology, for example, have created (or are creating) ISDN protocol conformance and SS7 test procedures. Many manufacturers of ISDN equipment have also created proprietary tests for internal use.

There are many protocol analyzers, monitors, and simulators available, testing the entire range of protocols from BISYNC to ISDN. Table 10.3 lists many of those devices that are available for ISDN and SS7 analysis and conformance testing.

10.7.3   Switch Simulators

Simulators are needed not only for ISDN CPE but for ISDN switches as well. This is particularly important for a product supplier or application developer in the early stages of product development. Individual users cannot monopolize an ISDN switch that is part of the public network and most product developers cannot afford to purchase switches for in-house development activities. Switch simulators solve this problem. They can then also be used as sales and marketing aids, providing a way for portable product and applications demonstrations.

Many CPE and application developers use switch simulators, although most of these devices are proprietary. Some companies, however, build these simulators as a product.

Teleos Communications, for example, builds a portable device that simulates the ISDN circuit switched capabilities of class 4 and 5 switches, simulating BRI and PRI access and some supplementary services. This simulator is based upon their IAP6000 Adjunct Processor, mentioned earlier. Siemens Components and Tekelec also build ISDN switch simulators.

10.7.4   Test Facilities

Testing laboratories are becoming increasingly important for the acceptance of new vendors' equipment and to test the interoperability of devices from different manufacturers. One of the purposes of Southwestern Bell's Advanced Technology Laboratory, for example, is to test the interoperability of switches from AT&T, Ericcson, Northern

TABLE 10.3   Protocol Analyzers and Monitors
for ISDN and/or SS7 Protocols

VENDOR	MODEL	Protocol Tests		
		ISDN	SS7	X.25[1]
Ando	AE-5120	●	-	●
Atlantic Research	Comstate II	-	●	●
	Interview 7000	●	●	●
CXR Telcom	841A/845A	●	●	●
Digilog	320/420/620/820	●	●	●
DSP Technology	PRIDE-100	●	-	-
Frederick Engineering	FELINE	●	-	●
Hard Engineering	645i	●	-	-
Harris	ISDN Protocol Analyzer[2]	●	-	-
Hewlett-Packard	HP 4954A/4955A	-	●	●
	HP 37900A/B	-	●	-
Idacom	IPT 468	●	-	-
	MPT 368.2	●	-	●
	PT 300	●	-	●
Kamputech	KAT-1000	●	●	●
Navtel	9440/9460	●	-	●
Network Communications Corp.	Network Probe 6640	●	-	●
Progressive Computing	Tel/scope[2]	●	-	●
	LM1[2]	●	-	●
Tekelec	Chameleon 32	●	●	●
Tektronix	TC 1000/TC 2000	●	-	-
Telenex	Autoscope	●	●	●
Wandel & Golterman	DA - 20	●	-	-

KEY: ● Available (possibly an option)   - Not supported
NOTES:
1) Analyzers that test X.25, but not ISDN nor SS7, are not
   listed in this table.
2) PC-based protocol analyzer.

Telecom, and Siemens. Bell Atlantic, Bellcore, BellSouth, NYNEX, and other LECs also have test facilities with which to examine new CPE and applications, as well as to test multivendor interoperability.

The First Application System Test (FAST) office in Research Triangle Park, NC, was built by Northern Telecom to test ISDN terminal equipment from any manufacturer. It is a complete, self-contained telephone network, offering laboratory facilities to test all network components and services. Engineers from any manufacturer, assisted by engineers from Northern Telecom, can test their equipment using BRI or PRI access to a DMS-100 switch or Meridian SL-1 PBX.

U.S. Sprint also operates a test laboratory. One of their primary goals is to test the interoperability of several models of PBX, including AT&T's System 85, NTI's SL-1 and SL-100, Fujitsu's Focus 9600, IBM/Rolm's 9750, NEC's 2400, and Siemens' Saturn 2E. In addition to interoperability, they will test PRI access, SS7, and their operation with NTI DMS-250 switches.

AT&T's Feature Interactive Verification Environment (FIVE) is a customer facility for testing, verifying, evaluating, and demonstrating a wide variety of network capabilities from a 5ESS switch. Their Product Engineering Control Center (PECC) support group and Bell Laboratories Field Support personnel are part of the team providing support for customers' ISDN trials and other service offerings.

Other protocol and application test facilities have been developed or proposed by a number of sources other than service providers. User's groups such as the North American ISDN Users Forum, as well as individual users such as North Carolina State University, have proposed to specific manufacturers that such laboratory facilities be developed. It is possible that central ISDN testing laboratories will be built that contain ISDN C.O. equipment, customer premises equipment, test equipment, and applications from several sources. This would provide a testbed for developers, as well as potential new users.

Conclusion

In the 1870s, so the story goes, a newspaper editorial noted that:

> ...carrying human voice over copper wires is impossible and even if was possible, the thing would have no practical use.

Nevertheless, telephones were developed and did find many applications. Indeed, early use was for business purposes, but telephones soon found their way into the home. While telephones became an important communications medium, they did not obviate the need for the primary communications network of the day because the telegraph was able to handle some types of communication better than the telephone (e.g., lists of names, numbers, and places). What did occur was a huge growth in the amount of communication between people and the way in which it occurred.

Many critics of ISDN doubt that multiple digital channels can effectively and economically be carried over twisted pair. Others have already pronounced ISDN dead, noting that we should be implementing broadband ISDN instead of the current narrowband version. Other critics wonder how anyone will use this technology or why.

Indeed, users typically try to fit new technologies into old ways of doing things because it does not make sense to invest in a new technology for a given application that doesn't work at least as well as the old technology and because it is much easier to envision new applications of a new technology after the technology is in place.

Before the introduction of telephones, for example, a doctor might dictate a message for a doctor in another town to his or her receptionist. The receptionist, in turn, would give the message to a messenger, who would take it to the telegraph operator, who would send it to the other town. At the destination side, the process would work in reverse.

When telephones were first introduced into the above scenario, the initial reaction was "So what? By the time the telephone operator dictates the message to the other telephone operator, we could have telegraphed the message!" It took a while to look at the problem from a different viewpoint, to see that the telephone easily allowed direct, doctor-to-doctor communication.

In the early days of telephony, in fact, telephones were usually purchased in pairs. Within a community, the doctor and the pharmacist might share a telephone line, as might the butcher and the general store. Later, "closed user groups," such as all of the doctors and pharmacists in town, shared a party line. Eventually, everyone wanted to talk to everyone else and telephone switching was invented.

ISDN is coming. It is a natural outgrowth of the 30-year-old evolution toward digital telephone networks. While the technology currently exists to build ISDNs, this will undoubtedly be the easiest part of introducing the network.

ISDN's initially must offer the same set of services that we have today; no one will buy this new service (PANS) if it offers fewer features than the old service (POTS). New applications will be developed for this technology as they have been for other technologies; look at what spreadsheet software did for the PC industry. As ISDN service becomes more available, more people will use it; this will prompt new applications and products to be developed, in turn bringing more users online. Ironically, the new applications that are promised by ISDN will, by necessity, be among the last ones developed.

This bootstrapping process will continue for many years until ISDN becomes commonplace. Most people today do not remember using crank telephones to obtain basic telephone service or calling the operator to obtain long distance service. In another 50 years, voice-data-image communications will be the norm and people then will wonder how we existed with the old-fashioned communications that we have today.

Abbreviations and Acronyms

ACCS	Automated Calling Card Service
ACD	Automatic call distribution
ADPCM	Adaptive differential pulse code modulation
AMI	Alternating mark inversion
ANI	Automatic number identification
ANS	American National Standard
ANSI	American National Standards Institute
ATM	Asynchronous transfer mode
AU	Access unit
Bellcore	Bell Communications Research
B-ISDN	Broadband ISDN
BOC	Bell operating company
bps	Bits per second
BRI	Basic rate interface
B8ZS	Bipolar 8 Zero Substitution
CCIS	Common Channel Interoffice Signaling
CCITT	Comité Consultatif International Télégraphique et Téléphonique (International Telegraph and Telephone Consultative Committee)
CCS	Common channel signaling
CEPT	Conference of European Postal and Telecommunications Administrations
CLASS	Custom Local Area Signaling Services
C.O.	Central office

CODEC	Coder/decoder
CPE	Customer-premises equipment
CRC	Cyclic redundancy check
CRV	Call Reference Value
DCE	Data circuit-terminating equipment
DLCI	Data Link Control Identifier
DMI	Digital Multiplexed Interface
DSL	Digital subscriber line (or loop)
DSS 1	Digital Subscriber Signaling System No. 1
DTE	Data terminal equipment
DTMF	Dual-tone multifrequency
DUP	Data User Part (SS7)
ECH	Echo Canceller with Hybrid
ECMA	European Computer Manufacturers' Association
ECSA	Exchange Carriers' Standards Association
ESF	Extended superframe format
ET	Exchange termination
E911	Enhanced 911 service
FAS	Frame alignment sequence
FAX	Facsimile
FCC	Federal Communications Commission
FCS	Frame check sequence
FDM	Frequency division multiplexing
FFS	For further study or for future standardization
Gbps	Gigabits, or billions of bits, per second (10^9)
GOSIP	Government OSI Profile
HDB3	High-Density Bipolar—3 zeroes
HDLC	High-level Data Link Control
Hz	Hertz (cycles/second)
IAN	Integrated analog network
IA5	International Alphabet No. 5
IDN	Integrated digital network
IEC	Interexchange carrier
IN	Intelligent network
ISDN	Integrated Services Digital Network
ISO	Organisation International de Normalisation (International Organization for Standardization)
ISPBX	Integrated services private branch exchange
ISUP	Integrated Services Digital Network User Part (SS7)

ITC	Independent telephone company
ITU	International Telecommunication Union
IVDT	Integrated voice/data terminal
kbaud	Thousands of signals per second (10^3)
kbps	Kilobits, or thousands of bits, per second (10^3)
kft	Kilofeet, thousands of feet (10^3)
kHz	Kilohertz, thousands of cycles per second (10^3)
km	Kilometer, thousands of meters (10^3)
LAN	Local area network
LAPB	Link Access Procedures Balanced (X.25)
LAPD	Link Access Procedures on the D-channel
LATA	Local access and transport area
LE	Local exchange
LEC	Local exchange carrier
LIDB	Line information database
LT	Local termination
Mbps	Megabits, or millions of bits, per second (10^6)
MFJ	Modification of Final Judgment
MHS	Message Handling System
MHz	Megahertz, millions of cycles per second (10^6)
modem	Modulator/demodulator
ms	Millisecond, thousandths of a second (10^{-3})
MTP	Message Transfer Part (SS7)
mV	Millivolt, thousandths of a volt (10^{-3})
mW	Milliwatt, thousandths of a watt (10^{-3})
NANP	North American Numbering Plan
NIST	National Institute of Standards and Technology
NIUF	North American ISDN Users' Forum
NT	Network termination
NTI	Northern Telecom Incorporated
NT1	Network termination type 1
NT2	Network termination type 2
OAM	Operations, administration, and maintenance
OMAP	Operations, Maintenance, and Administration Part (SS7)
OSI	Open Systems Interconnection
PABX	Private automatic branch exchange
PAD	Packet assembly/disassembly
PANS	Pretty amazing new stuff

PBX	Private branch exchange
PC	Personal computer
PCM	Pulse code modulation
PDN	Public data network
PH	Packet handler *or* packet handling
PLP	Packet Layer Protocol (X.25)
POTS	Plain old telephone service
PRI	Primary rate interface
PSAP	Public Safety Answering Point
PSN	Packet switched network
PSPDN	Packet switched public data network
PSTN	Public switched telephone network
PTN	Public telephone network
PTT	Postal, Telephone, and Telegraph administration
PVN	Private virtual network
RBOC	Regional Bell operating company
RDI	Restricted digital information
SAP	Service Access Point
SAPI	Service Access Point Identifier
SCCP	Signaling Connection Control Part (SS7)
SCP	Service control point (SS7)
SG	CCITT study group
SMS	Service Management System
SNA	Systems Network Architecture (IBM)
SP	Signaling point (SS7)
SPC	Signaling point code (SS7)
SS6	Signaling System No. 6
SS7	Signaling System No. 7
STP	Signal transfer point (SS7)
TA	Terminal adaptor
TCAP	Transaction Capabilities Application Part (SS7)
TCM	Time compression multiplexing
TDM	Time division multiplexing
TE	Terminal equipment
TEI	Terminal Endpoint Identifier
TE1	Terminal equipment type 1
TE2	Terminal equipment type 2

TUP	Telephone User Part (SS7)
UDI	Unrestricted digital information
VAS	Value-added service
WAN	Wide area network
WATS	Wide area telecommunications services
2B1Q	Two binary, one quaternary
μs	Microsecond, millionths of a second (10^{-6})

B

CCITT ISDN
Recommendations

B.1 ORGANIZATION OF I-SERIES RECOMMENDATIONS

Part I—General structure—I.100-series

Section 1—Frame of I-series Recommendations
  I.110: Preamble and general structure of the I-series Recommendations for the integrated services digital network (ISDN)
  I.111: Relationship with other Recommendations relevant to ISDNs
  I.112: Vocabulary of terms for ISDNs
  I.113: Vocabulary of terms for broadband aspects of ISDN

Section 2—Description of ISDNs
  I.120: Integrated services digital networks (ISDNs)
  I.121: Broadband aspects of ISDN
  I.122: Framework for providing additional packet mode bearer services

Section 3—General modeling methods
  I.130: Method for the characterization of telecommunication services supported by an ISDN and network capabilities of an ISDN

Section 4—Telecommunication network and service attributes
  I.140: Attribute technique for the characterization of telecommunication services supported by an ISDN and network capabilities of an ISDN
  I.141: ISDN network charging capabilities attributes

Part II—Service capabilities—I.200-series

  I.200: Guidance to the I.200-series of Recommendations

Section 1—General aspects of services in ISDN
I.210: Principles of telecommunication services supported by an ISDN and the means to describe them

Section 2—Common aspects of services in the ISDN
I.220: Common dynamic description of basic telecommunication services
I.221: Common specific characteristics of services

Section 3—Bearer services supported by an ISDN
I.230: Definition of bearer service categories
I.231: Circuit-mode bearer service categories
I.232: Packet-mode bearer service categories

Section 4—Teleservices supported by an ISDN
I.240: Definition of teleservices
I.241: Teleservices supported by an ISDN

Section 5—Supplementary services in ISDN
I.250: Definition of supplementary services
I.251: Number identification supplementary services
I.252: Call offering supplementary services
I.253: Call completion supplementary services
I.254: Multiparty supplementary services
I.255: Community of interest supplementary services
I.256: Charging supplementary services
I.257: Additional information transfer

Part III—Overall network aspects and functions—I.300-series

Section 1—Network functional principles
I.310: ISDN—Network functional principles

Section 2—Reference models
I.320: ISDN protocol reference model
I.324: ISDN network architecture
I.325: Reference configurations for ISDN connection types
I.326: Reference configurations for relative network resource requirements
I.32x: ISDN hypothetical reference connections (FFS)

Section 3—Numbering, addressing and routing
I.330: ISDN numbering and addressing principles
I.331: Numbering plan for the ISDN era (Published in the E-series as Rec. E.164)
I.332: Numbering principles for interworking between ISDNs and dedicated networks with different numbering plans
I.333: Terminal selection in ISDN

I.334: Principles relating ISDN numbers/subaddress to the OSI reference model network layer address

I.335: ISDN routing principles

Section 4—Connection types
I.340: ISDN connection types

Section 5—Performance objectives
I.350: General aspects of Quality of Service and network performance in digital networks, including ISDNs

I.351: Recommendations in other Series including network performance objectives that apply at T-reference points of an ISDN

I.352: Network performance objectives for call processing delays

Part IV—ISDN user-network interfaces—
I.400-series

Section 1—ISDN user-network interfaces
I.410: General aspects and principles relating to Recommendations of ISDN user-network interfaces

I.411: ISDN user-network interfaces—Reference configurations

I.412: ISDN user-network interfaces—Interface structures and access capabilities

Section 2—Application of I-Series Recommendations to ISDN user-network interfaces
I.420: Basic user-network interface

I.421: Primary rate user-network interface

Section 3—ISDN user-network interfaces: Layer 1 Recommendations
I.430: Basic user-network interface—Layer 1 specification

I.431: Primary rate user-network interface—Layer 1 specification

I.43x: Higher rate user-network interfaces (FFS)

Section 4—ISDN user-network interfaces: Layer 2 Recommendations
I.440: ISDN user-network interface data link layer—general aspects (Published in the Q-series as Rec. Q.920)

I.441: ISDN user-network interface data link layer specification (Published in the Q-series as Rec. Q.921)

Section 5—ISDN user-network interfaces: Layer 3 Recommendations
I.450: ISDN user-network interface layer 3—general aspects (Published in the Q-series as Rec. Q.930)

I.451: ISDN user-network interface layer 3 specification for basic call control (Published in the Q-series as Rec. Q.931)

I.452: ISDN user-network interface layer 3 specification—generic procedures for the control of ISDN supplementary services (Published in the Q-series as Rec. Q.932)

Section 6—Multiplexing, rate adaption and support of existing interfaces
   I.460: Multiplexing, rate adaption and support of existing interfaces
   I.461: Support of X.21 and X.21 *bis* and X.20 *bis* based data terminal equipments (DTEs) by an ISDN (Published in the X-series as Rec. X.30)
   I.462: Support of packet mode terminal equipment by an ISDN (Published in the X-series as Rec. X.31)
   I.463: Support of data terminal equipments (DTEs) with V-series type interfaces by an ISDN (Published in the V-series as Rec. V.110)
   I.464: Multiplexing, rate adaption and support of existing interfaces for restricted 64 kbit/s transfer capability
   I.465: Support by an ISDN of data terminal equipment with V-series type interfaces with provision for statistical multiplexing (Published in the V-series as Rec. V.120)

Section 7—Aspects of ISDN affecting terminal requirements
   I.470: Relationship of terminal functions to ISDN

Part V—Internetwork interfaces—
I.500-series

   I.500: General structure of ISDN interworking Recommendations
   I.510: Definitions and general principles for ISDN interworking
   I.511: ISDN-to-ISDN layer 1 internetwork interface
   I.515: Parameter exchange for ISDN interworking
   I.520: General arrangements for network interworking between ISDNs
   I.530: Network interworking between an ISDN and a public switched telephone network (PSTN)
   I.540: General arrangements for interworking between circuit switched public data networks (CSPDNs) and integrated services digital networks (ISDNs) for the provision of data transmission (Published in the X-series as Rec. X.321)
   I.550: General arrangements for interworking between packet switched public data networks (PSPDNs) and integrated services digital networks (ISDNs) for the provision of data transmission (Published in the X-series as Rec. X.325)
   I.560: Requirements to be met in providing the telex service within an ISDN (Published in the U-series as Rec. U.202)

Part VI—Maintenance principles—
I.600-series

   I.601: General maintenance principles of ISDN subscriber access and subscriber installation

I.602: Application of maintenance principles to ISDN subscriber installation

I.603: Application of maintenance principles to ISDN basic accesses

I.604: Application of maintenance principles to ISDN primary rate accesses

I.605: Application of maintenance principles to static multiplexed ISDN basic accesses

B.2 OTHER CCITT RECOMMENDATIONS RELATED TO ISDN

General tariff principles (D-series)
D.93, D.200-series

Telephone network and ISDN—Addressing, routing, quality of service, network management, and traffic engineering (E-series)
E.163-E.167, E.170-E.172, E.184, E.330, E.331, E.502

Telegraph and mobile services (F-series)
F.69

International telephone connections and circuits, transmission media, and digital transmission systems (G-series)
G.100-series, G.601, G.700-series, G.800-series, G.900-series

Protection against interference (K-series)
K.20, K.22, K.23

General maintenance principles (M-series)
M.20, M.21, M.22, M.24, M.30, M.36, M.40, M.122, M.125, M.250, M.251, M.550, M.555, M.557, M.770, M.782

Telephone transmission quality (P-series)
P.31, P.56, P.66, P.84

Telephone switching and signaling (Q-series)
Q.65, Q.71-Q.99, Q.120-Q.180, Q.251-Q.300, Q.310-Q.490, Q.500-series, Q.600-series, Q.700-series, Q.920, Q.921, Q.930, Q.931, Q.932, Q.940

Telematic services (T-series)
T.70, T.90

Telegraph switching (U-series)
U.12, U.201, U.202

Data communication over the telephone network (V-series)
V.25, V.32, V.100, V.110, V.120, V.230

Data communication networks (X-series)
X.1, X.2, X.10, X.15, X.21, X.21 bis, X.25, X.30, X.31, X.71, X.75, X.81, X.110, X.121, X.122, X.180, X.181, X.200, X.300-series

Functional Specification and Description Language (SDL) (Z-series)
Z.100-series

Messages and Information Elements from Recommendations Q.931 and Q.932

C.1 Q.931 AND Q.932 MESSAGES

The following paragraphs will briefly describe the messages found in Recommendations Q.931 (I.451) and Q.932 (I.452). Scenarios describing the use of all of these messages and details about coding them are beyond the scope of this book; readers are encouraged to refer directly to the CCITT recommendations.

In the message descriptions below, the significance, or relevance, of the message is indicated in parentheses. Possible options for message significance are:

- *Local:* Relevant only at the originating or terminating access points

- *Access:* Relevant at the originating and terminating access points but not in the network

- *Dual:* Relevant at either the originating or terminating access points and in the network

- *Global:* Relevant at the originating and terminating access points and in the network

If more than one type is listed, it means that the significance of the message depends upon the application. Unless otherwise noted, more information on the messages described below can be found in Recommendation Q.931.

Call Establishment Messages

- *ALERTING (global or local):*   Sent by the called user to the network and by the network to the calling user to indicate that the called user has initiated an alert procedure.

- *CALL PROCEEDING (local):*   Sent by the called user to the network or by the network to the calling user to indicate that the requested call establishment or access connection has been initiated and that no more call establishment information is needed or will be accepted.

- *CONNECT (global or local):*   Sent by the called user to the network and by the network to the calling user to indicate call acceptance by the called user.

- *CONNECT ACKNOWLEDGE (local):*   Sent by the network to the called user to indicate that the user has been awarded the call or access connection. It may be sent by the calling user to the network to allow symmetrical call control procedures.

- *PROGRESS (global or local):*   Sent by the user or the network to indicate the progress of a call or access connection in the event of interworking, in relation with the provision of in-band information, or within a private network.

- *SETUP (global or local):*   Sent by the calling user to the network and by the network to the called user to initiate call or access connection establishment.

- *SETUP ACKNOWLEDGE (local):*   Sent by the network to the calling user or by the called user to the network to indicate that call establishment has been initiated but that additional information may be required.

Call Information Phase Messages

- *RESUME (local):*   Sent by the user to request that the network resume a suspended call. A new B-channel and CRV must be allocated to the call (see SUSPEND; compare RETRIEVE).

- *RESUME ACKNOWLEDGE (local):*   Sent by the network to the user to indicate completion of a request to resume a suspended call.

- *RESUME REJECT (local):*   Sent by the network to the user to indicate that the network cannot comply with a request to resume a suspended call.

- *SUSPEND (local):*   Sent by the user to request that the network suspend a call. The B-channel and CRV associated with the call are released and may be used for other calls (see RESUME; compare HOLD).

- *SUSPEND ACKNOWLEDGE (local):* Sent by the network to the user to indicate completion of a request to suspend a call.

- *SUSPEND REJECT (local):* Sent by the network to the user to indicate that the network cannot comply with a request to suspend a call.

- *USER INFORMATION (access):* Sent by the user to the network to transfer information to the remote user or sent by the network to the user to deliver information from the other user. This message may also be used if the user-to-user transfer is part of an allowed information transfer.

- *HOLD (local):* Sent by the network or the user to request the hold function for an existing call (Q.932). The B-channel may be retained or released, per arrangement with the network, and the CRV is retained for possible retrieval of this call (see RETRIEVE; compare SUSPEND).

- *HOLD ACKNOWLEDGE (local):* Sent by the network or the user to indicate that the hold function has been successfully performed (Q.932).

- *HOLD REJECT (local):* Sent by the network or the user to indicate that the request to hold a call has been denied (Q.932).

- *REGISTER (local):* Sent by the user or the network to assign a new call reference for non-call-associated transactions (Q.932).

- *RETRIEVE (local):* Sent by the network or the user to request the retrieval of a held call (Q.932). The CRV of the retrieved call is the same as before it was put on hold (see HOLD; compare RESUME).

- *RETRIEVE ACKNOWLEDGE (local):* Sent by the network or the user to indicate that the retrieve function has been successfully performed (Q.932).

- *RETRIEVE REJECT (local):* Sent by the network or the user to indicate the inability to perform the requested retrieve function (Q.932).

Call Clearing Messages

- *DISCONNECT (global or local):* Sent by the user to request that the network clear an end-to-end or access connection or sent by the network to indicate that the end-to-end or access connection is cleared.

- *RELEASE (local):* Sent by the user or the network to indicate that the equipment sending the message has disconnected the channel and intends to release the channel and Call Reference Value and that the receiving equipment should release the channel and prepare to release the CRV after sending a RELEASE COMPLETE message. This message may also be sent by the network to the user to indicate that the access connection is awarded on the D-channel or an existing channel and that the network intends to release the CRV.

- *RELEASE COMPLETE (local):* Sent by the user or by the network to indicate that the equipment sending the message has released the channel and CRV, the channel is available for reuse, and the receiving equipment shall release the CRV.

- *RESTART (local):* Sent by the user or the network to request that the recipient restart (i.e., return to an idle state) the indicated channel(s) or interface.

- *RESTART ACKNOWLEDGE (local):* Sent to acknowledge the receipt of a RESTART message and to indicate that the requested restart procedure is complete.

Miscellaneous Messages

- *SEGMENT:* (This message is specified in Recommendation Q.931, but its use and format are not defined.)

- *CONGESTION CONTROL (local):* Sent by the user or the network to indicate the establishment or termination of flow control on the transmission of USER INFORMATION messages.

- *FACILITY (local):* Sent to request or acknowledge a supplementary service (Q.932).

- *INFORMATION (local):* Sent by the user or the network to provide additional information for such purposes as information for call establishment (e.g., the telephone number) or miscellaneous call-related information.

- *NOTIFY (access):* Sent by the user or network to indicate information pertaining to a call.

- *STATUS (local):* Sent by the user or the network in response to a STATUS ENQUIRY message or at any time during a call to report certain error conditions.

- *STATUS ENQUIRY (local):* Sent by the user or network at any time to solicit a STATUS message from its peer layer 3 entity. Sending a STATUS message in response to a STATUS ENQUIRY message is mandatory.

C.2 Q.931 AND Q.932 INFORMATION ELEMENTS

The information elements listed below are defined in Recommendation Q.931 (I.451). Table C.1 shows the relationship between the messages and information elements. Messages may comprise different information elements for different applications; furthermore, information elements may be mandatory in messages for some applications and optional in others. The order of the information elements listed here indicates the relative order in which the information elements will appear in a message if they are used.

- *Shift:* The information elements listed here are defined by CCITT recommendations. The Shift information element provides a means for other information elements to be used, as defined by a national standard, local network (public or private), or user-specific application. This information element is not included in Table C.1 but may be a part of any message.

- *More data:* Sent by the user to the network in a USER INFORMATION message and delivered by the network to the destination user(s) in a corresponding USER INFORMATION message. Indicates to the destination user that another USER INFORMATION message will follow that contains information belonging to the same block.

- *Sending complete:* May be used to indicate the completion of the called party number.

- *Congestion level:* Describes the congestion status of a call (i.e., receiver ready or receiver not ready).

- *Repeat indicator:* Indicates how repeated information elements shall be interpreted when included in a message. Several information elements, such as Bearer capability, Cause, and Channel identification, may be legally repeated within one message; most information elements cannot be repeated.

- *Segmented message:* Indicates that the current message is part of a segmented (i.e., fragmented) message. This information element also contains information so that the destination user can allocate sufficient buffer space for the entire message.

- *Bearer capability:* Indicates the profile of bearer service characteristics to be provided by the network. This includes the information transfer and access attributes (described in Chap. 3) with the exception of the access channel to use.

- *Cause:* Describes the reason for generating certain messages, provides diagnostic information in the event of procedural errors, and indicates the location of the cause originator.

TABLE C.1 (a) Relationship between Q.931/Q.932 *Call Establishment* Messages and Information Elements

A dot means that the information element may be mandatory or optional in some use of the specified message, depending upon application.

I.451 AND I.452 MESSAGES

Application and Direction — Information Elements (Single Octet and Variable Length)

(● indicates that the information element may be used with the message.)

Message	Type (hex)	Circuit-mode connection control	Packet-mode connection control	Temporary signalling connection control	Global Call Reference	I.452 (Q.932) Supplementary Service	More data	Sending complete	Congestion level	Repeat Indicator	Segmented message	Bearer capability	Cause	Call identity	Call state	Channel Identification	Facility	Progress Indicator	Network-specific facilities	Notification Indicator	Display	Date/time	Keypad facility	Signal	Switchhook	Feature activation	Feature indication	Information rate	End-to-end transit delay	Transit delay selection and indication	Packet layer binary parameters	Packet layer window size	Packet size	Calling party number	Calling party subaddress	Called party number	Called party subaddress	Redirecting number	Transit network selection	Restart indicator	Low layer compatibility	High layer compatibility	User-user
Alerting	01	both	u→n	both												●	●	●			●			●		●	●																●
Call Proceeding	02	both	both	both												●	●	●			●																						
Connect	07	both	both	both												●	●	●			●	●		●		●	●														●		●
Connect Acknowledge	0F	both	both	both												●					●			●	●																		
Progress	03	both	u→n										●					●			●																					●	●
Setup	05	both	both	both				●		●		●				●	●	●	●		●		●	●		●	●	●	●	●	●	●	●	●	●	●	●	●	●		●	●	●
Setup Acknowledge	0D	both														●		●			●																						

DIRECTION: u→n = User-to-network only   n→u = Network-to-user only   both = Sent by either network or user

TABLE C.1(b) Relationship between Q.931/Q.931 *Call Information Phase* Messages and Information Elements

I.451 AND I.452 MESSAGES

CALL INFORMATION PHASE MESSAGES

Message	Type (hex)	Application and Direction	More data	Cause	Call identity	Channel identification	Display	User-user
Resume	26	u→n			●			
Resume Acknowledge	2E	n→u				●	●	
Resume Reject	22	n→u		●			●	
Suspend	25	u→n			●			
Suspend Acknowledge	2D	n→u					●	
Suspend Reject	21	n→u		●			●	
User Information	20	both	●					●
Hold	24	both					●	
Hold Acknowledge	28	both					●	
Hold Reject	30	both		●			●	
Retrieve	31	both					●	
Retrieve Acknowledge	33	both				●	●	
Retrieve Reject	37	both		●		●	●	

Application and Direction categories: Circuit-mode connection control, Packet-mode connection control, Temporary signalling connection control, Global Call Reference, I.452 (Q.932) Supplementary Service

INFORMATION ELEMENTS:

Single Octet: More data, Sending complete, Congestion level, Repeat indicator, Segmented message, Bearer capability

Variable Length: Cause, Call identity, Call state, Channel identification, Facility, Progress indicator, Network-specific facilities, Notification indicator, Display, Date/time, Keypad facility, Signal, Switchhook, Feature activation, Feature indication, Information rate, End-to-end transit delay, Transit delay selection and indication, Packet layer binary parameters, Packet layer window size, Packet size, Calling party number, Calling party subaddress, Called party number, Called party subaddress, Redirecting number, Transit network selection, Restart indicator, Low layer compatibility, High layer compatibility, User-user

DIRECTION: u → n = User-to-network only   n → u = Network-to-user only   both = Sent by either network or user

263

TABLE C.1(c) Relationship between Q.931/Q.932 *Call Clearing* and *Miscellaneous* Messages and Information Elements

I.451 AND I.452 MESSAGES — INFORMATION ELEMENTS

Message (I.451/I.452)	Type (hex)	Circuit-mode connection control	Packet-mode connection control	Temporary signalling connection control	Global Call Reference	I.452 (Q.932) Supplementary Service	More data	Sending complete	Congestion level	Repeat indicator	Segmented message	Bearer capability	Cause	Call identity	Call state	Channel identification	Facility	Progress indicator	Network-specific facilities	Notification indicator	Display	Date/time	Keypad facility	Signal	Switchhook	Feature activation	Feature indication	Information rate	End-to-end transit delay	Transit delay selection and indication	Packet layer binary parameters	Packet layer window size	Packet size	Calling party number	Calling party subaddress	Called party number	Called party subaddress	Redirecting number	Transit network selection	Restart indicator	Low layer compatibility	High layer compatibility	User-user
CALL CLEARING MESSAGES																																												
Disconnect	45	both	both										●				●	●			●			●			●																●
Release	4D	both	both	both									●				●				●			●			●																●
Release Complete	5A	both	both	both									●				●				●			●			●																●
Restart	46				both											●					●																			●			
Restart Acknowledge	4E				both											●					●																			●			
MISCELLANEOUS MESSAGES																																												
Segment [1]	60																																											
Congestion Control	79	both							●				●								●																							
Facility	62					both											●				●																							
Information	7B	both	both					●					●								●																							
Notify	6E	both										●								●																							
Status	7D	both	both	both									●		●						●		●	●	●	●	●									●							
Status Enquiry	75	both	both																		●																						
Register	64					both											●				●																							

DIRECTION: u→n = User-to-network only   n→u = Network-to-user only   both = Sent by either network or user

NOTE 1: The SEGMENT message is listed in I.451, but its use and corresponding Information Elements are not defined.

- *Call identity:* Provides a unique identification of a suspended call across the user-network interface.

- *Call state:* Describes the current state of a call or access connection.

- *Channel identification:* Identifies the requested channel within the interface(s) controlled by these signaling procedures.

- *Facility:* (This information element was a part of Q.931 in 1984. Most of the description of this information element has been moved out of the 1988 version of Q.931 and moved to Q.932. See the Q.932 description below.)

- *Progress indicator:* Describes an event that has occurred during the life of a call. For example, this information element may indicate that the origination or destination address refers to a non-ISDN party, the call is not over an end-to-end ISDN path, or in-band signaling is being used.

- *Network-specific facilities:* Indicates that network-specific facilities are being invoked.

- *Notification indicator:* Carries information pertaining to a call, such as user suspended, user resumed, or a change in the bearer service.

- *Display:* Supplies information that may be displayed by user equipment.

- *Date/time:* Provides date and time information to the user. Indicates when the message was generated by the network.

- *Keypad facility:* Used to convey IA5 characters, e.g., characters entered from a terminal keyboard.

- *Signal:* Allows the network to convey information to a user regarding tones and alerting signals, e.g., can indicate the absence of any tone or the presence of a dial tone, busy or network congestion (reorder) signal, call waiting tone, or various ringing patterns.

- *Switchhook:* Indicates the status of the terminal switchhook to the network for use in supplementary services (i.e., on-hook or off-hook).

- *Feature activation:* (See the Q.932 description below.)

- *Feature indication:* (See the Q.932 description below.)

- *Information rate:* Notifies the terminating user of the throughput that is indicated in the incoming X.25 CALL REQUEST packet.

- *End-to-end transit delay:* Used to request and indicate the nominal maximum permissible transit delay applicable on a per-call basis to that X.25 virtual call.

- *Transit delay selection and indication:* Used to request and indicate the nominal maximum permissible transit delay applicable on a per-call basis to that virtual circuit.

- *Packet layer binary parameters:* Indicates the requested layer 3 (e.g., X.25 PLP) parameter values for the call. These include the modulo of DATA packet sequencing, and whether Fast Select, expedited data (e.g., an X.25 Interrupt), or delivery confirmation service (e.g., X.25 D-bit procedures) is required.

- *Packet layer window size:* Indicates the requested layer 3 transmit window size for DATA packets (i.e., the allowable number of outstanding DATA packets). The window size for both directions of transmission is specified.

- *Packet size:* Indicates the requested packet size to be used for the call. The packet size for both directions of transmission is specified.

- *Calling party number:* Identifies the network address of the originating party of a call.

- *Calling party subaddress:* Identifies the subaddress associated with the origin of a call. (Subaddresses are defined in CCITT Recommendation I.330.)

- *Called party number:* Identifies the network address of the called party of a call.

- *Called party subaddress:* Identifies the called party's subaddress. (Subaddresses are defined in CCITT Recommendation I.330.)

- *Redirecting number:* Identifies the number from which a call diversion or transfer was invoked.

- *Transit network selection:* Identifies a transit network for the establishment of this call, e.g., allows a user to select the interexchange carrier when placing a call across LATA boundaries in the United States or allows the selection of an international carrier.

- *Restart indicator:* Identifies the facility (i.e., channel or interface) to be restarted.

- *Low-layer compatibility:* Provides a means which should be used for compatibility checking of low-layer protocols by an addressed entity.

- *High-layer compatibility:* Provides a method which should be used by the remote user for high-layer protocol compatibility checking. This information element is passed transparently through the ISDN from the call originator to the addressed party.

- *User-user:*   Conveys information between ISDN users. The user information in this information element is carried transparently by the ISDN and is delivered to the remote user.

ISDN user-network messages to support supplementary services are defined in Recommendation Q.932 (I.452), a new recommendation in 1988. Recommendation Q.932 defines six additional information elements, also shown in Table C.1:

- *Endpoint identifier:*   Indicates the user service identifier and terminal identifier for the purpose of terminal identification or to indicate a specific terminal for the purpose of terminal selection.

- *Facility:*   Indicates the invocation and operation of supplementary services.

- *Feature activation:*   Used to invoke a supplementary service.

- *Feature indication:*   Allows the network to convey feature indications to the user regarding the status of a supplementary service.

- *Information request:*   Provides the capability for requesting additional information and signaling completion of the information request.

- *Service profile identification:*   Allows the user to initiate automatic assignment of the user service identifier and terminal identifier.

Standards Sources

American National Standards Institute
Sales Department
1430 Broadway
New York, NY 10018
212-642-4900

AT&T Customer Information Center
P.O. Box 19901
Indianapolis, IN 46219
800-432-6600 (within continental U.S.)
317-352-8557 (outside continental U.S.)

Bell Communications Research
Documentation Coordinator
60 New England Avenue
Piscataway, NJ 08854
201-699-5800

CCITT
United Nations Bookstore
Room GA-32B
UN General Assembly Building
New York, NY 10017
212-963-7680

Exchange Carriers' Standards Association
5430 Grosvenor Lane
Bethesda, MD 20814-2122
301-564-4505

U.S. Department of Commerce
National Technical Information Service
5285 Port Royal Road
Springfield, VA 22161
703-487-4650

United States Telephone Association
900 19th Street, N.W., Suite 800
Washington, D.C.
202-835-3100

Glossary

access protocols The set of procedures which enable a user to obtain services from a network.

access unit (AU) Device providing ISDN access to a packet switched service or network.

adaptive differential pulse code modulation (ADPCM) Voice compression scheme that converts 8-bit pulse code modulation bit streams to 4 bits, providing a digital voice rate of 32 kbps (rather than PCM's 64 kbps); defined in CCITT Recommendation G.721.

alternating mark inversion (AMI) Digital data signaling scheme where 0s are sent as 0 V and 1s are sent as signals with alternating positive and negative polarity.

American National Standards Institute (ANSI) U.S. coordinator of national standards activity and U.S. representative to ISO.

analog Signals or data that are continuous; that is, they may take on any value within some range of values (e.g., human voice).

application layer Layer 7 of the OSI Reference Model; provides specific network services and applications to the user, such as message handling systems, directory services, virtual terminal emulation, and network management.

application part Protocols corresponding to higher-layer functions in SS7.

associated signaling Signaling mode in a CCS network where messages related to adjacent signaling points are carried over a link directly interconnecting the two points. One of the modes supported by SS7.

asynchronous transfer mode (ATM) A transmission scheme that assigns time to users as needed, providing service for time-sensitive and time-insensitive applications; ATM will be used in broadband ISDN.

asynchronous transmission Transmission scheme where each octet is preceded by a single Start bit and followed by a Stop interval lasting for at least one bit-time; typically used in terminal-to-computer communications. The term *asynchronous* refers to the variable timing between characters and is sometimes used to refer to any time-insensitive application.

Automated Calling Card Service (ACCS) Telephone company service that allows automatic billing to a telephone company calling card.

automatic call distribution (ACD) Service or devices that automatically route calls to customers in geographically distributed locations, usually served by the same central office.

Automatic Number Identification (ANI)   Ability of the network to notify the called party of the calling party's number and/or directory listing. Also called Calling Party Line Identification (CPLID) service and Calling Line Identification Presentation (CLIP).

B-channel   Bearer service channel operating at 64 kbps, carrying user voice and data.

bandwidth   The width of a channel's passband; e.g., the bandwidth of a channel with a 300 to 3400-Hz passband is 3100 Hz, or 3.1 kHz.

basic rate interface (BRI)   One of the access methods to an ISDN, comprising two B-channels and one D-channel (2B + D); described in CCITT Recommendation I.430.

bearer service   The basic set of services offered over the B-channel that provides the capability to exchange signals between two user-network interfaces.

Bell Communications Research (Bellcore)   Main research and development organization for regional Bell operating companies after the breakup of AT&T.

Bell operating company (BOC)   The 22 local telephone companies formed after the breakup of AT&T.

Bipolar 8 Zero Substitution (B8ZS)   A signaling method used in the 1.544-Mbps PRI to ensure that no octet contains all 0s, thus satisfying the ones density requirements; an all-zero octet is filled with a special signaling pattern.

bit-oriented protocol   A type of data link layer protocol commonly used in ISDN applications, based upon ISO's High-level Data Link Control (HDLC) protocol. Bit-oriented protocols usually use this frame format or a variant: a Flag (01111110) to indicate the beginning of the frame, an Address field to indicate the sender or intended receiver, a Control field to indicate the frame type and carry sequence numbers, an Information field to carry the data, a Frame check sequence field for bit error detection, and another Flag to indicate the end of the frame; to ensure that an unwanted Flag bit pattern does not occur, zero-bit insertion is used for transparency. LAPD (ISDN), LAPB (X.25), V.120 (rate adaption), and the Signaling Link protocol (SS7) are all bit-oriented protocols based on HDLC.

bit-stuffing   See *zero-bit insertion*.

broadband   In ISDN, channels supporting rates above the primary rate (1.544 or 2.048 Mbps). In general data communications, usually refers to analog, modulated signals, and a bandwidth greater than that of the voiceband.

broadband ISDN (B-ISDN)   ISDN services using broadband channels.

broadcast   Unidirectional transmission from a single point to one or more subscribers.

C-plane   The control plane within the ISDN protocol architecture; these protocols are for the transfer of information for the control of user connections and the allocation/deallocation of network resources; C-plane functions include call establishment, call termination, changing service characteristics during the call (e.g., alternate speech/unrestricted 64-kbps data), and requesting supplementary services. (See *U-plane.*)

Call Reference Value (CRV)   A number carried in all Q.931 (I.451) messages, providing a local identifier for a given ISDN call.

central office (C.O.)   Telephone company switching office providing local access to the telephone network and services. Also called an end office, local office, or class 5 office.

Centrex (or central exchange)   A service offering from the LEC that provides local switching applications similar to those provided by an on-site PBX; with Centrex, there is no on-site switching and all customer connections go directly back to the C.O.

circuit-mode   *Circuit switching* bearer services offered by an ISDN.

circuit switching   A switching procedure where two devices are connected by a physical resource that is dedicated to the parties for the duration of the call.

class 5 office   See *central office.*

code violation   In alternating mark inversion signaling schemes, a code violation occurs when two signal pulses in a row have the same polarity; often used for synchronization, timing, or the indication of a special event.

coder/decoder (CODEC)   Device used to convert analog signals to digital bit streams and vice versa; used to allow voice and video communication over digital networks.

Common Channel Interoffice Signaling (CCIS)   North American version of Signaling System No. 6 (SS6) introduced by AT&T.

common channel signaling (CCS)   Out-of-band network signaling whereby several voice trunks share a common signaling channel. CCS networks include SS6 (CCIS) and SS7.

companding   The algorithm specifying how the amplitude of the voice signal is mapped onto a nonlinear scale in *pulse code modulation (PCM)*; two such algorithms are specified in CCITT Recommendation G.711, namely, the A-law (used in most parts of the world) and the μ-law (used mostly in North America).

Custom Local Area Signaling Services (CLASS)   A set of services that can be offered by a telephone company that has implemented SS7; CLASS services are based upon the network's knowledge of the calling party's telephone number.

customer-premises equipment (CPE)   According to the FCC, any communications equipment placed on the customer's site.

cyclic redundancy check (CRC)   Mathematical algorithm used to detect bit errors in data transmission; implemented in chips with shift registers and exclusive-OR gates, thus adding no processing delay.

D-channel   The ISDN out-of-band signaling channel, carrying ISDN user-network signals; it can also be used to carry packet-mode user data. The D-channel operates at 16 kbps in the BRI and 64 kbps in the PRI.

data circuit-terminating equipment (DCE)   In X.25, network nodes terminating the user's access circuit, i.e., a packet switch. In some uses, DCE refers to data communications equipment, or modems.

Data Link Control Identifier (DLCI)   The logical link identifier, comprising the Service Access Point Identifier (SAPI) and Terminal Endpoint Identifier (TEI) subfields of the LAPD Address field.

data link layer   Layer 2 of the OSI Reference Model; responsible for error-free communication between adjacent devices in the network.

data terminal equipment (DTE)   In X.25, the host computer connected to a PSPDN. In general, any data device generating digital data, including computers, PCs, terminals, or printers.

Data User Part (DUP)   Higher-layer application protocols in SS7 for the exchange of circuit switched data; not supported by ISDNs.

delay insensitive   See *time insensitive.*

delay sensitive   See *time sensitive.*

demand service   A bearer service in which the communications path is established immediately, at the time of the user's request.

digital   Signals or data that are discrete; that is, they may only take on specified values within a range of values (e.g., binary data streams containing only 0s and 1s).

Digital Multiplexed Interface (DMI)   A standard for PBX-computer communications that is compatible with the ISDN PRI.

digital subscriber line (or loop) (DSL)   A local loop carrying digital signals.

Digital Subscriber Signaling System No. 1 (DSS 1)   The ISDN user-network interface, comprising a data link layer and network layer; described in CCITT Recommendations Q.920/Q.921 (LAPD) and Q.930/Q.931/Q.932, respectively.

disassociated signaling   Signaling mode in a CCS network where signaling messages are carried on paths totally separate from the voice trunks; the signaling network, then, is entirely separate from the network that it is controlling. Not one of the modes supported by SS7.

dual-tone multifrequency (DTMF)   The tones generated by a tone-dialing telephone.

duplex   See *full-duplex.*

E.164   CCITT recommendation defining the ISDN numbering plan; also called Recommendation I.331.

E-channel   A 64-kbps channel defined in the CCITT 1984 ISDN recommendations for PBX-to-SS7 connections; dropped from the 1988 recommendations.

Echo Canceller with Hybrid (ECH)   A device that will be used to allow full-duplex, digital communication over a two-wire local loop. ECH is a part of ANSI standard T1.601 describing the two-wire U reference point BRI.

enbloc The ability of an ISDN terminal to send the called party's ISDN number in a single SETUP message. (See *overlap.*)

end office See *central office.*

Enhanced 911 service (E911) A service allowing a single 911 dispatch center to cover a large regional area, using SS7 signaling between several local exchanges.

European Computer Manufacturers' Association (ECMA) An organization in Europe comprising computer manufacturers and vendors, forming standards in many areas related to computers and communications.

Exchange Carriers' Standards Association (ECSA) A U.S. organization comprising the common carriers; secretariat for ANSI T1-series standards on telecommunications.

exchange termination (ET) That portion of the local exchange (LE) with responsibility for the LE's communication with the rest of the ISDN.

extended superframe format (ESF) A multiframing strategy for T1 carriers that is nearly identical to the 1.544-Mbps PRI multiframing format; an ESF multiframe comprises 24 T1 frames.

E1 carrier In the digital TDM hierarchy used in Europe and many other parts of the world (outside of North America and Japan), a 2.048-Mbps digital carrier multiplexing 30 voice channels; a single E1 frame carries an 8-bit voice digitization sample from each of the 32 channels plus an 8-bit signaling channel plus an 8-bit framing channel; 8000 256-bit frames are transmitted each second.

facsimile (fax) A communications service allowing documents to be transferred through the telephone network over voice-grade lines; designated Group 1, 2, 3, or 4, depending upon capabilities. Group 1 through 3 fax uses analog facilities and requires 10 or more s to transmit a page of information. Group 4 digital facsimile can transmit a page in 3 to 4 s over 64-kbps digital channels.

Feature Key Management protocol An ISDN protocol invoked when a user presses a feature key on the ISDN terminal but not on the dialing pad. (See *stimulus protocols.*)

Federal Communications Commission (FCC) The U.S. federal commission with primary responsibility to regulate the telephone industry.

frame In ISDN, the unit of transmission at the physical layer or data link layer; physical frames are fixed-size blocks of transmitted signals and contain some sort of frame delimiters; data link frames are variable-length groups of octets, typically delimited by a special 8-bit pattern called a Flag (01111110).

frame alignment sequence (FAS) A bit sequence used to ensure that receivers maintain synchronization of incoming physical layer frames.

frame check sequence (FCS) The portion in a data link frame containing the remainder from the cyclic redundancy check (CRC) bit-error detection calculation.

frame relay   An ISDN packet-mode service using a minimal set of LAPD procedures across the user-network interface, providing unacknowledged transfer of frames between users; additional layer 2 and layer 3 functions must be provided by the end users. In frame relay 1, the additional layer 2 functions are provided by any data link protocol of the user's choosing; in frame relay 2, additional layer 2 functions are provided by Recommendation I.441 Extended (I.441*). The layer 3 protocol is always specified by the user. Frame relay is described in Recommendation I.122.

frame switching   An ISDN packet-mode service using an extension to the LAPD protocol across the user-network interface, called I.441 Extended (I.441*). Layer 3 procedures must be provided by the end users. Frame switching is described in Recommendation I.122.

frequency division multiplexing (FDM)   A form of multiplexing where users share a communications facility by splitting the bandwidth; each user is assigned a specific frequency passband.

full-duplex   Bidirectional communications facility where transmissions may travel in both directions simultaneously. Also called duplex.

Functional protocol   An ISDN protocol that is invoked when the user presses certain keys on the ISDN terminal and the terminal exchanges a set of defined messages with the network; differs from *stimulus protocols* since the intelligence to request services is in the ISDN terminal.

general attribute   Those attributes of a bearer service describing additional features of the service, such as supplementary services, performance, and quality of service.

H-channel   Higher bandwidth ISDN channels. H_0-channels are equivalent to 6 B-channels and operate at 384 kbps, H_{11}-channels are equivalent to 24 B-channels and operate at 1.536 Mbps, and H_{12}-channels are equivalent to 30 B-channels and operate at 1.920 Mbps. H_2- and H_4-channels have also been proposed for B-ISDN applications.

half duplex   Bidirectional communications facility where transmissions may travel in either one direction or the other at any given time. Sometimes called simplex outside of North America.

High-Density Bipolar—3 zeroes (HDB3)   A signaling method used in the 2.048-Mbps PRI to ensure that no octet contains all zeroes; an all-zero octet is filled with a special signaling pattern.

High-level Data Link Control (HDLC)   The ISO standard for bit-oriented protocols; LAPD, LAPB, V.120, and the SS7 data link layer protocol are all based upon HDLC.

host   An end-communicating system in a network, e.g., a telephone in the telephone network or a computer in a data network.

I.331   See *E.164*.

I.430   A CCITT recommendation describing the physical layer aspects of the basic rate interface (BRI).

I.431   A CCITT recommendation describing the physical layer aspects of the primary rate interface (PRI).

I.440   See *Q.920.*

I.441   See *Q.921.*

I.450   See *Q.930.*

I.451   See *Q.931.*

I.452   See *Q.932.*

I.462   See *X.31.*

I.463   See *V.110.*

I.465   See *V.120.*

independent telephone company (ITC)   In the United States, those telephone companies that were not part of the Bell system; non-Bell operating companies.

information access attribute   Those attributes of a bearer service relating to how the user will access the network across the local user-network interface, such as the channel to use, rate adaption algorithm, and required protocol support; information access attributes do not have to be the same at all user-network interfaces.

information transfer attribute   Those attributes of a bearer service relating to the transfer of information across the network, such as the transfer rate, transfer mode, structure, etc.

integrated analog network (IAN)   A telephone network where all components, from telephones to trunk lines to switches, are analog in nature.

integrated digital network (IDN)   A telephone network where all components, from telephones to trunk lines to switches, are digital in nature.

Integrated Services Digital Network (ISDN)   A digital network that provides a wide variety of services, a standard set of user-network messages, and integrated access to the network.

integrated services private branch exchange (ISPBX)   A CCITT term describing an ISDN-compatible PBX.

integrated voice/data terminal (IVDT)   An ISDN terminal that allows both voice and data communications.

intelligent network (IN)   In ISDN, an expanded set of services that are available to the user from the network. IN deployment will closely track that of SS7 but requires major advances in network switch architecture, signaling network capabilities, and intelligent peripheral capabilities.

interexchange carrier (IEC)   In the United States, a long distance telephone company, specifically, a communications carrier that can provide inter-LATA (i.e., long distance), but not intra-LATA (i.e., local), service. Also abbreviated *IC* and *IXC*.

International Alphabet No. 5 (IA5)   An ISO standard character code, nearly identical to the American Standard Code for Information Interchange (ASCII).

International Organization for Standardization (ISO)   An international organization forming standards in many areas. Data communications standards include HDLC, the OSI Reference Model, and OSI protocols.

International Telecommunication Union (ITU)   An agency of the United Nations, the parent organization of the CCITT.

International Telegraph and Telephone Consultative Committee (CCITT)   A committee of the International Telecommunication Union (ITU) concerned with recommendations regarding public telegraph, telephone, and data networks.

ISDN number   The address of a user's ISDN interface, i.e., what we today call a telephone number; routing of calls through the ISDN will be based upon the called ISDN number, while ANI-type services will deliver the calling ISDN number.

ISDN User Part (ISUP)   Higher-layer protocols for SS7 that support signaling for ISDN applications.

Keypad protocol   An ISDN protocol invoked when a user presses a sequence of keys on the ISDN terminal's dialing pad (0–9, #, *). (See *stimulus protocols*.)

Line Information Data Base (LIDB)   A telephone company database that allows customized services, such as credit card calling.

Link Access Procedures Balanced (LAPB)   The X.25 data link layer protocol.

Link Access Procedures on the D-channel (LAPD)   The ISDN data link layer protocol specified for the D-channel; described in CCITT Recommendation Q.920 (I.440) and Q.921 (I.441).

local access and transport area (LATA)   U.S. local telephone service areas, defined after the breakup of AT&T.

local area network (LAN)   A communications network interconnecting devices over a geographically small area; characteristics typically include high speeds (>1 Mbps), small geographic area (<10 km), low error rate, and limited to several hundred devices.

local exchange (LE)   An ISDN central office.

local exchange carrier (LEC)   In the United States, a local telephone company; specifically, a communications carrier that can provide intra-LATA (i.e., local) but not inter-LATA (i.e., long distance) service.

local loop   The physical connection between the central office and telephone network customer; the local loop usually uses 22 to 26 AWG twisted pair wire, although optical fiber is being used in some areas.

local office   See *central office.*

local termination (LT)   That portion of the local exchange responsible for functions related to termination of the local loop.

M-channel   A 4-kbps maintenance channel defined in ANS T1.601 for NT1-LE communication over the two-wire BRI.

maximum service integration scenario   See *X.31 Case B.*

Message Handling System (MHS)   A standard electronic mail system based on CCITT X.400-series recommendations.

Message Transfer Part (MTP)   SS7 protocols equivalent to the physical layer, data link layer, and lower sublayer of the network layer. These layers are the Signaling Data Link, Signaling Link, and Signaling Network Management and Message Handling protocols, respectively.

minimum service integration scenario   See *X.31 Case A.*

Modification of Final Judgment (MFJ)   The U.S. Department of Justice decree (1982) settling the U.S. Government's 1974 antitrust suit against AT&T, resulting in the breakup of AT&T in 1984.

modulator/demodulator (modem)   A device that converts digital data into analog tones, and vice versa; used to allow data communications over the analog telephone network.

multiframing   A mechanism to logically group together sets of individual physical layer frames, allowing for the definition of channels for physical layer signaling; CCITT Recommendations I.430 (BRI) and I.431 (PRI), as well as ANS T1.601, define multiframing formats.

multiplexing   The ability of many users to share a single communications facility; common approaches are frequency division multiplexing, time compression multiplexing, and time division multiplexing.

narrowband   In ISDN, usually taken to mean the opposite of broadband, i.e., ISDN channels operating at speeds up to the primary rate (1.544 or 2.048 Mbps). In general communications, usually means a channel with a bandwidth less than the 3.1-kHz voiceband.

National Institute of Standards and Technology (NIST)   Formerly the National Bureau of Standards (NBS), a U.S. Department of Commerce agency responsible for creating standards and policies related to high-technology issues.

network   A collection of communicating devices, switches, and links that are interconnected and autonomous.

network layer   Layer 3 of the OSI Reference Model; primarily responsible for congestion control, routing, and network accounting.

network termination type 1 (NT1)   The ISDN device responsible for the termination of the ISDN transmission facility at the customer premises.

network termination type 2 (NT2)   An ISDN device responsible for on-premises communication distribution, such as a PBX, LAN, or host computer.

node   A device in a network that is not functioning as an end-communicating device; e.g., a switch in the telephone network or a store-and-forward multiplexer in a data network.

nonassociated signaling   Signaling mode in a CCS network where signaling between two offices may not follow the same path as the user information between those two offices; this mode is not supported by SS7.

North American Numbering Plan (NANP)   Numbering plan for North American telephone networks; every telephone number is ten digits in length, where the first three digits identify the area code, the next three digits identify the central office, and the final four digits identify the user's line.

octet   An 8-bit quantity; used in lieu of the term *byte*.

ones density   A requirement of T1 networks and the PRI that a certain number of 1 bits occur per unit time so that physical layer timing and synchronization is maintained. Current T1 specifications do not allow more than 15 contiguous 0s in a transmission and require approximately 23 1s in every frame.

Open Systems Interconnection (OSI) Reference Model   A 7-layer model architecture for open systems, allowing communication between computers from different vendors using different network architectures; initially proposed by ISO, adopted by CCITT and most major computer manufacturers around the world; model and protocols defined in CCITT X.200-series recommendations.

Operations, Maintenance, and Administration Part (OMAP)   Higher-layer protocols for SS7, providing network management, operations, and maintenance functions.

overlap   When an ISDN terminal sends the called party's ISDN number in separate messages, one digit at a time. (See *enbloc*.)

packet assembly/disassembly (PAD) facility   In X.25, provides access to a PSPDN by an asynchronous terminal; at the sender's side, the PAD collects a series of asynchronous characters and builds an X.25 packet; at the receiver's side, the PAD accepts an X.25 packet and delivers individual asynchronous characters to the terminal; the PAD facility is based upon Recommendations X.3, X.28, and X.29.

packet handler (PH)   A packet switch (or X.25 DCE equivalent device) in an ISDN.

Packet Layer Protocol (PLP)   The X.25 level 3 protocol.

packet mode   *Packet switching* bearer services offered from an ISDN. (See *X.31, X.31 Case A,* and *X.31 Case B.*)

packet switched network (PSN)   A data communications network that uses packet switching technology.

packet switched public data network (PSPDN)   A public data network using packet switching technology; commonly supports the X.25 interface.

packet switching   A switching procedure whereby two parties have a logical connection across a network, but no dedicated facilities, and where units of transmission have a maximum size (usually 128 or 256 octets); this is a store-and-forward technique where nodes in the network may store a packet for some time before forwarding it to the next node in line.

pair gain   A device in a network that provides multiplexing so that more conversations can be carried by fewer twisted pair; these devices are usually electronic systems positioned somewhere between the central office and the customer premises; a T1 line is a type of pair gain since 24 voice conversations can be carried over two twisted pair.

passband   The frequency spectrum that can pass through a channel, which may be limited by the characteristics of the medium or by load coils; the passband of the telephone local loop is 300 to 3400 Hz.

perfect scheduling with fairness   Contention resolution scheme used on the D-channel in the point-to-multipoint BRI, ensuring that all collisions (i.e., the result of multiple transmitters) have a winner; in this way, transmissions are never lost because of collisions and the D-channel is always busy as long as one TE wants to transmit. Fairness is employed to ensure that no transmitter(s) can dominate the channel.

permanent circuit service   A bearer service in which the communications path is established at subscription time and remains available for a predetermined amount of time.

phantom power   In the CCITT BRI standard, the ability of the NT1 to provide power to the TE1/TA over the transmit and receive wire pairs.

physical layer   Layer 1 of the OSI Reference Model; primarily responsible for the transport of bits between adjacent devices in a network, describing electrical and mechanical characteristics of the connection and media.

plain old telephone service (POTS)   The ability of the public telephone network to offer basic telephone service only; i.e., call setup, connection, and termination.

point-to-multipoint ISDN configuration   A physical connection in which a single network termination supports multiple terminal equipment devices.

point-to-multipoint connection   The connection established between one user-network interface and more than one other user-network interface, e.g., a conference call.

point-to-point ISDN configuration   A physical connection in which a single network termination supports one terminal equipment device.

point-to-point connection   The connection established between two specified user-network interfaces, e.g., an ordinary telephone call.

Postal, Telephone, and Telegraph (PTT) administration   The government agency that controls and/or regulates the public communications networks in most countries outside of the United States.

presentation layer   Layer 6 of the OSI Reference Model; primarily responsible for general user services and the representation of user data, such as encryption, text compression, code conversion, and file format conversion.

primary rate interface (PRI)   One of the access methods to an ISDN, comprising either 23 B-channels and one D-channel (23B + D), 24 B-channels (24B), or 30 B-channels and one D-channel (30B + D); described in CCITT Recommendation I.431.

private automatic branch exchange (PABX)   An automatic PBX.

private branch exchange (PBX)   A customer-site telephone switch; common usage today implies that a PBX is an automatic switch, although a PBX could be under the control of an operator (or attendant).

Private Virtual Network (PVN)   An SS7 service that allows a subscriber to create a private subnetwork over public facilities.

protocol   In communications, the set of rules that governs the exchange of information between two devices, allowing them to effectively communicate with each other.

Protocol Discriminator   The first octet of every ISDN layer 3 protocol transmission, identifying the specific layer 3 protocol being used; Q.931 and X.25 are the current choices.

pseudo-ternary signaling   Digital data signaling scheme used across the BRI S/T reference points, where 1s are sent as 0 V and 0s are sent with alternating positive and negative voltage.

public data network (PDN)   A public network offering data communications service.

Public Safety Answering Point (PSAP)   Centralized dispatch center for E911 services.

public switched telephone network (PSTN)   The public circuit-switched telephone network.

public telephone network (PTN)   A public network offering telephone service (see *public switched telephone network*).

pulse code modulation (PCM)   Voice digitization scheme that samples the analog voice signal 8000 times per second and converts each sample to an 8-bit stream, yielding a digital voice rate of 64 kbps; defined in CCITT Recommendation G.711.

Q.920   A CCITT recommendation describing the general aspects of the Link Access Procedures on the D-channel (LAPD); also called Recommendation I.440.

Q.921   A CCITT recommendation describing the operational procedures of the Link Access Procedures on the D-channel (LAPD); also called Recommendation I.441.

Q.930   A CCITT recommendation describing the general aspects of the D-channel level 3 protocol; also called Recommendation I.450.

Q.931   A CCITT recommendation describing D-channel user-network messages for basic call control; also called Recommendation I.451.

Q.932   A CCITT recommendation describing D-channel user-network messages for supplementary services; also called Recommendation I.452.

Q-channel   An 800-bps maintenance channel defined in CCITT Recommendation I.430 for use with the BRI.

quantization error   The difference between the actual analog voice signal and the digital representation of that signal; this error is the result of mapping an analog (continuous) signal onto a digital (discrete) scale.

quasi-associated signaling   A special case of nonassociated signaling; a signaling mode in a CCS network where all messages related to a given call will follow the same, nonassociated path. One of the modes supported by SS7.

R reference point   The protocol reference point between non-ISDN terminals (TE2) and terminal adaptors (TAs); the actual protocols used here are determined by the TA manufacturer.

rate adaption (or adaptation)   Algorithms used to map a user's actual bit transfer rate (from 50 to 56 kbps, synchronous or asynchronous) to the 64-kbps speed of the B-channel. (See *V.110* and *V.120*.)

reference point   A conceptual interface between two types of ISDN devices. (See *R, S, T, U,* and *V reference points*.)

regional Bell operating company (RBOC)   The seven regional holding companies formed after the breakup of AT&T.

reserved circuit service   A service in which the communications path is established at a later time, in response to a user's request.

restricted digital information (RDI)   64-kbps bit streams where the eighth bit of each octet is always set to 1, thus ensuring that the bit stream never contains all-zero octets. (Compare *unrestricted digital information*.)

S reference point   The protocol reference point between ISDN terminals (TE1) and network termination equipment (NT1 or NT2); these ISDN protocols are written by the CCITT.

service access point (SAP)   An address or other access point at a host where higher-layer services may be obtained by lower layers.

Service Access Point Identifier (SAPI)   A subfield in the LAPD Address field which indicates the type of level 3 service being obtained.

Service Control Point (SCP)   An SS7 database that controls routing and special services.

session layer   Layer 5 of the OSI Reference Model; primarily responsible for process-to-process communication between two machines.

Signaling Connection Control Part (SCCP)   An SS7 protocol corresponding to the upper sublayer of the OSI network layer.

signaling point (SP)   An SS7 end-office; the SS7 signaling network interconnects SPs.

Signaling System No. 6 (SS6)   The CCITT version of CCIS, one of the first common channel signaling networks.

Signaling System No. 7 (SS7)   The high-speed, digital common channel signaling network required for ISDN applications; also provides a myriad of services based upon the calling party's ISDN number. Described in CCITT Q.700-series recommendations; the U.S. national version is described in ANSI T1.110-series standards.

signal transfer point (STP)   An SS7 switching point.

simplex   In North America, one-way transmission, such as a TV or radio broadcast. In some places, simplex is used as a synonym for *half-duplex.*

stimulus protocol   Protocols that are invoked when the user presses a sequence of keys on the ISDN terminal *and* the terminal passes the identity of the keys on to the network; the network determines what action to take based upon the identity of the keys that were pressed; unlike *functional protocols,* the terminal has no knowledge of the procedures used to invoke the service. (See *Keypad protocol* and *Feature Key Management protocol.*)

study group (SG)   CCITT committees with specific standard-setting tasks.

subaddress   Additional addressing that may be used in an ISDN call to identify a specific terminal at an ISDN interface, such as a specific phone on a PBX; subaddresses do not identify the ISDN interface in any way, thus are not used by the network for routing purposes.

superframe   An ANS T1.601 (two-wire BRI) multiframe. (See *multiframing.*)

supplementary services   Additional services offered to an ISDN customer that are based upon information known to the network, such as the calling party's ISDN number; these are not enhanced services because they do not manipulate user-supplied data in any way.

switching   The process of interconnecting two devices on a network; two common approaches are circuit switching and packet switching.

synchronous transfer mode (STM)   A transmission scheme that assigns time to users on a fixed, scheduled basis.

synchronous transmission   Transmission scheme where octets are grouped together for transmission into units called *frames*; typically used in computer-to-computer communications; the term *synchronous* is sometimes used to refer to any *time-sensitive* application.

T reference point   The protocol reference point between NT1 and NT2; these ISDN protocols are created by the CCITT.

telecommunication   The transmission of signals representing voice, video, data, or images.

telecommunication service   See *teleservice*.

telecommuter   A person who commutes to the office via a telecommunications link rather than by physically traveling; the telecommuter works at home and communicates with colleagues via such devices as the telephone, PC, and/or fax machine.

telemetry service   A teleservice that typically uses short messages at very low transmission speeds.

Telephone User Part (TUP)   A set of higher-layer protocols for SS7 supporting signaling for telephone communications; although they are being defined in many parts of the world, they will not be supported in the North American SS7 networks.

teleservice   ISDN value-added services that may be offered to a subscriber by another ISDN user or by the network itself.

terminal adaptor (TA)   A protocol converter used to allow a non-ISDN terminal (TE2) to access the network using ISDN protocols and procedures.

Terminal Endpoint Identifier (TEI)   A subfield in the LAPD Address field that identifies a given TE device on the ISDN interface.

terminal equipment (TE)   Any ISDN-compatible device that may be placed on the network, such as a telephone, IVDT, PBX, TV, PC, computer, etc.

terminal equipment type 1 (TE1)   ISDN-compatible terminal equipment.

terminal equipment type 2 (TE2)   Non-ISDN-compatible terminal equipment.

time compression multiplexing (TCM)   A multiplexing scheme where the communications facility operates at high speed in half-duplex mode, simulating lower-speed, full-duplex operation; used in some two-wire digital services.

time division multiplexing (TDM)   A multiplexing scheme where several users are assigned a specific time slot on a communications facility.

time insensitive   Those applications where a slight delay in transmission will not change the inherent meaning of the data, e.g., most interactive data communication. Also called delay insensitive.

time sensitive   Those applications where a variable network-induced delay will change the meaning of the data and, therefore, cannot be tolerated, e.g., voice, video, and real-time data. Also called delay sensitive.

Transaction Capabilities Application Part (TCAP)   A set of higher-layer protocols for SS7 to provide transaction-oriented services, such as credit card billing.

transport layer   Layer 4 of the OSI Reference Model; primarily responsible for error-free communication between two hosts across the subnetwork comprising the intermediate nodes.

twisted pair   A pair of 22 to 26 American wire gauge (AWG) (0.036 to 0.016 in) insulated copper wires that are twisted in a helix around each other to reduce noise and electrical interference; typically used for the telephone local loop and ISDN digital subscriber line.

two binary, one quaternary (2B1Q)   The signaling method used across the two-wire BRI, U reference point according to ANSI standard T1.601; 2B1Q is a four-level line code, associating 2 bits to each line signal.

T1 carrier   In the digital TDM hierarchy used in North America and Japan, a 1.544-Mbps digital carrier multiplexing 24 voice channels; a single T1 frame carries an 8-bit voice digitization sample from each of the 24 channels plus a single framing bit; 8000 193-bit frames are transmitted each second.

T1.601   An ANSI standard describing the basic rate interface over two-wire digital local loops.

U-plane   The user plane within the ISDN protocol architecture; these protocols are for the transfer of information between user applications, such as digitized voice, video, and data; user plane information may be carried transparently by the network or may be processed or manipulated (e.g., A-law to μ-law conversion). (See *C-plane.*)

U reference point   The protocol reference point between ISDN network termination (NT1) equipment and the LE; the actual protocols across this transmission line are not subject to CCITT standardization.

Unrestricted Digital Information (UDI)   Bit streams that may contain any sequence of 0s and 1s, including all-zero octets. (Compare *restricted digital information.*)

user-network interface   The boundary between user equipment (TEs) and network termination equipment (NTs), at which the access protocols apply; the ISDN S and T reference point(s).

user part   Protocols corresponding to the higher layer functions in SS7.

user-user protocols   Higher-layer protocols used between two or more users which enable them to intercommunicate; user-user protocols are typically transparent to the network.

V reference point   The protocol reference point between the local termination (LT) and exchange termination (ET) functions in the LE; the actual protocols used here are determined by the LE manufacturer and are not subject to CCITT standardization.

V.110   A rate adaption scheme to convert asynchronous or synchronous transmission at rates from 50 bps to 19.2 kbps to the B-channel 64-kbps rate; widely used outside of North America; also called Recommendation I.463.

V.120   A rate adaption scheme to convert asynchronous, synchronous, or bit transparent transmissions at rates from 50 bps to 19.2 kbps to the B-channel 64-kbps rate; also provides error correction and statistical multiplexing of multiple low-rate channels onto a single B-channel using an HDLC-like protocol; widely used in North America; also called Recommendation I.465.

value-added service (VAS)   A service provided by a network above and beyond the mere transport of user-originated information, such as message storage for later delivery, code conversion, electronic mail, etc.

virtual circuit   In packet switching, refers to a connection between two hosts where packets are guaranteed to be delivered to the destination and are guaranteed to be delivered in sequence, but no physical lines are dedicated to the connection.

voiceband   A communications channel with a passband of approximately 300 to 3400 Hz, or a bandwidth of 3.1 kHz; the equivalent of the passband necessary for a single voice conversation.

wide area network (WAN)   A network that spans a large geographic scope, such as a national or international telephone or data network.

Wide Area Telecommunications Services (WATS)   A telephone network service that allows a subscriber to pay a flat fee for unlimited outgoing calls (OUTWATS) and/or provides the public with toll-free numbers (800 numbers) where the charges are made to the subscriber (INWATS).

wideband   See *broadband*.

X.25   A CCITT recommendation describing layers 1 through 3 of the user-network interface for PSPDNs.

X.31   A CCITT recommendation describing the support of X.25 DTEs on an ISDN; also called Recommendation I.462.

X.31 Case A   The X.31 case where the packet switching network is totally separate from the ISDN and where packet-mode service can only be offered on the B-channel; the ISDN gives a user a pathway to the PSPDN only; also called minimum service integration scenario.

X.31 Case B   The X.31 case where the packet service is available from the ISDN and where packet-mode service is available on either the B- or D-channel; also called maximum service integration scenario.

X.75   A CCITT recommendation describing layers 1 through 3 of the interface between PSNs, including PSPDNs and ISDNs.

zero-bit insertion   The transparency technique used in bit-oriented protocols; to ensure that an unwanted Flag bit pattern (01111110) does not occur, the transmitter will automatically insert a 0 after any string of five contiguous 1 bits while sending data.

2B1Q   See *two binary, one quaternary*.

Bibliography

Aaron, R. and R. Wyndrum. "Future trends." *IEEE Communications,* March 1986.

Adams, D. E. "U.S. Telecommunications Policy: Directions for the Next Five Years." *IEEE Communications,* January 1989.

Anderson, C. P. "ISDN market opportunity." *IEEE Communications,* December 1987.

ANSI. *American National Standard for Telecommunications - Integrated Services Digital Network - Basic Access Interface for Use on Metallic Loops for Application on the Network Side of the NT - Layer 1 Specification,* Draft ANS T1.601-1988.

AT&T. *AT&T Integrated Services Digital Network (ISDN) Basic Rate Interface Specification.* Technical Reference, PUB 801-802-100, April 1988.

———. *AT&T Integrated Services Digital Network (ISDN) Primary Rate Interface Specification.* Technical Reference, PUB 41449, March 1986.

———. *ISDN Marketing Guide.* AT&T Technologies, 1986.

———. *ISDN Planners Guide.* AT&T Technologies, 1987.

Axner, D. H. "Powerful Tools Inspect, Probe User Networks." *TPT* (Telecommunication Products + Technology), August 1988.

Bellcore. *Advanced Intelligent Network Release 1 Proposal.* Bell Communications Research Special Report SR-NPL-001509, Issue 1, November 1989.

———. *ISDN System Plan.* Bell Communications Research Special Report SR-NPL-000224, Issue 1, June 1985.

———. *Switching Systems Requirements for Call Control Using the ISDN User Part.* Bell Communications Research Technical Requirement TR-TSY-000317, Issue 1, August 1987.

Bendel, J. E. "ISDN: The Learning Continues." *IEEE Communications,* December 1987.

Berberi, N. "T1 to ISDN: How to Get There from Here." *Data Communications,* February 1988.

Bhusri, G. S. "Considerations for ISDN Planning and Implementation." *IEEE Communications,* January 1984.

Boehm, R. J. "SONET: An International Standard." *Telecommunications,* March 1988.

Bosik, B. S. "Time-Compression Multiplexing: Squeezing Digits through Loops." *AT&T Bell Laboratories Record,* February 1984.

Brackett, J. "Fast Packet Switching: A Tutorial." *Telecommunications,* November 1988.

Braue, J. "Will the Local Loop Choke ISDN?" *Data Communications,* October 1988.

Brown, H. R. "British Telecom's ISDN Experience." *IEEE Communications,* December 1987.

Byrne, W. R., T. A. Kilm, B. L. Nelson and M. D. Soneru. "Broadband ISDN Technology and Architecture." *IEEE Network,* January 1989.

Carney, D. L. and E. M. Prell. "Planning for ISDN on the 5ESS Switch." *AT&T Technical Journal,* January/February 1986.

CCITT. Recommendations from the E-, G-, I-, Q-, V-, and X- series. Geneva: ITU, 1989 (CCITT 1988 Blue Books).

Chen, P. "How to Make the Most of ISDN's New LAPD Protocol." *Data Communications,* August 1987.

Chen, T. M. and D. G. Messerschmitt. "Integrated Voice/Data Switching." *IEEE Communications*, June 1988.

Cooper, R. W. "The Moving Target: Marketing ISDN to Businesses." *IEEE Communications*, December 1987.

Delatore, J. P., H. Oehring, and L. C. Stecher. "Implementation of ISDN on the 5ESS Switch." *IEEE Journal on Selected Areas of Communication*, November 1986.

Derfler, F. J., Jr. "Is ISDN Tomorrow's Interoffice Network?" *PC Magazine*, February 13, 1990.

Dicenet, G. *Design and Prospects for the ISDN*. Boston: Artech House, 1987.

Donohoe, D. C., G. H. Johannessen, and R. E. Stone. "Realization of a Signaling System No. 7 network for AT&T." *IEEE Journal on Selected Areas of Communication*, November 1986.

Duc, N. Q. and E. K. Chew. "ISDN Protocol Architecture." *IEEE Communications*, March 1985.

Eigen, D., N. Huang, and R. Koch. "Broadband ISDN and the Central Office." *Telephone Engineer & Management*, December 1, 1986.

Falek, J. I. and M. A. Johnston. "Standards Makers Cementing ISDN Subnetwork Layers." *Data Communications*, October 1987.

Freuck, P. and J. Kutney. "An Approach to Introducing ISDN Basic-Access Terminal Adapters." *Telecommunications*, February 1988.

Gansert, J. A. "Intelligent Network Evolution Issues." *IEEE Communications*, December 1988.

Gantz, J. "SS#7: Its Promises and Pitfalls." *TPT* (Telecommunication Products + Technology), September 1988.

———. "Standards: What They Are. What They Aren't." *Networking Management*, May 1989.

———. "White Paper to Management: ISDN Takes Shape." *TPT* (Telecommunication Products + Technology), January 1989.

Glen, D. V. *Networks, Signaling, and Switching for Post-Divestiture and the ISDN*. Washington, D.C.: U.S. Dept. of Commerce, National Telecommunications and Information Administration, 1986. (NTIA Report 86-191)

———. *Reference Manual for Packet Mode Standards*. Washington, D.C.: U.S. Dept. of Commerce, National Telecommunications and Information Administration, 1987. (NTIA Report 87-211)

Graciosa, H. M. M. "Telecommunications Research and Development in Brazil." *IEEE Communications*, September 1989.

Gulick, D. "What ISDN Brings to the Office of the Future." *Data Communications*, August 1988.

Habara, K. "ISDN: A Look at the Future through the Past." *IEEE Communications*, November 1988.

Händel, R. "Evolution of ISDN Towards Broadband ISDN." *IEEE Network*, January 1989.

Herman, J. G. and M. A. Johnston. "ISDN When? What Your Firm Can Do in the Interim." *Data Communications*, October 1987.

Iffland, F. C., G. D. Norton, and J. M. Waxman. "ISDN Applications: Their Identification and Development." *IEEE Network*, September 1989.

Information Gatekeepers, Inc. *ISDN Field Trial and Implementations in the United States and Around the World*. Boston: IGI, 1988.

Kenedi, R. and C. L. Wong. "Architecture for Implementation." *IEEE Communications*, March 1986.

Kessler, G. C. and R. K. Gojanovich. "Before ISDN: C.O. LANs Offer Voice and Data Networking Now." *LAN*, February 1989.

Kobayashi, K. *Computers and Communications - A Vision of C&C*. Cambridge (MA): The MIT Press, 1986.

Koenig, R. L. "How to Make the PBX-to-ISDN Connection." *Data Communications*, May 1989.

Komiya, T., Y. Suzuki, H. Yamada, and K. Tomita. "An Approach to the Multifunction Graphic Terminal for the ISDN Environment." *IEEE Network*, September 1989.

Lahti, W. G. and S. Kelly. "The Impact of ISDN on the CPE Market." *Telecommunications,* August 1988.

Lamont, J. and M. H. Hui. "Some Experience with LAN Interconnection via Frame Relay." *IEEE Network,* September 1989.

Lechleider, J. W. "Line Codes for Digital Subscriber Lines." *IEEE Communications,* September 1989.

Levin, D. "Private Branch Exchanges: The Best Time to Shop May Be Right Now." *Data Communications,* August 1987.

Lin, N.-S., and C.-P. J. Tzeng. "Full-Duplex Data over Local Loops." *IEEE Communications,* February 1988.

Malek, M. "Integrated Voice and Data Communications Overview." *IEEE Communications,* June 1988.

Mantelman, L. "Tips from Europe's ISDN Pioneers." *Data Communications,* May 1989.

McDonald, J. C. "Constraints Shaping ISDN." *IEEE Communications,* March 1986.

McDonald, J. C. "The Regulatory Challenge of Broadband Technologies." *IEEE Communications,* January 1989.

McNamara, J. E. *Technical Aspects of Data Communication* (3rd ed.). Maynard (MA): Digital Press, 1988.

Mier, E. E. "PBX Trends and Technology Update: Following the Leaders." *Data Communications,* September 1985.

Minzer, S. E. "Broadband ISDN and Asynchronous Transfer Mode (ATM)." *IEEE Communications,* September 1989.

———. and D. R. Spears. "New Directions in Signaling for Broadband ISDN." *IEEE Communications,* February 1989.

Mizuki, K. and R. Hall. "T1 and CEPT Rates Boost Flexibility." *Telephone Engineer & Management,* August 15, 1988.

Mulqueen, J. "In with the New: ISDN Spawns Own Test Gear Market." *Data Communications,* September 1988.

Nesenbergs, M. and P. M. McManamon. *An Introduction to the Technology of Intra- and Interexchange Area Telephone Networks.* Washington, D.C.: U.S. Department of Commerce, 1983. (NTIA Report 83-118)

Nolle, T. "Has Time Bypassed Packet Switching?" *Telecommunications,* July 1988.

Northern Telecom, Inc. *DMS-100 ISDN Implementation,* Issue #3. Research Triangle Park (NC): NTI, 1987.

Ohkoshi, S., K. Matsumoto, and S. Nakano. "A Digital Telephone Set for ISDN." *IEEE Journal on Selected Areas of Communication,* November 1986.

O'Toole, T. J. "ISDN: A Large User's Perspective." *IEEE Communications,* December 1987.

Ramesh, N. S. and Y-L Su. "Chip-Level Solutions for All-Digital ISDN Networks." *Data Communications,* December 1986.

Rey, R. F. (tech. ed.). *Engineering and Operations in the Bell System* (2d ed.). Murray Hill (NJ): AT&T Bell Laboratories, 1984.

Roberts, M. M. "ISDN in University Networks." *IEEE Communications,* December 1987.

Roehr, W. C., Jr. "Inside SS7: A Detailed Look at ISDN's Signaling System Plan." *Data Communications,* October 1985.

Roehr, W. "Knocking on Users' Doors: Signaling System 7." *Data Communications,* February 1989.

Rudigier, J. J. "Army Implementation of ISDN." *IEEE Communications,* December 1987.

Schwartz, M. *Telecommunications Networks: Protocols, Modeling and Analysis.* Reading (MA): Addison-Wesley, 1987.

Seligman, D. R. "Signaling System 7: Mastering It Takes a Special Vocabulary." *Data Communications,* February 1989.

Shafer, T. C. "Packing Data for the ISDN Migration, and Avoiding Costly Baggage." *Data Communications,* November 1984.

Sheridan, P. F. and J. A. Weitzen. "Evaluation of Network Planning and Design for Corporate Internetworks." *IEEE Network,* November 1989.

Skrzypczak, C. S. "The Intelligent Home of 2010." *IEEE Communications,* December 1987.

Snelling, R. K. "Environmental Aspects of ISDN." *IEEE Communications,* December 1987.

———— and K. W. Kaplan. "Services and Revenue Requirements." *IEEE Communications,* March 1986.

Stallings, W. *Data and Computer Communications* (2d ed.). New York: Macmillan, 1988.

————. "Digital Signaling: Which Techniques Are Best—and Why It Matters to You." *Data Communications,* November 1988.

Stephenson, R. W. and S. A. McGaw. "Southwestern Bell Telephone's ISDN experience." *IEEE Network,* September 1989.

Stine, L. L. "Why Are ISDN Standards Important?" *IEEE Communications,* August 1988.

Stoffels, P. R. "Update on 911." *Telephone Engineer & Management,* December 15, 1987.

Strathmeyer, C. "Voice/Data Integration: An Applications Perspective." *IEEE Communications,* December 1987.

Strauss, P. R. "An Update on U.S. Services and Standards." *Data Communications,* May 1989.

Tanenbaum, A. S. *Computer Networks* (2d ed.). Englewood Cliffs (NJ): Prentice-Hall, 1988.

Town, R. S. "Evolving North American Switching Systems with Fast Packet T-1 Carriers." In: *Proc. of INTERFACE '88,* March 28–31, 1988. New York: McGraw-Hill, 1988.

Trouvat, M. "The RENAN Project: Opening up ISDN in France." *IEEE Communications,* December 1987.

Tsuji, H., H. Kawamura, K. Wakayama, and S. Kikuchi. "A Mail and Protocol Conversion Node for ISDN Facsimile Application." *IEEE Network,* September 1989.

United States Telephone Association. *Planning Considerations for Common Channel Signaling Networks Using Signaling System No. 7 Protocol.* Network Planning Subcommittee/CCS-SG, Technical Bulletin NPL 87-106 (June 22, 1987).

Unsoy, M. "How Packet-Mode Transmission Services Will Evolve in ISDN." *Data Communications,* April 1988.

Watanabe, H. "Integrated Office Systems: 1995 and Beyond." *IEEE Communications,* December 1987.

Weissburger, A. J. "The Evolving Versions of ISDN's Terminal Adapter." *Data Communications,* March 1989.

Weisser, F. J. and R. L. Corn. "The Intelligent Network and Forward-Looking Technology." *IEEE Communications,* December 1988.

Woinsky, M. N. "National Performance Standards for Telecommunications Services." *IEEE Communications,* October 1988.

Wolf, D. and S. S. King. "Making the Most of ISDN Now." *Data Communications,* August 1989.

Index

ABOUT THE AUTHOR

Gary C. Kessler currently operates a data communications
training and consulting firm in Colchester, Vermont.
Previously, he held a number of professional positions
including Coordinator of Academic Computing at St.
Michael's College, Winooski, Vermont, Software Engineer
at Lawrence Livermore National Laboratories, Livermore,
California, and Member of the Technical Staff at Hill
Associates, Inc., Winooski, Vermont. Since 1984, Mr.
Kessler has been developing courses, teaching, and
consulting in the area of data communications and
computer networking for numerous communications firms,
including AT&T Bell Laboratories, Ameritech, Bell
Atlantic, NYNEX, Southwestern Bell, and United
Telecommunications. His primary areas of interest include
ISDN, packet switching and X.25, communications
standards and protocols, and local area networks. Mr.
Kessler is a member of the ANSI X3S3.7 Task Group,
creating U.S. national standards for packet switching and
public data network access.